AT THE
HANDS
OF A
STRANGER

AT THE
HANDS
OF A
STRANGER

LEE BUTCHER

PINNACLE BOOKS
Kensington Publishing Corp.
http://www.kensingtonbooks.com

PINNACLE BOOKS are published by

Kensington Publishing Corp.
119 West 40th Street
New York, NY 10018

All Kensington Titles, Imprints, and Distributed Lines are available at special quantity discounts for bulk purchases for sales promotions, premiums, fund-raising, and educational or institutional use. Special book excerpts or customized printings can also be created to fit specific needs. For details, write or phone the office of the Kensington special sales manager: Kensington Publishing Corp., 119 West 40th Street, New York, NY 10018, attn: Special Sales Department, Phone: 1-800-221-2647.

Pinnacle and the P logo Reg. U.S. Pat. & TM Off.

ISBN-13: 978-0-7860-2193-2
ISBN-10: 0-7860-2193-4

First Printing: May 2012

10 9 8 7 6 5 4 3

Printed in the United States of America

I would like to thank Barbara Taylor
for helping keep me informed of new developments
and reminding me of old ones.
Thanks also to all of the law enforcement officers
who helped, and many thanks to Bonnie Fruchey,
who was my Friday.

Chapter 1

On New Year's Day, 2008, the killer watched a young woman with shoulder-length blond hair as he waited for a chance to strike. It was a cold day on Blood Mountain in Georgia's Vogel State Park; the temperature was just above freezing, in the crisp afternoon light. The woman was accompanied by a mixed-breed black dog, which seemed to be part Labrador retriever. His own dog was a red Irish setter named Dandy, and the canine had not had a bath or brushing in a long time.

The killer had come to Blood Mountain two or three days before—he had lost track of time—because it was a good place to hunt women. He considered himself to be a professional soldier who was always on combat maneuvers; he used his training and keen powers of observation to scrutinize his surroundings in detail. He was always on high alert. The woman's unleashed dog was of no concern to him, because he had been attacked by canines many times in the past. Usually, it was the other way around: He attacked dogs when he disapproved of their behavior. The dogs didn't have a chance against him. Sometimes pepper spray would be enough to chase a dog off; but if one was determined, he always had his butcher knife, bayonet, and a collapsible police-style baton, which snapped into a yard-long club that could crush bone.

"It's easy to kill a dog," he would say, even to strangers. He boasted that for a man with his fighting skills, it was also easy to kill a human being.

Blood Mountain, about ninety miles northwest of Atlanta, was an ideal setting for the killer. It rises 4,458 feet into the air and is thick with trees and hiking trails so narrow that in some parts two hikers can't walk side by side. There were still smudges of gold, brown, and red on the poplar, birch, oak, and maple trees—although the height of the color season had passed and most of the deciduous leaves were on the ground. During the peak of autumn, Blood Mountain trails were thick with hikers who wanted to walk among this splendid beauty.

With the colorful foliage almost gone, there were fewer hikers than usual, but that suited the killer's purpose. The less populated the trails, the better his chances were of not being seen by someone who could identify him later. He wasn't famous yet, except in his own mind, but it seemed to him that he attracted attention like the Lone Ranger, who wore a skintight outfit, a fancy two-gun holster rig, and rode a palomino. That was all staging and show business designed to draw attention so that when people asked, "Who was that masked man?" everyone knew that it was the Lone Ranger. None of that shit for him. Once he drew attention to himself, and his picture was published in a newspaper, he was done for; and he had already been "screwed, blued, and tattooed" by society in every way imaginable.

People invariably remembered him because of his brightly colored, expensive hiking clothes, a weird demeanor, scary appearance, and general attitude of menace.

"I'm the fucking Lone Ranger," he sometimes told people to describe the attention he generated.

The killer was Gary Michael Hilton, a former paratrooper and career criminal, who had been hiking and running for years along the Appalachian Trail and in remote mountain forests of the Northwest region of the United States. Except for a two-year enlistment as a U.S. Army paratrooper, Hilton had been a drifter most of his life. He had chosen to become homeless about fourteen years earlier. At five feet ten inches tall and 160 pounds, Hilton was lean and strong, with whipcord muscles connecting tendons like steel cable beneath his weathered brown skin.

Although only a fringe of gray hair formed a horseshoe on his head, he was tougher than a pine knot and could run through the mountains for hours and walk all day and all night toting a seventy-pound backpack. No one had better mess with him, and people seldom did because he looked mean. A former roommate had described Hilton as being "a sociopath with a mean streak." He was insulted at first, but then he realized it was true—and he liked it. He was mean and he knew it. The unkempt gray goatee on Hilton's face and lack of all but one jagged, brown front tooth accented his menacing appearance: when he smiled, there was only a black hole with the jagged tooth between his lips. Hilton had pulled most of his teeth out with a pair of pliers rather than get dental care. It was something else he bragged about. Hilton was also a sociopath—and he knew that, too. This self-awareness made him superior to other people who were also mean and sociopathic, but were unable to recognize it in themselves.

He had told an acquaintance that he had no conscience

and felt sorry for people who did, because having one made life too complicated.

The woman he had decided to hunt today was Meredith Emerson, a twenty-four-year-old graduate of the University of Georgia, who was employed in an executive-training position by an Atlanta company that sold shipping boxes in bulk. An avid hiker and outdoorswoman, Emerson started to walk up a "feeder" trail with her dog frolicking around her, but she almost immediately met another couple coming from the other direction with their dog on a leash. They stopped and Hilton watched as they took turns petting the dogs and chatting. People with dogs were the easiest targets, he believed, because they were more likely to be approachable. All you had to do was start talking about what a good-looking dog they had—*blah, blah, blah*—and they became instant buddies. This was something he had learned during the forty years that he had been on perpetual combat control.

Hilton's money supply had dwindled to forty dollars. He figured he had to spend at least thirty dollars to put gasoline in his filthy, dilapidated 1996 Chevrolet Astro van. The vehicle, which he called home, had been running on fumes. He was hungry, and he needed more money; that was why he had driven to Blood Mountain. Although it was against park rules to camp in the parking lot, Hilton had managed to get away with it for the past two or three nights by unloading his equipment after sundown and long before sunrise. At these times it was too late or too early for anyone to be at the park. It was another carefully thought-out tactical maneuver, and he enjoyed his clever deceit.

The van was dented and rusty, muddy, filled with empty food cans, rotten fruit peelings and cores, and cargo bags filled with camping gear. The back door was held on with bungee cords, because the hinges were broken. It attracted as much attention as Hilton did. The camper was careful to move the van to a new spot every day and park in the space that was in an out-of-the-way spot, to lessen the chances of the van being noticed by others walking to the Blood Mountain hiking area.

Although Hilton had been homeless for the past decade, he still needed money to eat and buy incidentals. Any kind of work, of course, was beneath his status as a perpetual soldier and professional criminal, and he wouldn't be caught dead in some of the cheap, inadequate hiking gear that others wore. He wore the best microfiber clothing that was available, and that was one of the reasons people noticed him. Anyone seeing him today, he knew, would remember the bright yellow jacket, with the black stripes and patches on the elbows, and the black backpack that he carried, and they would wonder how such a dirty, strange, unkempt man could afford such expensive clothing. It was seldom that anyone asked about the clothing; if they did, Hilton told them that he had a marketing arrangement with the manufacturers. Or he would freak them out with a glare and say, "Because I'm Microfiber Man." He never revealed how he *really* got the clothing. The hiking clothes and gear were the best money could buy, and the clothing drew attention to him, but that was the risk he had to take for being a professional.

Hilton also had an edge over others because of his intelligence and awareness that life was filled with nothing but meaningless activity. Among all men, he knew that life was a shifting, meaningless charade to keep people so busy that they wouldn't have to think about the inevitability of their impending deaths. Hilton was terrified of his own death, and his earliest memory was of looking at his hand when he was a four-year-old boy and realizing that one day it would be nothing but a skeleton.

The two hikers who chatted with Emerson started to go their separate way from her. She sat on the ground at the intersection of the Byron Herbert Reece Trail and the Appalachian Trail in order to rest and eat some trail mix. She gave her dog a drink of water and some treats. Hilton saw the departing couple glance at him as he went to the same path the girl had chosen. Ordinarily, he would have abandoned the mission because, when he went out to kill, he didn't want anyone to remember having seen him in the area. He would be screwed. However, he was desperate, so he ignored the warnings that told him to abandon the mission and just go for a hike with his dog and have fun. Hilton told himself he should be patient and wait for more suitable prey, but he needed food and money. He had to kill someone.

Hilton believed he had found prey the day before yesterday on Blood Mountain when he spotted a young woman hiking toward the summit. He passed a group of hikers about thirty yards behind her. Hilton closed the gap between them and started up a conversation with her about the dog trotting beside her. They rounded a bend, and the people behind them were out of sight. This could be his chance.

"Are you hiking alone?" he had asked.

"No. That group behind me is my family."

Hilton had grunted in anger, got off the trail, and walked into the woods and stayed there until it was dark enough to sneak back to his van in the parking lot and make camp. He had come up empty. So here he was again today, still hunting.

Blood Mountain was one of the best places Hilton knew to hunt because it was one of the most popular daytime hikes in Georgia. There were a lot of potential targets. People came to the roughly 24,000-acre Dawson Forest Wildlife Management Area to hike, watch birds, hunt, fish, camp, ride horses, or canoe on the scenic Amicalola and Etowah Rivers. It was only about sixty miles from the Atlanta urban area. Conversely, Blood Mountain's popularity was also bad news for Hilton because it increased the danger of being seen. Even the most efficient professional couldn't anticipate every Tom, Dick, and Harry who might pop out of the woods onto the trail.

He took the same trail that Emerson did and noticed with satisfaction that her dog was a female. It was unleashed, as was his male dog. As he followed the woman, they encountered a few hikers coming back down the mountain. Hilton realized that he should have hidden in a blind off the trail and waited for someone to come along. It was too late for that now, so he lagged several feet behind the woman and began to talk about her dog. The dog's name was Ella, the girl said, but didn't offer her own name. That was a mistake in his opinion, because he believed that if she feared abduction, she should do everything she could to make herself seem more human. She ought to try and make him like her, personalize her, to be more than an object, so she might elicit feelings of sympathy from her abductor.

But she was not a professional like him. After a while the girl told him she wanted to hike alone and he dropped back, but he kept talking to her. He asked her what kind of music she liked as he tagged along, going deeper into the woods. She took a branch off the main trail and walked onto a path wide enough for only one person at a time. The killer continued tailing her and continued to talk; he was garrulous or stone-cold silent by nature, and it didn't matter to him if she answered or not.

He dropped back farther and she was soon out of sight as she headed toward the summit. There were no other trails she could take to get back. He knew he would meet her once more when she came back down. She would be tired from the hike and he would be relatively fresh. Not that he needed to be. He could whip almost anybody's ass because he was one hell of a stud, but he was glad he had found a petite woman. A man would be more likely to put up a fight, and then you never knew what might happen. He wanted it to be nice and easy.

Hilton got off the narrow trail and hid in the deep woods, where he could still see her, but he would be out of her line of vision when she returned. About an hour later, Emerson and her dog came into view. Now that she was on the way back to the parking lot, the woman seemed to feel more at ease. Emerson walked happily along, half jogging, and talking to her dog. Hilton burst out of the woods with his bayonet drawn and blocked her way.

"Give me your credit cards and PIN number," he snarled, "and I won't hurt you."

Hilton approached her, threatening with the bayonet, hurrying, because he thought that Emerson would try to run. Instead, she faced him in a defensive stance and started to fight. She wrested the bayonet from his hand and it tumbled down a ravine into a pile of leaves.

The bayonet had sliced her palm and the webbing between her thumb and forefinger and blood flowed. In spite of this, Emerson continued to face Hilton in a defensive position. He was afraid he had picked the wrong target. This woman was not weak. Having lost the bayonet, Hilton pulled out his favorite weapon, the collapsible baton, and snapped it out to full length. He was an expert with the baton and was proud of how well he could use it. He had beaten men much larger than himself senseless. He swung at her, but the woman dodged and the baton missed. Her hand slammed into his face and the baton flew out of his grasp and fell down the ravine with the bayonet. Hilton could not believe how fast she was and how well she could fight.

She's kicking my ass! he thought in disbelief. *This woman is kicking my ass.*

"I've got a gun!" he yelled. "Stop fighting or I'll shoot."

The woman screamed and continued to fight, kicking and flailing. He slammed a fist to the side of her head and she hit him back. They were grappling when they slipped and went tumbling down a steep ravine on the opposite side of the trail, where the bayonet and baton had tumbled. Hilton hoped she wouldn't break away and run, because he knew most women could run faster than he. The woman fought so hard and long that Hilton almost gave up. He had another large knife in a sheath strapped to his leg, but he couldn't get to it. The woman feinted, and then hit him from the other side. When he grabbed her around the body and pinned her arms, she became limp and he thought he was in control. And then he found himself being thrown into the air and landing hard on the ground.

After he got to his feet, he managed to hit her in the face several times with his right fist. It felt like he had broken several of his fingers. But the woman kept fighting, until he found a heavy limb on the ground and smashed it against her face. The woman went limp and the killer felt a thrill of triumph because he finally had subdued her.

Emerson groaned and ceased to struggle. Hilton held her down for a few minutes and continued talking. He assured her that he had no intention of hurting her. All he wanted was her identification, ATM bank card, and PIN code. And then he heard hikers on the main trail and squatted down, partly behind a tree, to hide from them. They passed without saying anything, and Hilton hoped they had not seen him. If they had, perhaps they thought he was having a bowel movement.

When he believed Emerson could resist no more, he

tied a rope in a slipknot around her neck and told her to walk ahead of him onto a contour trail, where they would be less likely to meet anyone. It was a trail that couldn't be seen by anyone from the Byron Herbert Reece Trail. The woman didn't scream or yell, but suddenly she turned again and attacked. The force of her body hitting him sent both tumbling out of control down another ravine. He managed to hold on to the limb after they stopped rolling, but Emerson avoided his first swing at her and kicked him. The fight lasted for several minutes. The killer wished that he had not chosen this woman because she was strong, fast, brave, and seemed to have training in martial arts. He repeatedly clubbed her head until she could fight no more and then dragged her down the mountain, where he used black plastic zip ties to fasten her to a tree. Emerson was not unconscious, but there was a lump on her forehead, her nose looked broken, and both of her eyes were black and swollen almost shut.

"I'm not going to hurt you," Hilton said. "Stop fighting and be quiet or you *will* get hurt. Listen, honey, I ain't going to spend my life in prison, so you better be quiet. I've got a gun and I'll shoot your ass."

Hilton was the professional soldier again, in control, showing what he called his command presence. "You wait here and I'll be back. I have to get something."

He wanted to clean up the crime scene where he had first attacked the girl. He needed to retrieve the knife, bayonet, water bottle, scraps of clothing, the girl's dog leash, and anything else that could tie him to the crime scene. The baton was the killer's favorite weapon, and he knew where it had fallen. However, there was nothing at the crime scene when he arrived. He assumed that one of the hikers he had seen had found everything and would report suspicious behavior to the authorities. That was a stroke of really bad luck.

Now he had to hurry to get out of the park because the woman had fought so long that he was afraid a park ranger would find his van, which was supposed to be out of the park by nightfall. He needed to load the woman into the van and get away from Vogel Park fast.

"Hon, we got to get out of here," he told Emerson. "This place is gonna be crawling with cops. Give me the keys to your car."

She told him the keys were in her fanny pack. He got them. "What kind of car is it?"

"A white Chevrolet Caprice."

"Where's your purse?"

"Under the driver's seat."

It was dusk when he approached his van, which was half filled with sleeping bags, shoes, socks, toiletries, a small cooking stove, pornographic magazines, and a cooking kit. A heavy metal chain, about eight feet long, lay across a pile of cargo bags. One end was locked to a steel seat support, secured with a padlock. There was also a padlock on the other end. Another chain, four feet long, was padlocked to a different seat support; and a nylon rope, about five feet long, was tied with a series of square knots to a metal eyelet welded on the floorboard. Hilton drove the van and parked it so that the sliding side door was next to Emerson's car; then he returned to where she was secured to a tree.

The young woman saw him approaching and said, "No. No."

He leaned close.

"Honey, don't worry," he said. "I'm not going to hurt you. I just want your credit cards and PIN numbers. But if you try to run away, I'll shoot your ass down. If I was going to hurt you, I'd have already hurt you. Understand, hon?"

The girl didn't answer but offered no resistance as he grabbed one end of the rope with a slipknot noose around her neck and cut the straps that held her to the tree. He marched her like a dog down a steep ravine, following behind her. She stumbled and fell once and moaned, but she did not yell. Ella, Emerson's dog, was frightened and confused as she trotted next to her owner. The sun had dropped below the horizon and it was getting cold, so Hilton put one of his extra jackets around the girl's shoulders and led her up a steep ravine. They waded across a creek, climbed down a boulder field, and walked several yards through thick brush in the direction of where he had parked his van next to her car.

He asked about her purse with the credit cards and she told him again that it was beneath the driver's seat. Hilton kept a tight grip on the leash around Emerson's neck and continually warned her to keep quiet or he would kill her. Emerson had made a lot of noise during their struggle; he feared an army of cops would be arriving any minute.

Just a few yards inside the woods, but near the parking lot, Hilton strapped Emerson to another tree outside of view. He took Emerson's car keys from her fanny pack and slid the side door of his van open. The purse was beneath the passenger seat. He thought the woman was brain-dead for trying such a stupid trick by trying to fool him by saying it was under the driver's seat. Did she think he wouldn't look there? Dumb. Going back to the tree, he cut the straps free and led her to the vehicles and told her to get into his van. Ella followed along uneasily, obviously afraid of Hilton.

"Get in," Hilton ordered.

"No," Emerson said, resisting. "They told me never to get into a vehicle."

"Get in, bitch!" He shoved her inside and pointed to several cargo bags. "Lie down on those."

The young woman did as she was told. Hilton looped the longer chain around her neck so that she could not slip her head out of it. He secured it with two padlocks. He tied a rope from an eyelet on the floorboard around her ankle and secured it with seven square knots, one on top of the other. She could untie the square knots, he knew, but it would take a long time to undo so many. He would hear her before she got loose. Even if she untied her ankle, she wasn't going anywhere with the chain around her neck. Emerson lay on her side, trussed in heavy chains like a piece of equipment.

Ella was nervous and ran in circles outside the van, barking and whining, but not threatening him. Hilton didn't want the dog to be found running loose, because someone might know to whom it belonged. Worse, the dog might have an identification microchip embedded beneath its skin. Just one more problem for him. He forced the dog into Emerson's car and closed the doors.

"No!" the woman said. "You can't leave her like that. She'll die."

Disregarding the woman's protests, the killer drove away and headed north on Highway 129, moving toward Blairsville, about fifty miles away. Emerson continued to worry about the dog and begged Hilton not to leave Ella in the car to freeze to death. A few miles down the road, he began to be concerned that the woman's aggravation might cause her to start making more trouble for him. He wanted her to be nice and compliant. He was amazed at how quickly *they* always became compliant: unaware that in his observations he had used the plural "they" instead of the singular "she."

"You want me to turn around and go back to get your damn dog?" he asked.

"Yes. Please."

He turned the van around, drove back to the park, took Ella from the car, and put her inside the van. The dog immediately lay down beside the girl and started to lick her face. Hilton thought he had once more demonstrated his professionalism. The dog's presence helped keep his prisoner quiet, and his decision to go back and get it would make the woman think he was kind. It was important for her to think of him as just a harmless guy with a couple of screws loose who wouldn't really hurt her. He wanted her to see him as quirky, intelligent, intuitive, well-read, and essentially a decent human being who cared about her. Hilton talked nonstop as he drove toward Blairsville and asked about her job and hobbies. He complimented her combat skills. He learned that she studied judo and karate and held a green belt in judo and a brown belt in karate. That meant she was fairly advanced in karate. No wonder she almost kicked his ass.

He had determined that her name was Meredith Hope Emerson, but he never used it. He called her "hon," "honey," "bitch," or "cunt." It was unprofessional to form an attachment to her; he had to think of her as just a faceless person whom he was going to kill. That was easy because he hated people. At the very gut level, he was filled with rage against society, especially women, because they tried to turn a man into a domestic faggot. A man was meant to be wild and free, not sit at home in a house with frilly curtains and cute little whatnots. A man might protest against this by having a few manly tools in the garage to fool him into thinking he was still a man, but he was really a neutered faggot.

Women controlled men because they had the pussy and knew how much men valued it. Women could threaten to withhold it, which increased the pussy's value. They could threaten to give it to someone else, and that increased its value, too. The only time the pussy lost value was when women threatened to give it away and actually did. Males were safe when they were kids; but when puberty kicked in, they were trapped and led around the rest of their lives by the pussy.

Hilton pulled the van to a stop opposite a convenience

store and warned Emerson to be quiet. He pumped thirty dollars of gasoline into his van. He was down to ten bucks now. Then he drove to the Appalachian Community Bank in Blairsville and checked the surroundings. Inside Emerson's purse he had found not just one ATM card, but three: Frontier Visa, Capital One Visa, and MasterCard. He had struck the mother lode. There were just enough people on the street, for him not to arouse suspicion at the ATM. This was the tricky part. You couldn't try to get money when there were *too few* people or *too many* people because, either way, you stood out. You couldn't go when it was too dark or some dickhead cop would drive by the ATM and become suspicious. The fuckers were born suspicious.

Holding a towel in front of his face, he walked over, inserted a card in the ATM, and punched the PIN code that Emerson had given to him. The ATM rejected the PIN and spit out the card, but no money. Growing increasingly frustrated, Hilton tried two more cards; they were rejected, too.

He walked angrily to the van. "Them's the wrong numbers. You better give me the right ones."

Emerson insisted that the PINs were correct. He tried again but received no money. Emerson suggested that he try another bank, so he drove to Gainesville, twenty-three miles away, and then another forty-two miles to Canton. He tried the cards at different banks. Still, no money. Emerson gave him different numbers and convinced him each time that she was telling the truth. The killer was nervous because of the television security cameras that recorded activities at ATMs. He concealed his face with a towel and a mask made of duct tape and goggles, but that was even more suspicious.

It became too late to try the ATMs without attracting a cop, if one should drive by on patrol. It had also turned bitterly cold. He returned to the van. Hilton was also feeling weak, like he was going to crash, physically, as if he couldn't keep going. His damn multiple sclerosis. He would crash and then the demons would come; and hours later he would find himself with shredded tires, wondering what the hell he had been doing all that time. The demons. Death chasing him since he was four.

"You're running me around like a fucking idiot," he said. "Keep this up and I'll shoot your ass. Make one sound and it's curtains."

Hilton laughed bitterly at himself. The woman had him running back and forth like a trained monkey. He knew she was lying about the PINs, but the eternal optimist, he just kept going. Finally he was exhausted, and it had become too risky that he would be spotted with a towel in front of his face. He needed to find a campsite somewhere in a remote area. He thought of some higher elevations in Dawson Forest. The problem with that was the ground had frozen and snow was coming in; it would be heavier at higher altitudes and accumulating rapidly on the ground. He didn't want to have a wreck or get stuck in a snowbank.

Two inches of ice and snow were already on the road, and Hilton's tires had little, if any, treads. He almost lost control several times. The snow slashed parallel through the twin beams of the headlights, and the wipers labored to keep two half-moons of the windshield clear of slush. It was nerve-wracking in the dark, and then there was a heart-stopping incident.

Hilton's van was sliding out of control as he drove around a curve. In the stabbing beams of the headlights, he saw that another car was stalled on the shoulder. Worse, there was a sheriff's patrol car beside it, with the blue lights flashing. Hilton's van continued to struggle up the hill as he fought panic and weighed the situation. The cop was only a few feet away and his attention was riveted on the car that had slid off the road. Emerson was quiet and didn't seem to know what was happening. If she started to make a ruckus, though, the cop might hear her and make Hilton stop the van. The van's windows were black and opaque from the outside, but you could still see in from the outside of the windshield.

Hilton struggled to maintain control of his emotions—and the vehicle—and he knew conditions would only be worse at higher elevations. The deputy would more than likely stop him, put up a roadblock, and tell him not to go up any higher. If he didn't turn around and start back down, Hilton believed, the cop would stop him and tell him he was nuts. And he might see or hear Emerson in the van. He had no choice except to turn around and go down the hill and hope the cop didn't interfere with him.

I don't know what I'm doing, Hilton thought. *What the hell do I have in mind? How do I find a campsite? How do I keep the cop from coming over?*

In a panicked daze Hilton managed to turn the van around and start back down. He discovered that he had slid off the road into someone's yard, but his tires found traction and he was soon back on the road. Hilton passed within a few feet of the deputy sheriff on the way up and then again on the way back down. Hilton did not understand why Emerson had made no noise, unless she was afraid of the threat he had made to shoot her ass.

Hilton drove through the vast darkness toward a remote area of Dawson Forest, where he didn't think anyone would ever think to look. He had to move a ROAD CLOSED barrier before he could drive to where he would make camp, and then put it back in place after brushing away tire marks and footprints. Hilton was exhausted from his long day and all the hell that the woman had put him through. He felt himself coming down, ready to crash, and he needed to take an upper, downer, or anything he could find. Hilton made Emerson help him unload the camping gear, even though she complained of a severe headache and her eyes didn't seem to focus. Although he was angry, Hilton gave Emerson what he considered to be his best cold-weather sleeping bag. It was a high-quality bag, but it was filthy.

Hilton was infuriated by all of the hard work and nothing to show for it.

"Honey, I told you I was gonna let you go," he told her. "You've run me around. You've run me all over northern Georgia, made me put one hundred fifty miles on my van. You lied to me. You've run me around. Now you owe me some pussy."

He unzipped his pants and raped her while she was chained and on the lumpy cargo bags, surrounded by two dogs, empty food cans, banana peelings, and other trash. Emerson was unresponsive, but Hilton believed that she was enjoying herself and saw the kidnapping, beating, and rape as part of an unexpected and exciting adventure on what would otherwise have been a dull, routine day for her.

After all of this had transpired, Emerson lay on those same cargo bags inside the van with Ella. Her abductor and his dog, Dandy, slept in the front seats. It was bitterly cold and Hilton sometimes ran the engine for short periods to get heat inside the vehicle. Emerson had a heavy five-foot-long steel chain padlocked around her neck, which was also padlocked to a metal seat brace inside the vehicle. Her right ankle was tied with a short rope, which was also secured to a fixture inside the van.

"This is just in case you decide to wander away, cunt," the abductor had said before getting into his sleeping bag.

Emerson lay in the cold van, chained up, in the vast and lonely expanse of Dawson Forest.

Held captive by a homicidal maniac, she waited for whatever would happen.

Chapter 2

Julia Karrenbauer saw Meredith Emerson still asleep in her bedroom in their Duluth, Georgia, apartment on Tuesday morning, New Year's Day, 2008. Ella, Emerson's black rescue dog, part Labrador retriever, was asleep in the room with her. Karrenbauer had last seen Emerson awake on New Year's Eve, at about six o'clock at night. She had no reason to be concerned about her roommate not being home on New Year's Day afternoon. Emerson was gone, but she had left a note on the chalkboard saying that she had taken Ella for a hike. Not worried, Karrenbauer went to bed and slept until 3:30 P.M. that day.

It wasn't unusual for Emerson to go hiking, and Karrenbauer thought that Meredith had gone with her boyfriend, Steve Segars. Karrenbauer continued with her day and made preparations to watch the University of Georgia game, to be televised later that afternoon, with Brent Seyler, her boyfriend. What Karrenbauer didn't know was that Emerson had gone hiking with just Ella and that Segars was not with her.

Emerson and Segars had left a New Year's Eve fireworks display in Lawrenceville at about 11:30 P.M. because Emerson wanted to get home before the holiday traffic became too congested. Segars remembered that they had made plans to spend part of New Year's Day together, but he didn't hear from Emerson. He texted her twice that morning to remind her. He didn't receive an answer. At about 10:00 A.M., Emerson, whom Segars referred to as his "best friend and girlfriend," telephoned him to say that she had just awakened and had to take Ella for a walk.

Segars thought that Emerson didn't seem to care that their plans for the day were ruined because she had slept late. He said later that he was "terse and short" when he asked her to find something else to do. It was not a serious dispute, but Segars felt bad about the tone he had used with Emerson and telephoned back at about one o'clock to apologize. The call was transferred to Emerson's voice mail. Segars left a message and started to work on a bedroom that he was remodeling.

Segars tried numerous times to telephone Emerson that afternoon; each time the call was transferred directly to voice mail. None of the messages brought a response. He thought that Emerson might have turned her telephone off. Starting to be concerned, Segars went to Emerson's residence at about 7:00 P.M. He asked Brent Seyler about Meredith's whereabouts, and was told that they hadn't seen Emerson all day. Both Steve Segars and Julia Karrenbauer were starting to feel concerned now.

On Wednesday, January 2, at ten in the morning, Emerson's boss, Chris Hendley, telephoned Karrenbauer and told her that Emerson had not come to work and had not phoned in. Karrenbauer called Segars to pass on the information, but he had already received a call from Emerson's boss to tell him the same thing. Karrenbauer told Segars that Emerson had not come home Tuesday night, nor had she telephoned. For Meredith Emerson, this was completely out of character.

The situation suddenly escalated from the category of "unusual" to "alarming." Karrenbauer remembered that one of Emerson's friends in Colorado, where she had been visiting family over the Christmas season, had told her by telephone that Emerson said she had plans to go hiking on New Year's Day. Segars decided to start looking at some of her favorite hiking areas.

First he drove to DeSoto Falls, which was one of the areas where he and Emerson loved to hike together. He looked around the area but didn't see Emerson's car or any sign that she had recently been there. He continued driving and went to the Byron Herbert Reece Memorial Trailhead, at Vogel Park, and saw Emerson's Chevrolet Caprice in the parking lot. The car was dusted with snow and there were no footprints in the fresh snow around the vehicle. It didn't look as if the car had been moved since the snow fell.

Segars ran up the trail for a short distance and shouted Emerson's name, again and again. Failing to get a response, he hurried to a small store at the intersection of the Appalachian Trail and State Highway 129. He contacted Emerson's friends by text and cell phone and told them that he had found her car at Vogel Park. Friends arrived and they began to search the trail after Segars left a "sticky" note on Emerson's car window, telling her not to leave and that he would be back.

Emerson's family was told about what had happened, and Margaret Bailey, of Athens, Georgia, who was a close family friend and Emerson's godmother, telephoned the Gwinnett County Police Department (GCPD) and spoke with Officer Jeff Legg. Legg also spoke with Emerson's mother, Susan. Both women told him that this type of behavior was "unlike" Meredith.

During her initial contact with the police, Bailey didn't know that Emerson's car had been found at Vogel Park in Union County. Bailey had also learned, for the first time, that Emerson had a boyfriend and that he and Emerson had plans to hike together on New Year's Day. Somehow, those plans had fallen through. Legg elicited additional information and filed a report that read in part: *(Bailey) also stated she was told that there was a witness in the area of Blood Mountain that saw the victim and her dog hiking in the area and also saw a male walking down the trail with some sort of police baton. During the search effort, the baton and some of the victim's belongings were located but the victim and the victim's dog are still missing.*

No one, at the time, knew who this witness was.

Legg completed a form for missing persons and entered it into the Georgia Crime Information Center/National Crime Information Center (GCIC/NCIC) database and the information was immediately available to police officers throughout the United States. Meredith Emerson officially became a missing person at 11:37 A.M. on Wednesday, July 2, 2008. It would not be long before she was classified as an endangered kidnapping victim.

Emerson's friends, volunteers, Union County sheriff's deputies, Dawsonville police officers, fire and rescue personnel, and national and state forest rangers poured into Vogel Park. They faced the daunting task of combing thousands of acres where Emerson could be lying injured—or worse. Vogel Park was part of Dawson Forest, which included thousands of heavily wooded acres in the Blue Ridge Mountains. The Appalachian Trail, one of the longest and most scenic hiking trails in the world, stretched through it, running 2,160 miles from Mount Katahdin, Maine, to Springer Mountain in Georgia. Dedicated hikers sometimes took a lifetime to walk various parts of the scenic trail, until they traversed the full distance, following blazed trees that served as markers along the way.

Dawson Forest itself was huge and had trails that

were suitable for biking, horseback riding, and single-file walking. People came to the Edge of the World Falls; they canoed, fished, hunted, camped, and studied endangered land and water species. In 1956, ten thousand acres had been used for military research by Lockheed's Georgia Nuclear Aircraft Laboratory (GNAL) to try and develop a nuclear-powered warplane. Lockheed decommissioned the facility in 1971 and sold the property to the city of Atlanta.

Vogel Park, located near Dawsonville, was just more than thirty miles from Duluth, where Karrenbauer and Emerson lived. Had Emerson intended to hike up Blood Mountain with Ella and return straight home, she would have arrived home not long after dark on New Year's Day. She had climbed to the summit of the 4,458-foot-high mountain on many occasions and was familiar with the terrain. The origin of Blood Mountain's name was disputed. Some say it came about because of the color of the lichen and Catawba rhododendron that grow near the summit. Others claim the mountain was named for a fierce and bloody battle in the late 1600s between the Cherokee and Creek Indians near Slaughter Gap, when the two tribes were fighting for dominance. The Cherokees won the skirmish, and a tremendous amount of Native Americans died in the fight.

Hiking isn't without danger, and hiking solo poses even more hazards. You could slip, fall off a trail into a ravine, and be knocked unconscious. Nobody would be around to notice. You could be hurt during an encounter with a wild animal. Even in a park that is marked well, a hiker can wander off the trail and get lost. There is the danger of sudden extreme changes in the weather, especially in higher elevations, and dehydration is something that should always be considered. Furthermore, a lonely forest, far from civilization, is also a good place for sociopaths who are looking for easy targets to rob, hurt, rape, abduct, or kill. Emerson was aware of all of these pitfalls and had taken courses in both self-defense and hiking safety.

A college graduate with a degree and work experience in public relations, Julia Karrenbauer knew the value of people who use ink by the barrel and paper by the ton, and who send television news to millions of viewers around the world. According to the Georgia Bureau of Investigation (GBI), Karrenbauer and Steve Segars made telephone calls to dozens of friends, who agreed to meet at Vogel Park to start searching. Flyers with information and a photograph of Meredith Emerson with Ella were distributed. The GBI said Karrenbauer took a big step toward speeding the search for Emerson when she took the initiative to contact people in the media and tell them that Emerson was missing and what the circumstances were.

Time is critical in bringing an abduction case to a successful conclusion, and Emerson's friends and family had done all the things the police tell people to do in such matters. Maybe it was not too late to save Meredith Emerson.

Scores of people congregated at the entrance to Vogel Park to help search for the missing woman. Uniformed deputies from the Union County Sheriff's Office (UCSO), as well as members of the Union County Fire Department (UCFD), organized search parties. Now that Emerson's car had been found at Vogel Park, which was in Union County, the crime came under the jurisdiction of the UCSO. The Dawson County Sheriff's Office (DCSO) and Dawsonville Police Department (DPD) continued to help.

Several of Emerson's friends, who had hiked on Blood Mountain, had already started to comb the trails in search of the missing hiker. First Lieutenant Brad Niebrand, of the UCFD, found several volunteers with medical training who knew the park well. He immediately sent them out with his own men in case Emerson would need medical help when found. Deputies found Emerson's car, a 2000 white Chevrolet with the Georgia license plate number WX311S, abandoned at the Byron Herbert Reece Memorial Trailhead parking area near Blairsville. Segars's "sticky note" was still attached to the driver's-side window. The area was cordoned off with yellow tape with black letters that read CRIME SCENE to keep people away so crime scene investigation (CSI) officers would have an "uncontaminated" area in which to work their forensic wonders.

For a man who was trying to remain anonymous, Gary Michael Hilton might as well have been wearing neon lights for all the attention he attracted on Blood Mountain, not just on New Year's Day, but several days before. He stood out like a black spider on a white wedding cake. Deputies didn't have to wait long before finding evidence of a suspicious character on Blood Mountain the day that Meredith Emerson went missing.

Casey Smith noticed a man on Herbert Reece Trail who wore "a goofy furry hat" and had only one tooth in front. About sixty years old, the man wore a yellow windbreaker with black patches on the elbows and black stripes on the sides. The man carried a black backpack, carried a big knife on his waist and a collapsible nightstick, which looked like a police baton, and was accompanied by a red Irish setter. The man wasn't on the trail, Smith told a deputy, but that he had actually burst unexpectedly onto the trail from a heavily wooded area. He said the man was talking to himself.

Smith said he and the man talked together for a short time before they separated. Smith and his dog went to the parking lot. Just before he drove from the lot, Smith saw the same man come out of the woods, again off trail, with his dog and get inside a "dingy" white Astro van. The time was about five o'clock in the evening when Smith left. The unidentified man in the van was still in the parking lot.

Liz Porterwood and her husband, Randy, also remembered encountering a man on Blood Mountain on New Year's Day. Although the man looked scruffy and was missing at least two front teeth, Liz Porterwood described him as being "nice." Like the man Smith saw, the person with whom the Porterwoods talked wore a yellow windbreaker with yellow stripes and elbow patches. Even though he wore a fleece hat, the flaps were tied up, so they could tell he was balding and what little hair he had was gray, as was his beard. Liz Porterwood noticed that his skin was weathered and that he had numerous age spots on his skin. There were duct tape patches on the toes of both shoes. There was a scar above his upper lip, Porterwood said, and he had "really clear blue eyes."

The man said he hiked almost every day.

"Oh, you must live around here," Liz Porterwood had said.

The man didn't respond. Instead, he began to criticize other hikers for being ill prepared to hike the mountains and complained that the rescue personnel were "fat and lazy."

"I only packed for one day and I still didn't pack enough," he told Liz. He reached back and squeezed his partially filled backpack. "People aren't prepared enough. If anyone ever had a broken leg or any other trouble, they might not last through the night because of the weather. It gets down to forty degrees at night, even during the summer."

The man told Liz Porterwood that he had found a man with a broken shinbone who was being helped by a young firefighter, who was making little progress until Hilton stepped in to help.

"They send the young, inexperienced ones up because most of the ones who have experience are too fat to climb the mountain," he said.

The UCSO moved a mobile command post into Vogel Park to coordinate the search. They used a Global Positioning System (GPS) to divide the mountain into quadrants so that not one inch would be overlooked. Infrared heat-sensing devices, which can detect a person at night and in densely wooded areas, were used in the attempt to find Emerson. Helicopters patrolled the rivers, creeks, and lakes, where the lack of foliage allowed spotters to search from the air. The army of searchers came up empty.

But the police were gathering valuable information, especially with the consistency of witnesses who spotted the "creepy" bearded man, with his weathered skin and red dog. Emerson's friends had identified the dog leash, Eddie Bauer water bottles, and dog treats, which had been turned in by an as-yet-unidentified man on Blood Mountain late on New Year's Day, as belonging to Emerson. The hiker had found a collapsible police-type baton in the same area as the other evidence. The witnesses who described seeing the unidentified man had all said that he carried a baton of that type.

It was clear now that Emerson had been kidnapped. Her status was upgraded from "Missing Person" to "Kidnapped and Endangered." By sundown it was becoming too dangerous to continue a mass search. Walking on mountain trails under the best conditions requires careful attention to where you put your feet: when there is ice and snow and no light, it is easy to slip on something and go tumbling down a stony ravine. Except for some professional woodsmen familiar with the trails, the search was suspended for the night.

There were still a lot of people to be interviewed to try and establish a timeline that would help the police track Emerson and her abductor's path. The only thing they could do was continue to interview, search, investigate, and work backward to establish a path and perhaps determine where the abductor might be heading. With hard police work and a little luck, the police might find Emerson well and safe.

The police needed to find as many witnesses as possible and interview them. The man who had found the bottles, dog leash, and baton could have seen other things that had not seemed significant to him at the time. Under careful police questioning, the witness might mention other things he saw that he didn't realize had evidentiary value.

Apparently, several other witnesses had seen Emerson and Hilton on New Year's Day. They had to be found and questioned. There were no photographs and little information to release to the media, except to describe Meredith Emerson and ask the public for help if they had seen Emerson and her abductor. A sketch artist was preparing a drawing of the man described by the witnesses who had seen him on New Year's Day. When a photograph of Meredith was available, it would be televised, printed in newspapers, and sent to hundreds of sites on the Internet that are dedicated to finding missing persons. There would be a national "army" trying to find her and her abductor.

The police knew nothing about the suspect except what they had heard: he looked weird, acted strangely, had blue eyes, was weathered, and had an Irish setter, which one witness had heard him call Dandy. The two water bottles and brown leash were photographed by CSI and bagged for forensic testing.

The day had been bitterly cold and there was a light dusting of snow on the ground. The police were truly surprised at the large number of volunteers who had come to help look for the missing young woman. Although darkness made it too treacherous to continue searching the mountain, the investigative pace continued at full pace throughout the night.

Chapter 3

Hoarfrost covered the inside of the Astro van's windows at first light on the morning of Wednesday, January 2. It was bitterly cold and the thermometer showed that it was eleven degrees outside, tying a record low for that date. In the dim early light Hilton looked at Emerson and noticed that she was not bleeding, although there were scabs around her mouth and face from where he had beaten her with his fists and a club. Her eyes were black and puffy, and her nose was bruised so badly that he believed it was probably broken. Hilton asked Emerson if she was in pain and she asked for aspirin. Hilton gave her two aspirin and water to take it. He asked whether or not she had passed out during the night and if there was any ringing in her ears. No. Any double vision? She told him no, but said that she had a headache.

Hilton had given Emerson aspirin every time she asked for it and believed that he was being "very solicitous" of her health. He gave her water whenever she asked for it. That morning Hilton was exhausted, or "flagged out," as he thought of it, from the running around he had done trying to get cash from one of Emerson's ATM cards. He hardly remembered how he got to where he had made camp. It came to him that he had driven through the town of Dahlonega, and he wasn't sure why.

Now, starting the second day of holding Emerson captive, Hilton was no better off than when he had started this venture to get some fast money. He was still broke, needed gas, and he had at least three broken fingers. He looked at Emerson over a campfire.

"You had me running all over last night, hon," he said. "You didn't just try to convince me, you *did* convince me." He laughed. "Hell, I'm not even going to ask you why."

Hilton continued with a rambling monologue on how stupid people were, and how he knew so much more than almost anyone. People, even his criminal lawyers, were always commenting on his superior intelligence, his depth of knowledge in numerous areas, and his exceptional education. He loved it when people said, *You certainly are well-read. How many degrees do you have?*

They were both hungry, but Hilton had nothing for them to eat except two small cans of stew. He had water and dried food for both dogs. As Hilton pondered his next move, he decided that they would go to Canton later on in the day because he knew someone in that area who might be willing to give him some money. From Canton, he could drive on up to Cartersville after he telephoned Brenda Ayers (pseudonym), the woman who might give him money.

At least that was what he hoped. Like everyone else Hilton had known, Ayers wanted nothing more to do with him and had refused to talk to him on the telephone for more than three months. However, Ayers had known him for twenty years; in Hilton's mind Brenda was a longtime girlfriend. And then there was John Tabor, in Atlanta, for whom Hilton had done telemarketing, off and on, for more than ten years. They were far from being on the best of terms, and in his mind, Hilton figured that

Tabor owed him $250,000 from past sales commissions. Hilton had physically threatened Tabor more than once.

It was just after sunrise when Hilton decided to try Emerson's ATM cards a few more times and buy a cup of coffee and some bananas from his dwindling assets, which had shrunk to less than eight dollars. Hilton felt a familiar malaise coming over him—one that sometimes made him tremble and shake, or turned him into a limp blob of boneless protoplasm without the strength to move.

When he did not have those feelings, the emotion that dominated him was unbridled rage. Besides being a mean sociopath, which he thought made him superior, Hilton blamed these feelings of malaise on multiple sclerosis (MS)—a diagnosis he had made for himself—and for which he had convinced a doctor to write him a prescription for Ritalin.

According to the National Drug Intelligence Center (NDIC), which is a part of the U.S. Department of Justice (DOJ), Ritalin is a name for the generic drug methylphenidate, a central nervous system stimulant that is more powerful than caffeine and less potent than amphetamine. The doctor who wrote the prescription for Ritalin noted on Hilton's chart that the patient was more likely to be "schizophrenic" than to have multiple sclerosis, but that the patient had shown him a faded paper from a different doctor who offered the diagnosis of MS.

Ritalin is usually prescribed for children and teenagers to treat attention deficit disorder (ADD) or attention-deficit/hyperactivity disorder (ADHD), and is supposed to be monitored carefully for side effects. These can include insomnia, euphoria, increased focus and attentiveness, psychotic episodes, cardiovascular complications, and severe psychological addiction, according to the NDIC.

Hilton took other drugs at random, depending on their availability—uppers, downers, LSD, marijuana—but he rarely drank alcohol or smoked, except for a beer and a cigarette now and then. Hilton was glad that he had "trained" Emerson to help set up and break camp. She helped pack up without being told and he was pleased at how compliant she had become. Although he may not have realized it, Hilton always thought in the plural sense. *They always became compliant,* he thought—not *she* always became compliant.

Hilton felt desperate. His range of activity was limited and he was being hemmed in because the vehicle was running low on gasoline. One of Emerson's ATM cards and PINs *had* to work. He was also anxious to look at a newspaper to see if his photograph was in it or if he had in any way been associated with a missing hiker. Once the van was packed, Emerson was tied and chained inside and Hilton drove to Regions Bank on Marietta Highway, south of Canton. He pulled up near a building on what he thought was Moose Lodge Road.

"One of these better work," he told Emerson, gazing at her with his cold blue eyes. Then he laughed. "You're making a believer out of me."

Emerson gave him a PIN number and Hilton walked at what he believed was an inconspicuous pace toward the ATM. He inserted the debit card and punched in the PIN that Emerson had given to him. All the while he held a towel to obscure his face. No money came out of the ATM, so he went back to the van.

"It didn't work, bitch," he said. "Give me the right PIN."

Emerson gave him another PIN, but Hilton knew she was lying. What's more, he could tell that Emerson *knew* that *he knew* she was lying. But he ran back and forth four different times on fruitless trips to get the ATMs to stop rejecting the card and start spitting out money. He gave up on getting money but walked inside a Huddle House restaurant across the street and asked if he could use the telephone. The waitress thought he looked creepy and dirty, as if he had been sleeping in his clothing.

The waitress walked to the other end of the restaurant, where another waitress stood, while Hilton talked for a while on the telephone, seemingly getting more and more agitated. He had picked up a copy of the *Atlanta Journal-Constitution,* where he had seen a one-column story about a missing hiker and a short story with a photo of Emerson. There was no mention of him. He breathed a sigh of relief: he still wasn't famous yet, but it was only a matter of time.

Hilton finished his telephone conversation and ordered a cup of coffee to go and smiled as he paid the waitress.

"Things are looking up," he said cheerfully.

With that, he hurried to the van and drove back to the remote area of Dawson Forest where he had made camp the night before. He had at least another day to hold his victim because he wanted to ask her for different PIN numbers and try to find different banks to try each of her three different cards. Failing that, he had to rely on his acquaintances to give him money. In the daylight Hilton saw again what a good job he had done of picking a remote camping area. It was a great hiding place, several miles north on Shoal Creek Road, not far from Deer Creek Road, which had no designated camping areas. It was hidden away in the forest and far from any hiking trails. Hilton drove off into the woods, where the van couldn't be seen from any clearings, and set up camp.

The temperature was still just eleven degrees, and Hilton lit a gas cooking stove inside the van to help keep them warm. He ran the van's engine sparingly so he could also run the van's heater, but he was worried about burning too much gasoline. Hilton had expected a blitzkrieg: kidnap, get money, kill hostage, and flee. He had not counted on Emerson running him ragged any more by giving him incorrect PIN numbers. He was tired, cold, and hungry. It was about time to finish playing this string of cards.

Exercise might help him with his jitters, he thought, and ordered Emerson to put on a warmer jacket. After he was dressed in his warmest coat and hat, they headed into the woods for a hike. On a cold day like this, meeting someone else out hiking would be like finding a needle in a haystack. The exercise felt good to him as he, Emerson, and the two dogs hiked along Shoal Creek.

Hilton could tell that Emerson was having a good time because she kept chatting. It didn't occur to him that she might be talking because she was nervous, afraid, hungry, in pain, cold, and that she had just been beaten and raped hours earlier. No, she was not having a bad time—even though she had been kidnapped. He wouldn't say she was really *happy* about the situation, but consistent with his perception on her situation of being beaten up and kidnapped, he believed she was enjoying herself.

Of course, he had laid down the law before they started out on the hike. He wanted to make it perfectly clear that he was the professional, that he had the upper hand, and that she had no chance to escape.

"There's nowhere for you to go, honey," he said. "So remember two things. Number one, if you bust out running on me through the woods, I'll shoot your ass down."

He showed her a gun, which looked like a Colt Combat Commander, and she said, "No, no. Don't show me the gun. I don't want to see the gun."

"Just remember two things," he said. "If you bust out through the woods, the pursuer has the advantage. If you bust out running down the road or anywhere else, I'll shoot you down—and I'm a good shot, left- or right-handed." Hilton wasn't lying about that: he had earned expert sharpshooter medals when he was a paratrooper in the U.S. Army.

"If we come upon someone, don't do anything, or I'm gonna start shooting everybody," Hilton told Emerson. "Unless it's law enforcement. I won't shoot it out with law enforcement 'cause I won't win. But if it's anyone else, *everybody* is gonna get killed."

They started the hike, with Emerson walking ahead of Hilton. She was not wearing any restraints. *Where is she going to go?* he asked himself. *Nowhere,* he answered. There was absolutely nowhere Meredith Emerson could go from here.

He mocked the way the cops shot their guns when he watched them on TV, and he thought about this and many other things during his hours alone in the woods. The cops came out facing their opponent, holding the gun in front of themselves with both hands, giving the other shooter a wide target. The Western gunfighters stood face on, too, but used a single-handed grip. He, among all men, knew how brain-dead this was: you stood sideways, making yourself a small target, while taking steady aim with one hand. That was the way the pros, like himself, did it—not like the dumb-ass actor cops on television.

As he contemplated his situation, Hilton continued to believe that Emerson was having a good time and was in no mental distress. She commented time and again on how beautiful it was. So far as Hilton was concerned, she was a happy camper.

In fact, Meredith Emerson was cold and scared. Her abductor had stopped somewhere in Dawson Forest Wildlife Management Area to camp for the night, and she had spent the night without sleep. Emerson had intended to hike on Blood Mountain with her dog, Ella, for just a few hours and had brought no heavy clothing and had carried only a few necessities in a fanny pack.

She was bloody and sore as she shivered inside the ratty sleeping bag, which her abductor had provided for her. It was colder than usual. The temperature that time of year was usually fairly mild, but it had turned bitterly cold, dropping to eleven degrees, equaling a record low set there in 1940.

So far, Emerson had done everything she had been taught to fight against being abducted and how to behave if she was abducted. Getting into an abductor's vehicle increased the odds that things would end badly for the victim, and she had resisted as hard and as long as she could, using everything she had learned about self-defense in her judo and karate classes. She kept fighting, even when she thought she had no strength left, because getting under the abductor's control was the last thing she wanted.

But she had failed. He was too big and too strong and the blow to her head from a tree limb sent waves of pain and shock through her so that she could no longer resist. Then she had been chained and tied inside the abductor's dirty van and made to lie or sit on hard, lumpy cargo bags. She had been forced to listen to his manic voice and his vulgar and obscene railing against anything and everything, and she felt the lash of the vile names he called her.

Emerson was trying to stay alive because people would be looking for her. Before she left to go hiking on New Year's morning, she had left a note on the chalkboard, where she and her roommate, Julia Karrenbauer, used to leave messages for one another. Emerson had written a note telling Karrenbauer that she was taking Ella for a hike, and she tacked on a personal note about the New Year's Eve party Julia had attended: *Hope you had a good time*.

Karrenbauer would be expecting her to return during

the evening of New Year's Day. Her friend would not wait long to get word out that Emerson was missing, and then a search would soon be under way. People might already be looking for her. Emerson was doing her best to buy time, to give searchers a chance to find her. She had given her abductor false PIN numbers. When no cash came out, she convinced him that he had not entered the correct number. After several failed attempts to get cash, Emerson started telling her abductor that certain cards only worked at designated ATMs.

"You better not be lying to me, cunt," he said in his strange, chilling voice. "I'll shoot your ass."

The abductor looked mean and angry, and he had cold blue eyes with small pupils, which made him appear sinister. The eyes were colder than icicles and his face was frozen in an expression that was both menacing and without pity. How much longer could she keep him running from ATM to ATM before he decided to go ahead and do whatever he intended to do with her?

The Blood Mountain hiking area swarmed with an unprecedented number of people trying to find Meredith Emerson. Officials for more than a dozen federal, state, county, and city agencies—aided by scores of volunteers—looked for anything that might lead to Emerson's whereabouts. Although it was only a day after Emerson had been reported missing, word of mouth and a short newspaper notice had spread the news like wildfire.

Police departments throughout northern Georgia were being flooded by calls from people telephoning to report seeing Emerson, an older man, and two dogs matching Dandy and Ella on Blood Mountain.

Adam Linke told Special Agent Casey Smith that

sometime between 1:45 and 2:00 P.M. that he and his father-in-law, Dr. James Frazier, encountered a hiker named Seth Blankenship, who passed them on the trail going up Blood Mountain. Blankenship was walking a dog, and Linke had two dogs on leashes. After he passed the two hikers, Blankenship talked briefly with an older man wearing a yellow jacket with black stripes, fingerless gloves, and a knit hat. The man had moved about thirty feet off the trail and an Irish setter trotted beside him.

"Is your dog friendly?" Blankenship asked.

The man said that he was.

Blankenship stopped to pet the dog. "What's his name?"

"Dandy."

Blankenship, a former Florida police officer, noticed that the man carried an Armament Systems and Procedures (ASP) police baton at his side. He asked the man if Emerson, who was about thirty feet ahead of him, was hiking with him. The man said they weren't together, but that he had moved off to the side of the trail to let some other hikers pass.

Around 2:30 P.M., Linke and Frazier met Emerson, who was heading back down the mountain. An unleashed black retriever frolicked around her, tail wagging. The three hikers stopped and chatted for a few minutes while their dogs played together. Emerson wore a baby blue fleece jacket with black shoulders and black pants, with no pockets in the back. Linke described Emerson as being "very chipper and happy."

As they continued up the trail, Linke and Frazier met an older man in a yellow jacket with bold black stripes. The man was about twenty-five feet behind Emerson. When he saw Linke and Frazier, he immediately moved twenty feet farther off the trail, as if to avoid a close encounter. The man wandered off the trail and into the woods, still going downhill, but out of their line of vision. They noted, however, that the older hiker could still see Emerson from his vantage point. The other hikers thought it was strange, but they continued on to the summit and spent a few minutes exploring the Rock House, a shelter on top of the mountain, and chatting with Blankenship.

Blankenship started back down the trail, ten or fifteen minutes before Frazier and Linke began their descent. They met at the last creek that the trail crosses on the way down Blood Mountain. Blankenship was concerned because of some unusual items he had found at a switchback trail that split from the main trail: a dog's leather leash, an expandable baton made by ASP, a plastic bag of dog treats, a hair barrette, and two Eddie Bauer water bottles. Blankenship recognized the baton as the one the older hiker wearing the yellow jacket had carried at his side.

"Something's not right," he said.

At the bottom of the trail, the three men put the items down and Blankenship expanded the baton to examine it. He didn't see anything to make him think it had been recently used. Two women and a boy came down about five minutes later. They told Blankenship they saw the man in the yellow coat farther up the trail, but off into the woods. They agreed to show Blankenship where they had seen the man. It was about fifty feet from where Blankenship had found the baton and other items.

The three hikers left to drop the items Blankenship had found off at a store on Neel's Gap, while he, still feeling that something was wrong, decided to walk back up the trail and look around. He met Frazier and Linke again and asked about the older hiker. Both saw him and remembered him well because he had such "unusual eyes." Before leaving the park, Blankenship entered the Neel's Gap Store, gave his name and telephone number to the clerk, in case the police needed it, and then went home about 4:45 P.M.

Linke told a police officer that on his way back down the trail he had heard people yelling. He had expected to come upon some playing children, but they met no one else on the trail.

By the end of the day, police had consistent descriptions of the man who might have abducted Meredith Emerson. Perhaps the best one was from Nancy Linkes. Linkes told police she saw him when coming down from the summit on Reece Trail between three and four o'clock. He passed by her before going off into the woods to take a shortcut that put him farther ahead of her on the same trail.

According to Linkes, he had a black backpack and a dog named Dandy. He wore "parachute" pants and had duct tape around each shoe. She remembered seeing something black tied to his legs.

"He had light blue eyes and he looked weathered, like he had been in the sun a lot, old and wrinkly," she said. "He had very large, deep-set eyes, and was creepy-looking. The dog wasn't on a leash. He was saying how disgusted he was with how people came on the trail [and] were not prepared. They could get hurt easily, and he said I should have a sleeping bag with me. . . . When he went off the trail, the man complained about some hikers wearing shorts, and he was angry because they could step off the road and get hypothermia in minutes."

Jason Hill, who was hiking with his wife and little girl, saw the man on Blood Mountain and "he gave me the creeps. He was mumbling something and kept looking at my little girl at the very peak of the mountain. I thought the man was crazy. He was leering at women and would not look at me. He just looked at little girls and women. He was a freak."

That night, while Hilton was frantically deciding his next move, two specially trained police teams were still searching trails on Blood Mountain. Hilton was getting ever more tired and jittery and "felt the demons descending" on him. With each second that passed, the situation became more perilous for Meredith Emerson.

Chapter 4

Less than three months before Meredith Emerson went missing on January 1, 2008, two gruesome murders had occurred in Florida and in North Carolina. Another North Carolina hiker was missing and presumed dead. None of the police organizations in the different locations knew about the others, and none had a suspect.

The first to go missing were John Bryant and his wife, Irene, who hiked rigorous trails in North Carolina when many of their contemporaries were content to settle down and take things easy. John was seventy-nine years old and in robust health, except for painful arthritis in his back, which he refused to let change his activities. Irene, his wife for fifty-eight years, was a fascinating former veterinarian of eighty-four, with sparkle, verve, and insatiable curiosity.

They were both born in the Pacific Northwest and lived in Montana. Irene and John met there. Since they were both avid outdoors people, their dates were often hikes in the mountains. The first member of her family to attend college, Irene earned a doctorate from Washington State University (WSU) in veterinary medicine. She opened a clinic for large animals. Irene was the first female large-animal veterinarian in Montana, crashing the glass ceiling before most people had a name for it.

After a few years in Montana, the Bryants moved to the Finger Lakes district in Upstate New York, one of the most scenic areas in the Northeast. John was an engineer who worked on the Saint Lawrence Seaway while he earned a law degree at Cornell. After he passed the bar, he opened a practice in Syracuse. He served as the town attorney for Skaneateles, population 7,500, where they lived. He always underbilled for his services. Colleagues urged him to charge more. He told them that some people serve as volunteer firemen; this was his way of giving back to his community. Irene owned a large-animal clinic in New York, but she closed it to become a full-time mother to her daughter, Holly, and two sons. A woman with insatiable curiosity, Irene also took graduate courses in such things as psychology, forestry, and ichthyology.

The Bryants never lost their thirst for adventure and visiting new places. They traveled all over the United States and to various places around the world. They sent friends Christmas cards from their world travels, usually featuring photos of them posing in their hiking gear on the summit of a mountain. When they decided to retire, they still felt the call of the wild and moved to Horse Shoe, North Carolina, a small town near Pisgah National Forest, a place of steep climbs, wild rivers, and a variety of deciduous and coniferous trees. Wildlife was abundant.

Doctors told John that he should cut back on hiking because of the arthritis in his back, but John had other ideas. Hiking was his life. Instead of giving up, he took two years and conquered the Appalachian Trail in successive hikes; each one lasted about a week.

During retirement they hiked two or three times a week in Pisgah Forest, often choosing trails that were too difficult for inexperienced hikers to tackle. They roamed among the four-thousand-foot mountains, which were as colorful as a Claude Monet painting. The couple still enjoyed traveling and kept two full bags packed so they could take off at a moment's notice—should they find a special rate on a trip they couldn't resist.

On October 21, 2007, they decided to go for a hike in Pisgah Forest. They told friends and family and said they would call regularly so everyone would know they were fine. But something terrible happened near the Cradle of Forestry and Pink Beds in Transylvania County, near Brevard, North Carolina. There was a 911 emergency call from their cell phone, and it was abruptly disconnected. The call never reached the emergency dispatch office. No one even knew about the telephone call at the time, because there was no reason for anyone to worry about the Bryants, who were careful and experienced hikers.

And then the newspapers started to pile up in front of their house. Neighbors watched with growing alarm and telephoned Bob Bryant, their son, who lived in Austin, Texas. Bob telephoned his mother's sister, who usually talked with his mother once a week, and she had not heard from Irene Bryant, either. Bob caught the first flight he could from Austin and broke into his parents' locked house. Nothing seemed to be out of place, but the hiking gear was gone. Bob Bryant telephoned the Forsyth County Sheriff's Office (FCSO) and reported that his parents had not been seen in two weeks.

The sheriff's deputies found the Bryants' vehicle at a trailhead in Pisgah Forest, and a massive search was started. As is standard operating procedure (SOP) today, the area was divided into grids and marked by GPS. Hundreds of trained search-and-rescue people and volunteers combed the trails. Aircraft with spotters and infrared heat sensors streaked across the park looking for live or deceased bodies. Although unlikely, people clung to the hope that the Bryants had merely gotten lost.

That hope vanished on the second day of the search. Deputies discovered that Irene and John Bryant's ATM card had been used to withdraw three hundred dollars from their account at a People's Bank ATM at Five Points Drive in Ducktown, Tennessee. The bank's security camera showed a man in a yellow jacket, with the hood up to obscure his face, making the withdrawal. The jacket had black elbow patches and wide black stripes. Bob Bryant thought that the parka looked like one his father owned.

The unauthorized use of the Bryants' ATM card made it clear that this was more than a case of missing hikers. Sheriff David Mahoney assumed foul play and feared for the lives of the elderly couple.

On November 9, 2007, Mahoney's misgivings proved to be right. Irene's skeletal remains were found beneath a covering of branches and leaves. The remains were forty-six yards from their Ford Escape, on Yellow Gap Road.

Irene Bryant died from blunt trauma to the head and had defensive wounds on her right arm. There were three fractures on the right side of her face, and a massive fracture at the back of her head that crushed the skull. There were several fractures on her right arm, probably received when she tried to protect herself, and the right arm was severed and found several feet from the body. There was no sign of her husband; alarming fear mounted for his safety.

The Bryants' son Bob couldn't understand why a robbery had turned into a murder. At their age, he said, his parents posed no physical threat. Had they been confronted by someone who merely wanted money, Bob Bryant said, his parents would simply have handed over their wallets and money. Neither of them would have resisted, he said, unless one, or both of them, had been assaulted.

Mahoney called off the search for missing hikers and sent the volunteers home. This was clearly a homicide—maybe a double homicide—or possibly one homicide and one kidnapping, with assault and bodily harm. The search for John Bryant and his wife's killer would be continued by professionals. The Transylvania County Sheriff's Office (TCSO), North Carolina State Bureau of Investigation (NCSBI), and the Polk County Sheriff's Office (PCSO) searched for several more weeks without finding Bryant, alive or dead. There was little hope that he would be found alive. Bob Bryant was asked how he felt when he saw the picture of the man in the yellow parka. "I'm not consumed with hatred or anything like that. I want to find my dad, and I want law enforcement to find these people and give them a fair trial."

A newspaper delivery driver in Ducktown told the police that she saw a balding, bearded man in a yellow coat with black patches driving a white Astro van at about the same time that the card was used. In the area, during that same time, several people reported seeing a balding, bearded, scruffy-looking man, about sixty years old, weighing 160 pounds.

On October 26, 2007, Cherokee County deputy Will Ballard drove to a private hunting preserve to answer a complaint about an unauthorized camper. The hunting preserve is in northwestern Georgia, about seventy miles from Ducktown, Tennessee, where someone had used the Bryants' ATM card to withdraw three hundred dollars. Ballard's dashboard video/audio recorder was operating when he found the trespasser: a bald, weathered man about sixty years old, weighing about 160 pounds. He met Ballard in front of the deputy's car so that much of their twenty-minute conversation was recorded by the video/audio dashboard device. The man was talkative and animated, sometimes almost jumping in circles as he talked. He had blue eyes and no front teeth.

"Howdy, Deputy," he said. "How are you today?"

"Can I get your ID real quick?" Ballard asked.

"Yes, you sure can."

Ballard entered the information into his computer to search for outstanding warrants or BOLOs (be on the lookout for) and continued talking to the trespasser.

"You got any weapons on you? Anything in the van?"

"Oh, just the usual stuff." The deputy made a move toward the van, but the man hopped ahead of him. "Oh," he said, as if just remembering, "there's a backpack with an expandable police baton in it. I don't want you to get nervous. I'll get it for you."

He hurried to the van and retrieved the backpack and hopped back to the deputy. They were out of the dashboard video's range, but the audio was recorded.

"I was a paratrooper," the man said. "What I'm doing now is I'm on perpetual professional field maneuvers. You never know who or what you're gonna meet up here."

Ballard found no outstanding warrants on the man and told him he should leave.

"It's the first day of hunting season," Ballard said. "You should leave before you get shot."

"I'm leaving. I'm getting out of here!" the trespasser howled, flapping his arms. "God Almighty!"

"Have a nice day," Ballard said as he drove away.

"I love you!"

"Take care and be safe, Mr. Hilton," the deputy replied.

Ballard had just talked with Gary Hilton in northwestern Georgia, a day after a man fitting Hilton's description had used the Bryants' ATM card in Ducktown, Tennessee, about fifty miles away. In spite of an intense search, the police could not find John Bryant's body and had no suspect for the murder of Irene Bryant.

On December 1, 2007, Cheryl Dunlap left her house in Crawfordville, Florida, to take advantage of the one free day each week that she had to herself. Dunlap telephoned a friend about nine in the morning to say that she was going to the public library in Medart, just a few miles away. Crawfordville is in Wakulla County, a sparsely populated area that is a bedroom community for suburbanites who work in the state capital of Tallahassee, located about twenty miles farther north. The town is some three hundred miles south of Blood Mountain, from where Meredith Emerson would be kidnapped. The terrain in that area of Florida is heavily wooded and encompasses several parks, some of which bump shoulders with the Appalachian Trail.

Cheryl Dunlap was a healer, not just of the body, but of the spirit. Her long hours were not from obligation but from personal commitment. A registered nurse, Dunlap worked at Thagard Student Health Center at Florida State University (FSU), and was considered one of the best. According to the logbooks, she often saw patients right up to the last minutes of her shift.

Dunlap was the mother of two sons, Mike and Jake, and had been divorced from their father since they were little boys. Mike lived in Crawfordville and Jake was serving with the U.S. Army in Iraq. The other passion in Dunlap's life was her faith. She lived in Crawfordville all of her life and was a sixth-generation member of the White Church Primitive Baptist, a church with a congregation of a little more than sixty members. Jake won an award there for attending Sunday school every week for seven years. The church had a small congregation, but they were an active group of hardy souls.

They pitched in to help one another remodel homes; and even though it was small, the church had outreach programs and performed missionary work in foreign lands. Besides being a full-time single mother and nurse, Dunlap sang in the choir and taught Sunday school and Bible school. Dunlap was so passionate about her faith that she even made time to attend and graduate from the FIRE School of Ministry in Pensacola. Following graduation she made several trips to China and South America as a missionary, who worked in medicine and spread the Gospel.

When Hurricane Ivan threatened the central Alabama Gulf Coast in September 2004 with 165-miles-per-hour winds and lashing rain, more than two hundred thousand people in the area fled their homes in Florida and Alabama as the fifth strongest hurricane ever to develop in the Gulf Basin came closer. In spite of a slight weakening, Ivan was still a Category 3 hurricane, with sustained winds of 125 miles per hour, when the storm struck the Alabama and Florida coasts.

This killer storm produced a storm surge as high as ten to fifteen feet from Destin, in the Florida Panhandle, westward to Mobile Bay/Baldwin County in Alabama. One wave, which was measured by the buoy from the National Oceanic and Atmospheric Administration (NOAA), reached the monster height of fifty-two feet in the Gulf of Mexico, off the coast of Mobile, Alabama.

The storm caused catastrophic damage and loss of life from Florida through Nova Scotia. The worst damage was along the Alabama and Florida coasts with wind and water sweeping away buildings, ripping up trees, and even knocking down a huge section of a bridge on Interstate 10. Thousands were injured and left homeless without fresh water, utilities, medical aid, communications, and food.

Dunlap was one of the first to volunteer and spent several weeks in the most needful areas dispensing medical aid and spiritual comfort. It was a job for which she had unique qualifications. Dunlap was an important member of the River of Life Church. Everyone at the small church knew her.

The children whom Dunlap taught in Sunday and Bible school referred to her fondly as "Ms. Cheryl." It was surprising when Dunlap didn't appear on Saturday at the public library in Medart, where she usually went. Although a registered nurse with a good salary, Dunlap lived modestly and didn't have an Internet connection at her apartment. Surprise elevated to a mood of shock for the congregation at the River of Life Church when Dunlap didn't show up to teach her Bible studies class on Sunday morning. This type of behavior was totally out of character for her. She would never miss a class without making arrangements for a substitute and letting people know ahead of time. On Monday morning Dunlap didn't show up for work at Thagard Student Health Center.

Dunlap's friends and family began to worry when she missed Sunday-school class and were downright frightened when no one heard from her on Monday morning. Laura Walker, one of Dunlap's closest friends, didn't stand idly by. She drove past Dunlap's house on Monday morning and saw that her friend's Chihuahua was in the apartment. Alarm bells went off in her head: *Cheryl never goes anywhere without her dog. She certainly wouldn't leave it alone for so long.*

Walker considered going into the apartment, but she was afraid she might disturb evidence if the police were needed. Instead, she called the Wakulla County Sheriff's Department and advised them of the situation. "We talk pretty much every day," Walker told the police. "Even when she was away from her cell or home phone, she still called once a day to tell me she would be out and that she wouldn't have a phone for several hours."

Walker told Deputy Tim Ganey, of the Wakulla County Sheriff's Office (WCSO), that Dunlap had told her that someone broke into her apartment about a year ago. Walker said that the intruder stole Dunlap's underwear from the dresser drawers and "messed up" the bedsheets. Dunlap didn't report the incident, according to Walker.

Ganey talked with Dunlap's supervisor at Thagard and was told that it was unusual for Dunlap to miss work or not let anyone know where she was. "She calls if she's going to be a minute late," Ganey was told. The deputy issued a BOLO for Dunlap as her friends mobilized, telephoning anyone they could think of to alert them that Dunlap might be missing. They came up dry. The BOLO read:

Cheryl Hodges Dunlap, 46, of Crawfordville is described as 5'4", brown eyes, and brown hair.

Ms. Dunlap is a Sunday school teacher and did not show up for her bible class, which is very unusual. She is also a state employee and didn't show up for work this morning.

Just minutes after the BOLO went out, Dunlap's 2006 white Toyota was found abandoned in Leon County, just north of the Leon/Wakulla County boundary line. Highway 319, where the car was found, was a dark, isolated, two-lane road through a wild, forested area. There was no sign that a struggle had taken place where the car was found. Dunlap's purse was still in the car, but her wallet, which contained cash, identification, and credit cards, was missing. CSI taped off the crime scene and looked over the car, inside and out, checking for DNA, fibers, and anything else that might give them a clue as to what had happened. Dunlap was nowhere to be found.

The right rear tire was flat, with a puncture on the belt line about an inch and a half wide. CSI saw no indication that the car had been out of control when it pulled off the road. The way it was abandoned, closer to the forest than to the road's shoulder, was suspicious. There were no skid marks. One theory was that Dunlap had a flat tire, pulled over, and was abducted when she got out to fix it or to seek help. Major Morris Langston said police weren't sure: Dunlap could have been abducted elsewhere, and her car driven away and abandoned afterward.

The sheriff's office added an upgrade to its BOLO: *Authorities are processing the vehicle and Ms. Dunlap is considered a missing person.* Within an hour Dunlap's face was listed on dozens of "Missing Person" sites on the Internet, along with her description and where she was last seen. Diverse groups, such as the Texas Equusearch, were on the lookout, as were police officers throughout the nation.

In Wakulla and Leon Counties, scores of people mobilized, many from nearby cities, and began the same type of intensive search procedures that were being conducted in Pisgah Forest in North Carolina and in Georgia's Dawson Forest. Trey Morrison, Pat Smith, and Anthony Curles, members of the WCSO dive team, used underwater remotely operated vehicles (ROVs) to explore the murky waters of dozens of lakes and ponds in Florida as they looked for evidence. In addition to the "Video Rays," as the ROVs are called, the deputies also donned diving gear and searched. The small town of Crawfordville could talk about little else except—as one of her former Bible-school students put it—"Who in the world would want to hurt Ms. Cheryl?"

"I have been racking my brain to try to think of anything that was out of kilter for her," Laura Walker told

Wakulla County deputies. "I talked to her Friday. She was sweet, generous, and had no enemies. I can't think of anyone who would want to hurt her."

Dogs trained to find both the living and the dead searched hundreds of acres, and Leon County deputies and firefighters joined their counterparts in Wakulla County to comb the area. Even the Wakulla County Commission members, bank presidents, and the clerk of court joined in the search. They found no blood, no body, and not even field testing showed fingerprints on Dunlap's abandoned car. Air searches with spotters and infrared sensors found no sign of the missing nurse and missionary.

Members of the River of Life turned to God in prayer meetings; the fact that no body had been found kept them optimistic. Judy Brown noted that everyone was hoping and believed that Dunlap would be found alive. That hope suffered a severe setback when, on the fourth day of the search, deputies discovered that Dunlap's ATM card had been used at the Hancock Bank on West Tennessee Street on three consecutive days, starting on December 2. The bank's surveillance camera showed a man in a bizarre mask that appeared to be homemade, wearing a knit cap and thick goggles, making the withdrawals. He wore a long-sleeved shirt and gloves. Every square inch of his body was covered during the times he used the ATM card.

"The video isn't very telling," said Major Mike Wood, of the Leon County Sheriff's Office (LCSO). "The person that used it went to great lengths to disguise himself."

Hoping the man might return to the ATM again, the police established a weeklong stakeout to watch for him, starting the next week, but the man never returned. From the time Dunlap was reported missing, tips from people began to flood the Wakulla County and Leon County Sheriff's Offices.

Sandy Goff told deputies that she and her teenage

daughter met a man who fit Gary Hilton's description in a Laundromat at Crawfordville the first or second week in December 2007. The man drove a white Astro van, which she said was "junky" on the inside "because it had a lot of stuff in it." Goff reported seeing a rolled-up sleeping bag and yellow rope in the van. Accompanying the man was a large red dog. She thought it was odd that he didn't bring all of his laundry in at once, but rather carried in armloads at a time. He waited inside his van until the laundry needed tending.

"When he looked at you, it was a strange look," she told a Leon County deputy. "He just stared. He just wasn't acting like a normal person. It was just a weird vibe. He was giving me the creeps."

Hilton sometimes referred to himself as a parson, as well as a survivalist, Vietnam War veteran (he wasn't), and often attended church services while on his "maneuvers." In late November 2007, Delbert Redditt, pastor of the First Baptist Church of Madison, Florida, saw a stranger enter the sanctuary during services. The man was balding, with a fringe of gray hair, and looked disheveled. Redditt thought the man acted "kind of weird." Following the service, a member of the congregation prepared a meal for the man from food left over from the church's Saturday dinner. Redditt and several members of the congregation later identified the man as Gary Hilton.

There's no doubt that Hilton was in Leon County for several weeks in late November 2007 until sometime in mid to late December. On November 17, Mary King, a federal law enforcement officer, noticed a dirty white Chevrolet Astro parked not far from Moore Lake, in the Apalachicola National Forest. There was no one present. King ran a check on the van's license plate—Georgia AFQ1310—and discovered that the vehicle was registered to Gary Hilton, and its tag had expired five days earlier.

King found expired warrants issued by a Miami judge on Hilton for receiving stolen goods in 1972, as well as arson. She made marginal notes regarding warrants against Hilton in Miami for driving under the influence (DUI), and also cited: *arson, pistol without license, battery.* The warrants had been dismissed as part of a routine cleansing of old files. The report also showed that Hilton had a chauffeur's license revoked.

Hilton arrived after King had checked his record. She told him that she was just checking to make sure things were okay. Since there were no outstanding warrants on Hilton, King let him go after warning him not to violate the preserve's fourteen-day camping limit.

Two other forest rangers saw Hilton in the area, but the heavily redacted statements released by the police obscure the date. From the contents of the statements, it appears they saw him within days after his encounter with King. Ranger John Smathers reported that he saw a man fitting Hilton's description in the Apalachicola National Forest near a DUI checkpoint he had set up at the intersection of Dog Lake Tower and Silver Lake Road.

Smathers wrote that it was almost sunset, when he saw a man in a blue jogging suit with leg warmers on the outside of the lower pants. The man wore a cap pushed back on his head, so Smathers could tell he was bald. His body was thin and wiry, and he seemed to be approximately fifty-five to sixty years of age. The man was using poles to help propel him along the trail. He seemed to be speed walking. An unleashed dog, which seemed to be a reddish brown retriever mix, trotted with him. As the man drew closer to Smathers, the hiker leashed the dog. Smathers noticed that the man was also wearing a large black backpack. When the hiker was just twenty feet in front of Smathers, the officer asked him how he was doing. The man quickly explained that he had just been checked by a female officer before he left his campsite. Smathers asked if he just liked to walk. "I do this every day like a military hike," the man told him. Smathers said good-bye and told him to be careful because people were driving fast. The speed walker assured him that he would take care.

Ranger James D. Ellis saw Hilton as well—this time in the Osceola District of the Apalachicola Wildlife Preserve. Ellis found him in a remote part of the forest, west of Forest Service Road 212 and south of the Forest Service work center. Hilton had driven down a closed road and set up camp in an unauthorized area.

Hilton was surprised when the ranger approached. "How did you find me in this location?" he asked.

"I followed your tire signs."

"I like long-distance hiking," Hilton said, "but if you come to a WMA, you're going to get patted down." (WMA was shorthand for a Wildlife Management Area.)

The comment made no sense to Ellis and he asked Hilton what he meant.

"You can drive around town all day long but if you come to a WMA, you are going to get patted down."

Ellis told Hilton that he could only camp in designated areas and that he couldn't drive on roads that weren't designated by signs. Then he asked to see Hilton's driver's license. Hilton fumbled through his wallet, having trouble finding it; but when Ellis offered to help, he found the license right away. (The ranger's report has a heavily blacked-out redaction.) Hilton's driver's license had expired, and he had been cited for driving on closed roads and camping in unauthorized places. Ellis told Hilton he had to go back to Georgia and get his license renewed.

"I'm going to be driving back this way, and if I see you, I will issue you a one-hundred-seventy-five-dollar citation for your expired license and another one-hundred-seventy-five-dollar citation for driving with an expired license tag," Ellis told him.

Hilton continued talking and asked about various areas of Apalachicola Forest in Florida.

"You don't need to go to any national forest areas," Ellis told him. "You need to go back to Georgia and take care of your driver's license."

On December 15, William Kemp and Donald Trussell, employed by the Florida Fish and Wildlife Conservation Commission, were on patrol in the Apalachicola Forest, when Kemp received a call from the area command center. A group of hunters had found a dead body in the forest; Kemp and Trussell were directed to go there.

It was about eleven in the morning when the two wildlife officials met the hunters at Forest Road 381 and 381E. The hunters said the body was in the woods.

"Do you want us to show you where it is?" one hunter asked.

The officials followed the hunters as they drove a short distance into the woods and stopped. The hunters led the wildlife employees along the side of the road until they came to a pile of palmetto branches and leaves. That's when Kemp saw the body.

Approaching the scene, I observed, (HEAVILY INKED OUT) *was also vegetation type debris that appeared to be piled on top of the body,* Kemp wrote.

He and Trussell returned to Forest Road 381 to escort Sergeant Steve Norville and Deputy Alan Shepard, with the LCSO to the body, and then left. The crime scene was actually about a mile from where other responding units had stopped. The CSI from the LCSO taped off the crime scene; and with the help of CSI forensic experts from the Florida Department of Law Enforcement (FDLE), they began the tedious and time-consuming task of testing for even the most minute shred of evidence.

It didn't take an expert to tell that the woman was dead, but it was not so easy to identify her. Somebody had cut off her head.

Rumors, fueled by fear and horror, began to speed around Leon and Wakulla Counties. Some said that there was at least one serial killer, perhaps two, in the area on a murderous rampage, killing and dismembering women. Hundreds of women signed up and completed safety courses sponsored by LCSO. Compared to the previous six months, applications to carry concealed firearms increased by about one hundred.

Larry Campbell, the Leon County sheriff, held a press conference to dispel some of the rumors. It wasn't true that there were several killers on the loose. The police were following up on every lead, he said, and people should be cautious, but not frightened.

It was true that the police had no idea who had killed the woman believed to be Cheryl Dunlap.

The small communities were gripped by terror.

Chapter 5

Special Agent Clay Bridges, of the Georgia Bureau of Investigation, didn't know that a search was under way for a missing hiker in Vogel Forest until he received a telephone call at his district office in Cleveland from the Leon County Sheriff's Office on Wednesday afternoon, January 2. The LCSO deputy told him they needed help with the search.

"We think there's foul play involved," the deputy said.

"What makes you think that?"

"Because we found a police-style baton, water bottles, and a dog leash beside the trail. Someone else found it and turned it in. We have to suspend operations now because it's dark and there's snow falling."

Bridges told the deputy that he would be there as soon as possible. The agent wanted to have a meeting that night, but there were conflicts in timing. Bridges went to a breakfast meeting the first thing on Thursday morning. He explained the situation, picked up additional investigators, and left for Leon County.

* * *

Clay Bridges had known what he wanted to do with his life from his first memories. He wanted to be a police officer, but not just any police officer. Bridges wanted to be a special agent with the GBI, the crème de la crème of Georgia's law enforcement agencies, much as the Federal Bureau of Investigation is viewed as *the* top criminal investigative organization in the United States.

The GBI agent had not been born with a silver spoon in his mouth. Making it to the GBI had required dedication, hard work, and perseverance—all qualities that would serve him well if he ever managed to become a law officer. Bridges was hired as a rookie in 1991 by the Clarksville Police Department (CPD) and was recruited a short time later by the larger Gainesville Police Department (GPD).

Clarksville wanted him back again in 1995 and offered Bridges the job of chief of police for the seven-member force. Bridges had not given up on joining the GBI and told the city council that he would take the job with the understanding that he would continue his college studies and try to get hired by the GBI when he received his undergraduate degree.

"They were nice enough to do that," Bridges said. "I became a chief of police at age twenty-six. The council worked around it."

Bridge's life-long dream came true in 1999 when he graduated from college and was sworn in as a special agent with the GBI. Originally, the GBI put him to work in hard drug enforcement. He was undercover for the first two years before being assigned to a unit that concentrated on breaking large drug-smuggling operations. Bridges was transferred to the regional office in 2005 and had investigated about twenty homicides by the time he arrived to help find Meredith Emerson.

* * *

Arriving at the mobile command headquarters, Special Agent Bridges found good and bad news. The bad news was that the corrections officer who had found the baton did not wait longer to report it, or perhaps did not wait longer before he left. The abductor (police officers still didn't know his or her identity) had waited until after dark to bring Emerson to his van. During that time she had been secured to a tree just minutes away from help. There was no one to see Hilton drive away, and precious hours tracking him had been lost.

On the positive side, though, leads and tips were coming in by the hundreds. Special Agent Bridges credited Meredith Emerson's roommate, Julia Karrenbauer, for using her knowledge of public relations for getting the media involved on a large scale.

"She had reached out and talked to all kinds of media and notified them that her roommate was missing, and she got them mobilized," Bridges said. "That, in itself, was a good thing for us. She had already put out pictures and had people looking for her. Several groups were already searching when we arrived."

The media kept coming from throughout all of Georgia, until the entrance to Vogel Park bristled with television satellites and transmitting radio towers, as well as reporters from all around the country. Emerson's picture, description of her possible abductor, and other information soon found its way all across the United States. And more media units continued to arrive. Tips were coming in from people located as far away as California, who thought they had seen Emerson.

A psychic from New Orleans advised that the girl was in a culvert under a bridge. She was cold. She had hurt the man. The man had hurt her. She heard the searchers, but they couldn't hear her. She possibly broke the man's leg. The dog was not with her. She was possibly *harmed*.

Another tip came from a woman on Interstate 95 driving from Richmond, Virginia, to Washington, DC. Along the way she stopped at a gasoline station. There was a man in a white van. He was dressed in black and with a black dog. It looked like a bed had been built in the back of the van.

He got out, and the dog got out. He let it go pee, and then he put the dog back in the van. The dog seemed to be hyper. There was a possible spot of white on one paw. There may have been another dog in the van. It might have been an English pointer. The man was about the same size as the one described on TV.

There were also helpful communications from people who wanted to donate helicopters and other equipment to aid in the search.

Regardless of how trivial the tip might seem, none could be disregarded. They had to be written down and put in some kind of order. Bridges's first order of business was to establish what the GBI called a leads management system (LMS). The purpose of LMS was to filter through the leads and assign them priority. Bridges would decide how important the leads were and assign them to field agents to be checked out.

"There was already a lot of media there," Bridges said. "Once we got there and established a tip line and released it to the media, the leads started to flood in. There were a lot of people on the list to be checked out. We checked them out, sometimes by phone, to ask whether they had seen anything strange."

On a missing persons case, standard operating procedure called for Bridges to learn everything he could about the victim and the possible abductor. "I wanted to get to know Meredith as well as I could," Bridges said. "I wanted to know how she might react in any given situation. I wanted to learn anything at all that might help lead us to her." The same was true for the abductor, but the GBI did not yet know who that was.

As he learned about Meredith Emerson, Bridges came to know a lovely young woman with family and friends whom she adored and who returned her affection in kind. Although she was petite, Emerson was not a "girly girl," preferring to hike over rugged mountain terrain than to sit and sample high tea—although she would have been comfortable in such a social setting.

One characteristic about Meredith that people mentioned to Bridges was her burning desire to be a good person, to do good, and to make the world a better place. She often said: "I want to make a difference."

A native of South Carolina, Meredith Emerson had lived in North Carolina and Longmont, Colorado, with her parents and brother, Mark. She loved the South and its mountains and moved back to them when she enrolled in the University of Georgia to major in business. She changed her major to French literature. Emerson not only became fluent in French, but she also received the Joseph Yedlicka Scholarship for Study Abroad and earned the Cecil Wilcox Award for Excellence in French. A popular student, Emerson served as an officer for the French Honor Society (Pi Delta Phi) at the university's local chapter.

And although Emerson was fit and athletic, she was enchanted by such romantic frills as the book *Breakfast at Tiffany's* by Truman Capote. Emerson loved to read and spent many quiet hours being swept off on a sea of words to new worlds of adventure and learning. No one ever had to be at a loss as to what she would like as a gift: She would always be happy with a book. She read in English and in French. One of the books on her "wish list" was the French translation of the Harry Potter books by J. K. Rowling.

Friends described Emerson as being athletic and careful of her personal safety. She had earned a green belt and a brown belt in judo and karate, which she wore proudly around the waist of her *gi* at the dojo where she studied. Most of the students were men and they had a tendency to be gentle with the petite Emerson until she set them straight. She wanted no favoritism, no holding back. She once thanked a man for knocking the breath out of her when he threw her hard against the mat. Similarly, she gave as good as she got, and would be ecstatic when she sent a two-hundred-pound man flying over her shoulder and to the floor, or she sent him into a parallel free fall with a foot sweep.

Emerson enjoyed helping people, and she loved animals. She adopted from a shelter a mixed-breed dog, which was part Labrador retriever, and she showered the dog with love. Not wanting to be "babied" herself, she expected the dog, which she named Ella, to stay fit. No matter what the weather, Emerson and Ella took a daily walk. It could be raining buckets outside, but Emerson and Ella jogged together as they wore drenched but joyous expressions.

Emerson went out of her way to help her friends, even if she had to do things that weren't particularly appealing to her. She wasn't crazy about being photographed, but she agreed to model for a friend who was building a portfolio. Emerson had kidded that it amounted to "torture by photography." The efforts of the model and photographer resulted in a stunning display that highlighted various aspects of Emerson's personality.

There she was, in one picture, hanging upside down by her knees over a steel bar, wearing a white turtleneck and jeans, not a piece of clothing out of place. On the other hand, her long hair hung straight down, almost touching the ground. The pose accented Emerson's strength and athleticism. Although it would have been difficult for most people to maintain, the whimsical smile on Emerson's face, with her hands in her pockets, showed that the pose was a piece of cake for her.

Another photograph showed Emerson in a more glamorous, feminine light, with her long hair decorated with small, delicate beads and braids. There was a mischievous smile on her face, and her eyes were laughing. The photograph showed her with fairy wings, and the beautiful young woman looked as if she had plenty of fairy dust to share.

Brenda Porter (pseudonym) was filled with dread when her cell phone rang on January 3 and she recognized a chilling voice from the past. It was a man who terrified her, and who she had hoped would be out of her life forever.

"I'm in a fix," Gary Hilton told her. "I need some money. Can you lend me two hundred bucks?"

"No," Brenda said.

"Give me a hundred."

"The only reason I ever gave you money, Gary, was because I'm scared to death of you," Brenda told him.

"I need some gasoline. How about some money for that?"

"No, Gary. No."

Brenda hung up in a hurry but remembered to save the telephone number from where Hilton's call had originated. She trembled with fear. She lived in a wooded area and there were many nights she had spent in the house thinking, *God, he might be out in the woods right now.*

Brenda met Hilton twenty years ago when she lived in Atlanta with her mother, the manager of an apartment complex where Hilton rented a one-bedroom unit. Brenda was a star on the high-school girls' basketball team and regularly ran to stay in shape. She had noticed that Hilton ran almost every day, too. One day they struck up a conversation and started running together.

Brenda was fifteen years old and Hilton was forty-four when he persuaded her to have a sexual relationship with him. She had looked at him as a father figure and she admired his broad area of knowledge. They talked about everything, and the conversation eventually came around to sex. Hilton was in exceptionally good physical condition in those days, Brenda remembered, with taut muscles, a nice tan, "and the most beautiful blue eyes you've ever seen. He had hair and teeth then, and he could run circles around me. He really looked good."

Talking about sex increased their intimacy and she was curious about relationships between men and women. Having grown up without a father at home, Brenda found her affection toward Hilton growing. One thing led to another and she found herself having sex with him. Although he was often harsh with others, Brenda felt that he was kind to her.

"He was never mean to me and he could talk about anything," she said. "He was always reading magazines and encyclopedias."

Hilton gradually started talking to Brenda about intimate things and touching her. As a woman in her thirties, Brenda thought that Hilton took advantage of her inexperience. "I was a young girl and I was curious," she said.

"It was consensual sex in that he never hurt me. Now I know what a big deal it was to be an inexperienced teenager with a man in his forties."

Their relationship grew; and, after a time, when Hilton called, Brenda jumped. "'Hey, let's go for a five-mile run,' he would say, and I'd go right over."

Brenda never saw him pay much attention to anyone else on their excursions. He pretty much focused on her. His eyes didn't wander to other women, and he never made inappropriate comments about them. The world he encompassed during these runs seemed to be composed of nothing more than Brenda, the woods, and Ranger, the Irish setter he loved more than anything in the world.

Hilton was still living in the apartment complex when Brenda moved away to attend college in western Georgia. He called her occasionally, and over time she noticed a gradual change in his demeanor. Always a nonstop talker, Hilton started to rant at everybody and about everything. He never made much sense, and she felt incoherent vitriol flowing from him in torrents, like lava from an active volcano.

"He never threatened me, but he would go from happy to pissed off in a flash," Brenda noticed. "He just thought everybody in the world was stupid and incompetent, and that he was so much smarter than anybody else. He thought all men were faggots. He never made any direct threats to anyone, but his voice was so mean that he scared me. I told him to stop calling because I was afraid of him."

Brenda actually knew very little about Gary Hilton. He never spoke of his family life, except that he didn't like his mother because she had refused to loan him money to post bail. He had no brothers or sisters, so far as Brenda knew. Hilton was proud of having been a U.S. Army paratrooper and often performed combat demonstrations for her, advising her that "this is how the paratroopers do it." Hilton liked to brag that he had been in combat, but he confided to Brenda that he had not.

The telephone calls that Hilton made to Brenda after she left for college were not very revealing about him. They talked about the little things people do when they're catching up on news about each other. She told him about her college life, and Hilton related how he was raising money for various charities as a telemarketer. Brenda was proud of him for doing something so selfless. Of course, she didn't know that most of Hilton's telemarketing jobs were nothing more than scams: he got telephone pledges for a phony charity, had the pledges collected, and kept the money for himself. Brenda was on the college women's basketball team, and Hilton sometimes showed up to play one-on-one with her or to go for one of their power hikes.

Hilton's calls became fewer and angrier when Brenda told Hilton she had a serious boyfriend.

"He got scarier and scarier," Brenda said. "The way he talked about people was so mean and so ugly. Then he started to say mean things about me."

Hilton told Brenda that she was stupid and would never amount to anything. She was ugly and no man would ever want her. She was clumsy, silly, knew nothing about anything, and didn't know how to think analytically. The things she chose to read were worthless and a waste of time.

"He was never physically mean to me," Brenda remembered. "He was just verbally abusive. I was scared to death to be around him."

Hilton still continued to call; and like many women who suffer from battered woman syndrome (BWS), Brenda continued to take his calls, hoping things would get better. She believed she was so vulnerable because he was such a strong father figure to her. Hilton began to attack her boyfriend verbally and to make Brenda feel worthless.

"You're so stupid," he said. "He's in college with all those prettier girls around. You have to know he's fucking around on you. *La-de-da*. You're never going to amount to anything, and he's going to fuck all the pussy he can."

The only person Brenda remembered hearing Hilton speak kind words about was his second wife, Donna Coltrane (pseudonym), a former law enforcement officer at Stone Mountain Park. Hilton would praise Coltrane one minute and the next would eviscerate her with vile, cutting accusations. He didn't know why he had married the bitch. He believed she had married him because he qualified for a Veterans Administration (VA) home loan. She was a whore, who fucked anybody anytime. Oddly enough, Hilton said Coltrane had a lot of good qualities about her, but he never mentioned one specifically. He would rant for hours about her faults, but Coltrane still seemed to be the only person in the world about whom he ever said anything nice.

Following graduation from college, Brenda and Mack Porter (pseudonym) were married. She had not talked with Hilton for several months and Brenda thought that might be the end of it. But it wasn't. He telephoned her cell phone during the Christmas holidays and, on one occasion, she even met him for a hike, which she didn't tell her husband about. She insisted that it was nothing more than a hike.

About three years passed without Brenda seeing Hilton; then, one day, she was in her office building and looked up to see an unkempt, balding, almost toothless man sitting in the area that she supervised. His feet were propped on a desk and he was telling stories to three of Brenda's subordinates. Brenda was so startled at his appearance that she almost fainted. Her heart pounded. In a state of disbelief, she walked over to Hilton, looked at him closely, and asked, "Gary? Is that *you,* Gary?"

Once she got him into the privacy of an office, she looked at him closer and shivered. This man was weird and scary and had unkempt hair and a straggly beard. He had only one tooth in front. He had a maniacal look in his eyes, and he talked in an almost incomprehensible stream of disassociated thoughts. The old anger at the world had only festered with time and was now encapsulated in a thin veneer that seemed on the verge of erupting.

"I need money," Hilton said in a menacing voice.

Brenda couldn't hide a nervous tremor. She didn't recognize this man. He terrified her. He didn't look anything at all like the man she had known as Gary Hilton. She was scared to death. She summed up her courage and made her voice as firm as she could.

"Gary, I'm going to write a check and give you the money," she said. "But the only reason I'm doing it is because I'm afraid. You're acting really weird, Gary. I'm afraid of you and I don't want to talk with you again after I give you this money."

Brenda gave Hilton four hundred dollars, believing that he needed it to pay a fine after having been arrested for possession of marijuana.

"I never saw him take any other drugs, but I always knew he was a pothead," Brenda said. "He's been a pothead since I've known him."

In spite of his promise not to contact her again, Hilton had pushed his way back into her life, asking for more money. Brenda didn't know what to do. She didn't want to tell her husband about the telephone call because he had had a belly full of Gary Hilton.

About three months earlier, he was scheduled to leave his office and go on a short business trip, but he returned home a few hours later to get something he had forgotten. There was a familiar red Irish setter chained to a stake in the yard.

"Where's the owner of that dog?" he asked.

"I'm just keeping it for a friend," Brenda said.

"I know whose dog that is," Mack said. "He damn well better be gone when I get back."

Brenda saw no way out of the mess she was in now. She was afraid of Hilton and worried about her husband's reaction when he learned she had loaned Hilton four hundred dollars.

Hilton's current call could endanger her marriage. Mack had told Hilton to "leave my wife alone" four months ago. Brenda couldn't stop thinking about the situation all day. Brenda thought of Hilton possibly hiding in the dark woods at her house and trembled. She felt dazed by the danger she had placed her marriage in—all because she was too terrified of Gary Hilton.

When he came home from work, Brenda took a deep breath and told her husband about the telephone call.

"You've got to call the police," he said. "He's a wanted man now. You can't fool around."

"I know. I'm scared."

"Make the call. You might save that girl's life."

Brenda wrote down the number she had saved from Hilton's call and telephoned the GBI. Special Agent Clay Bridges answered the telephone.

"I know exactly who you're looking for," she said. "Gary Hilton. In fact, I just got through talking with him on the telephone."

"Do you know where he is?" Bridges almost jumped out of his chair.

"No, but I saved the telephone number."

Bridges had the number traced and discovered it designated a coin-operated telephone in Cumming.

"We have a patrol in that area," he told Brenda. "We're dispatching them now. Please stay on the line."

Two GBI agents received the assignment and started racing in silent mode toward the convenience store from where Hilton's call had originated. Less than half an hour later, they arrived at the telephone. No one was using the telephone, and there was no white van in the parking lot. They described Hilton and asked the clerk if he had been there.

"He was," the clerk said. "You just missed him. He left about fifteen minutes ago."

It was frustrating to have come so close to catching Hilton and to miss. The police didn't know if Meredith Emerson was still alive at this point, but everyone hoped and prayed that she was. There was no time to mull it over as the search for Emerson switched into the highest gear possible. At the command center, Bridges had also received telephone calls from three others who knew Hilton: a former wife, a former employer, and a former friend.

It was just January 3 and Bridges had established the GBI's LMS that morning. Police officers, however, had begun gathering information since Emerson was reported missing on January 2. As searches go, things were moving along at lightning speed.

"As soon as we established a tip line with the media, the calls started to pour in from people who were on Blood Mountain on New Year's Day," Bridges said. "A lot of calls started coming in about a strange individual named Gary Hilton. They said they had seen him hanging around the parking lot, with a red Irish setter named Dandy, and that he might be driving a white van. As soon as we released this information and named him as a person of interest, it was a train wreck."

Special Agent John Cagle, who was nearing retirement from the GBI, worked around the clock, as did Special Agent Bridges and most of the law enforcement officers. They felt they were drawing the noose tighter around Hilton's neck. Their main worry was about Emerson. The chances of finding her alive and unharmed faded with each passing minute. The police believed that Hilton might try to get back in touch again with Brenda and received permission to establish stakeouts at her home and workplace.

Meanwhile, Special Agent Matthew L. Howard interviewed Brenda at her home with her husband present. Matt Howard was careful to be delicate when asking about the sexual aspect of Brenda's past relationship with Hilton. The GBI needed all of the information it could get to help catch Hilton, and his sexual preferences could illuminate his personality and help anticipate his reactions.

"It would be hard for me to talk if I was in your shoes," Howard said. "You're embarrassed. We deal with this kind of thing all of the time, and there's nothing for you to be embarrassed about. It's very important that we know everything about him—when all this started, what made him tick, did something happen that triggered this behavior? Did he ever want to do something weird?"

"Why? Is he saying that?"

"No. We're just trying to find out everything we can about him. Do you know anything about his family?"

"Only that he had a mother he didn't like. He never mentioned her name. I think he must have had a tough childhood, but he never really talked about it."

"Did he ever try to pursue a physical relationship with you? Like boyfriend, girlfriend?" Howard asked.

Brenda hesitated and Mack voluntarily left the room. Howard resumed the interview. "I'm not trying to embarrass you. These are important questions."

Brenda said she was just a kid at the time.

"Obviously, there was an age difference," Howard said. "Was he pursuing younger women at the time?"

Brenda said she didn't know. She said that her physical relationship with Hilton began when she was fifteen or sixteen.

Howard asked: "How did he pursue that? What were his actions toward you?"

Brenda hesitated a long moment.

"This is totally confidential," Howard reassured her. "When we find out what he's all about, maybe we can even solve other crimes he may have been involved in— to try and get the families some closure."

"I don't know what to tell you."

"Was it something that he forced on you, or was it consensual?" Howard asked. "How long did it last? Did he say he was interested? Did he come on to you?"

There was a long pause. "I guess it was consensual."

"If it was forced, we need to know that."

"I was a kid and I was curious."

"There's nothing wrong with that," Howard said gently. "There are things that happen in college and high school that we're not proud of. We all make mistakes. That doesn't make anybody a bad person."

Brenda said, "I look at it like I was taken advantage of."

"Did he talk you into it?"

"Yes."

"What kind of things did he say? If he was preying on children, we need to know that."

Brenda told Howard she had never known or suspected that Hilton was sexually attracted to children. She reiterated that he was like a father to her and treated her differently after their sexual relationship began. He bought things for her, gave her a new bicycle, and called her regularly on the telephone to chat, mostly about her. He was often verbally abusive, she said, but not toward her. The telephone calls dwindled away when she left for college.

"So far as physical abuse, he never put a hand on me," she said.

Howard pursued the sexual aspect of the relationship further. Brenda's husband had come back into the room. Howard asked if there was anything involved in the sexual relationship besides sex, anything unusual. "What kinds of things did he talk about? What happened between you?"

There was a long, uncomfortable pause and Brenda made several false starts, clearly nervous and embarrassed.

"Go ahead, honey," Mack said. "It's no big thing."

"It is, too, a big deal!" Brenda snapped.

At her request Mack left the room again.

"This isn't easy," she said.

"Take as much time as you need, ma'am. Don't think you have anything to be ashamed of."

"We had a sexual relationship."

"Did he force you to try things during intercourse?"

"Persuaded, but he didn't force. He never did anything to me. He never hurt me. God, he was forty years older than me."

"He never tied you up or made you do anything?"

"No. I always believed he loved me."

Howard asked if Hilton had stalked her. Brenda replied that she believed she saw him in the crowd at several of her college basketball games, but they didn't acknowledge one another. After college, Brenda said, she received infrequent telephone calls from Hilton, and they usually occurred around Christmas. Then a few years would pass with no contact.

Once, after five years of being out of touch, Hilton telephoned and asked Brenda to go hiking with him. She accepted his invitation, and said it was not a date, just a hike, but that she never told her husband about it. Brenda told Howard how her husband came home early and found Hilton's dog staked in the yard.

"I never had a sexual relationship with him again and he never tried," she said. "He knew all about hiking. He was very, very smart and he knew all of the trails—Blood Mountain, Lookout Mountain, Stone Mountain. . . . He had spent most of his time in the mountains."

Since the last hike, Brenda said, she had not seen him in years. "And all of a sudden he just shows up at my office," she said. "He looked very weird. I didn't even recognize him, and I don't know how he knew where my office was. He freaked me out the minute he walked in. He didn't look anything like he did. I mean he had [no] teeth."

Hilton was homeless, so far as Brenda knew. She had never asked where he lived after he left the complex that her mother managed. Brenda said Hilton complained that he had multiple sclerosis and was dying. She said that Hilton hated John Tabor because he believed Tabor had cheated him out of sales commissions.

"When did he start to talk strange?" Howard asked.

Brenda laughed. "Gary's always been a talker. He talks loud, over himself, like he's in another world. Gradually he started being mean and saying things when he was mad. Each time it was a little worse. He would say things that scared me and I was afraid to be around him."

Howard asked if she could give some specific examples, but Brenda wasn't able to do so. She explained it like this: "He would say things that scared me. I don't know.

Just the tone of his voice. He'd be mad at the world. Everybody was stupid. It wasn't like he was mean to me, but to everybody. It was more like a gut feeling that I had."

"Was there a lot of anger?"

"He thought everybody was stupid and he thought all men were faggots. He thought John Tabor was a faggot."

"He actually thought that?"

"Oh, yeah."

Howard asked what he had said about Tabor.

"That he was a crappy salesman. That he was married, but he was a faggot. He said Tabor was too good-looking not to be a faggot."

Brenda explained that before she left for college, Hilton talked so mean and hateful that she "freaked. It got to the point that I didn't even want to talk to him."

"Did he ever make direct threats about harming somebody, like John Tabor, to you?"

"No. He talked bad about people, but he never said that."

Brenda said that he had worked for years for Tabor and had been criticizing him for most of the time. His criticism would be vitriolic.

Did you ever wonder why this guy was keeping him on if Hilton hated him so much? Howard asked.

"No. It was like Gary was a bright star doing his job, and Tabor was a total fuckup who couldn't sell. That's how Gary explained it."

Brenda told Howard that Hilton and she had hiked in all of the parks in Georgia, and that Hilton was an expert who knew about the most isolated places.

"Thinking back to those past years, and knowing what you know now, did he ever say or do anything that might have made you think he would do anything like this?"

"I've really thought about that and I can't think of anything," Brenda said. "I just kind of thought he was an outcast and didn't have anything to do with anyone. When he called, he said he was telemarketing. I wouldn't want to talk to him, but I was afraid not to. He was always talking bad about people. He would never say 'I'm gonna kill them.' I would have told somebody if I had heard that."

Thinking back, Brenda changed her mind about telling Howard that Hilton had not stalked her. Now she remembered that she felt that he stalked her most of the time she was in college. She said that Hilton would show up everywhere.

"Was there anything to indicate that he might have been doing [this] with other girls?"

"No, he never discussed anybody else."

Although the change she saw in Hilton was gradual, Brenda also remembered that there *had* been an abrupt change in his behavior. She said that Hilton had "talked mean" about everybody until she got married, and then there was a "distinct" change.

"He used to be happy and then, all of a sudden, about the time I got married, whenever I talked with him, he would always be mad. I could see his mood change from happy to pissed off really fast. He never forgot it if somebody crossed him, even on small things."

To illustrate, Brenda told Howard that Hilton took every rejection personally. Should he ask someone to walk to the store with him, and that person declined, Hilton would take it as a personal rejection, Brenda said, and would explode. And he would never let it go.

"Did he ever talk about a girlfriend?"

"He used to talk about his ex-wife, the lady who worked at Stone Mountain. He said she was a good woman."

When he returned to the room, Mack said he had met Hilton several times before he and Brenda were married.

The first time was at the apartment she shared with a girlfriend in Marietta. "Brenda had told me about Hilton, an older man who was just a friend. He wouldn't look me in the eye and kept his distance. He acted strangely," Mack relayed.

Mack said that just before he and Brenda were married, he found Hilton sitting in the house that he and Brenda shared. "He jumped up real quick and asked me if I was there to install an alarm system. I told him I wasn't. I didn't want an altercation because there were other people in the house, but I led him away and told him in no uncertain terms to get out of my house."

Brenda told the GBI agent that she had never seen Hilton with a gun, but that he always carried high-powered pellet guns and carried a baseball bat and pepper spray, explaining that it was to protect him from unleashed dogs.

Special Agent Matthew Howard concluded the interview and verified that Brenda's home and workplace would be under surveillance in case Hilton returned.

Chapter 6

On the morning of January 3, 2008, John Tabor was stunned when he saw the first news report about a young woman hiker missing on Blood Mountain and the circumstances surrounding it. The man whom the hiker had been seen with sounded like a former employee, who had threatened him numerous times over the past ten or twelve years: a drifter named Gary Hilton. He read the description several times with growing alarm and trembling hands.

According to witnesses, the man had a dark red Irish setter named Danny. Hilton had a red Irish setter whose name was Dandy. The man wore a utility belt and carried an extendable police baton, a knife, a bayonet, and cans of Mace. So did Hilton. The man's physical description also matched Hilton's.

Tabor's first thought was that it was Gary Hilton, a dangerous man with a hair-trigger temper, a man who had had altercations with residents of local parks.

A day earlier, before he knew that Hilton was in any way tied to the disappearance of a young hiker in the area, Hilton had telephoned Tabor. Hilton went into one of his maniacal rants, saying that he was starving and didn't even have money to buy dry dog food. Tabor said no and hung up on him.

Tabor wondered how his good intentions—his kindness, really—had managed to turn out so bad. One reason he had hired Hilton as a telemarketer twelve years ago was that he felt sorry for the pathetic, disheveled, and eccentric man, who seemed to have hit rock bottom. Tabor's good deed quickly blew up in his face, and he and his family had lived in fear of Hilton for years. Hilton had left veiled threats on Tabor's phone for a decade and had confronted him in Tabor's own yard, always keeping an estimated thirty feet away, having calculated that, if attacked, it would give Hilton time to grab one of his weapons and launch a deadly counterattack.

Tabor thought in alarm, *That young lady's life is in danger.* He quickly called the Forsyth County Police Department (FCPD) and reported his concerns. "I'm absolutely, one hundred percent certain it's Gary Hilton," he told the unidentified deputy. "He's got a red Irish setter named Dandy and he carries the same kinds of weapons as the man described in the story. He's very dangerous. He telephoned here yesterday, begging for money and his old job back. I hung up on him."

Tabor told the deputy that he and his wife were afraid for their lives. He had moved his wife and daughter into a relative's house following Hilton's latest telephone call. Given the opportunity, Tabor said, he was certain that Hilton would try to hurt them. He told the deputy that he was sure Hilton would contact him again to demand money.

The deputy took Tabor's telephone numbers, his home and business addresses, and said a GBI special agent would contact him right away. As he waited for the GBI to contact him, Tabor recalled meeting Hilton at a residence on Clermont Road in Chamblee that he used as the business office for his siding company. Tabor needed a telemarketer to make cold calls to solicit people who might want to have their homes re-sided. He had placed an advertisement in a local newspaper about the position.

Hilton showed up to interview for the job. Tabor was startled at his appearance. Hilton wore brightly colored hiking clothes, which were dirty and wrinkled. It appeared as if he had been sleeping in them. Hilton's skin was weathered and he had an unkempt beard, just longer than stubble, and was developing male-pattern baldness. Hilton wore a utility belt and carried a bayonet, knife, and two cans of Mace around his waist, a high-powered pellet pistol jammed into his waist, and held a leash attached to the collar of a large, friendly, tail-wagging dog, with his tongue flopping through what appeared to be a toothy canine grin. Hilton had good teeth, blue eyes, and looked exceptionally fit.

"I'm Mack Hilton," the man said. "I'm here about the job you advertised in the newspaper."

"I thought it was Gary."

"That's too sissified. Just call me Mack."

Tabor was surprised that anyone would apply for a job looking the way Hilton did, but, then again, a telemarketer didn't have to make a good physical impression on a prospective customer. All he had to do was read a prepared spiel and fill in pertinent information so that a salesman could call. It really didn't matter how he looked.

Tabor learned that Hilton was living in his van at a storage facility in Atlanta and had worked for various telemarketers in the past. The storage space Hilton rented had no running water or any other amenities, but he had no complaints. Moving would not be a problem for him. He told Tabor that he was a former paratrooper in the army and had been involved in transporting tactical nuclear weapons, which were designed for battlefield use.

Tabor knew that telemarketers jumped from one job to another and that some had shady pasts. Because of this, background checks were rarely made on prospective employees. Tabor came to regret this; but, since no one was knocking down the door to apply, Tabor hired Hilton. Working on a commission basis, Tabor told Hilton his telemarketers averaged about three to four hundred dollars a month.

Hilton agreed, but had two conditions: "I can't do it unless I can bring my dog to work, and I need a lot of time to be in the mountains."

Tabor was surprised at such unconventional demands, but he felt sorry for Hilton, who reminded him of a Vietnam War veteran suffering from post-traumatic stress disorder (PTSD). They agreed and shook hands on the deal. Later on, Tabor remembered something he had heard: *No good deed goes unpunished.* Hiring Hilton proved to Tabor just how true that was.

Hilton arrived for work with his dog, which lay quietly by his desk. Hilton caused a little curiosity because of the out-of-door clothes he wore and the weaponry on his utility belt. But he proved to be charismatic, charming, and very intelligent. The women almost swooned when Hilton's blue eyes captured their gaze, and he could talk about anything. Most of the people believed that Hilton was "very intelligent, probably at the genius level," according to Tabor.

Hilton also proved to be a gifted mimic. Sometimes he sounded like Cary Grant when he made his telephone calls. At other times the voices coming from his mouth seemed to be John Wayne, Jerry Lewis, or some other Hollywood celebrity.

A woman at a desk near his asked him why he did it. Hilton shrugged and explained that it made things more interesting.

Hilton told Tabor that he was living in a storage unit with two dogs, Dandy and Ranger, another Irish setter. Hilton slept on an air mattress and sleeping bags. A step up from the storage unit he had left in Atlanta, this shed had electricity and Hilton could watch television.

Hilton stayed at the telemarketing headquarters about two hours the first day, then disappeared. He always left with the cell phone Tabor provided and some contact sheets. For the next twelve years he would come and go sporadically, sometimes staying away for months at a time. The trouble he caused snowballed over the years.

And it got worse and worse for John Tabor. Special Agents Dustin Hamby and Matt Howard arrived to interview Tabor at his home in Duluth and could hardly believe the bizarre relationship Tabor described with Hilton. Even though Hilton rarely came to work, he began to accuse Tabor of cheating him out of commissions. Tabor almost always gave in because he was convinced that Hilton would have no qualms about killing him and his family.

"He always had weapons," Tabor said. "All the time. He would wear a belt and have a police baton, two pepper spray cans, and knives and a collapsible baton that he would buy at police utility stores. He ran with his dogs in the mountains for hour and hours, days at a time. That's pretty much all he did. After a few years he started to carry high-powered pellet guns. He knows how to use a firearm. He demonstrated his marksmanship on many occasions."

Hilton also boasted to Tabor of his expertise in the use of the baton. Sometimes he would show off his fighting skills and explain his method of using that weapon. "You got to know what to do, stay back, aim low," Hilton told Tabor. "I have good luck with the knees. You don't want to go up high, for the head, because once you've done that, brother, you've raised the level of violence and someone's going to get a world of hurt."

Tabor told the agents that he didn't think Hilton owned a real gun, "but he always craved one and mourned the fact that he couldn't get one as a convicted felon." Although he didn't care for guns, Tabor had once owned a .38-caliber Colt Special and an old single-shot twelve-gauge shotgun. He said that a couple of things caused him concern.

Tabor told the agents that he kept the Colt in his truck because a lot of his work was in high-crime neighborhoods. "I didn't look at it every day to see if it was there, but one day, several years ago, it disappeared. The shotgun was stolen from the house. I imagine he stole them."

Tabor said that although the Colt was stolen several years ago, he had never reported it to the police. The gun was still registered in his name. The shotgun, he said, was stolen within the past year from the house that Tabor had used for his telemarketing operations. "He probably still had a key to the house, and I imagine he has that."

Although he had known Hilton a dozen years, Tabor said, Hilton was an "off and on" employee, sometimes staying away as long as two years. That wasn't unusual, he said, because there is rapid employee turnover in the business. Hilton would disappear and then show up again without notice.

"The last time I saw him, he came to my house about three months ago," Tabor told the agents. "During the past couple of years, he said he was sick, needed money, medicine."

In what appeared to the agents to be an odd twist in Tabor's recollection was that, in spite of problems with him, Tabor allowed Hilton to use the bathroom at the house he used for his siding operation. Tabor said he shut down the telemarketing operation in 2000 and allowed

Hilton to live in the house for most of the past five years without having to pay rent or utilities.

"He just started staying there," Tabor said. "I didn't really object because I had no other use for it at the time. There might have been a time or two that he packed up and left for a few months."

During the periods Hilton was gone, Tabor didn't specifically know where he was, but thought that he spent most of his time in the North Georgia Mountains. He didn't limit his hiking to Georgia, but camped in forests from Florida to New England. Hilton spent a year in the Rocky Mountains but returned to the Appalachians because he liked them better. The mountains in the western part of America were too stark for his taste.

"He's been all over the area in the past thirty years," Tabor said. "He would be gone for weeks, if not months, at a time. He would violate the time limits on camping in parks, but he never got in trouble with the park rangers." Sometimes Hilton would want to look over a trail map for Tabor to see where he had been, but Tabor wasn't interested in such things.

Even when Hilton was on his mysterious disappearances, he took the cell phone that Tabor provided, the contact spiel and forms to record information on solid leads for siding, and made sure that Tabor got them. Hilton regularly argued with Tabor, claiming that he was being cheated out of commissions. For his part Tabor didn't know if Hilton had made the contacts or simply filled in the forms himself, using names from the telephone book. Tabor knew that Hilton was capable of violent behavior.

"Over the years he said lots of things, but they went in one ear and out the other," Tabor said. "He liked to talk like a big, tough guy. He had trained himself to fight and would show me little moves he had. He told me several times that over the years he had made a list of people he wanted to kill. When he got in a condition where he couldn't work, he was going to kill his dog, kill other people on the list, and then kill himself."

Howard asked if he knew who were the people on Hilton's "kill" list.

"It was pretty much just people who had caused him grief, and almost always the same thing," Tabor answered. "Anytime he went to a public park, he couldn't go without getting into an altercation with someone. People would come up to meet his dog, just wanting to be friendly. He would tell them, 'No, you stay away. Keep away.' He would do something inappropriate to cause them to get hostile. He would spray people in the face with pepper spray. He would spray dogs. Things would escalate to where people called the police. He never got arrested because he knew police procedures so well.

"He would make the threat indirect," Tabor continued. "He would never say that he was going to kill them, but he would imply it. When the police came, he twisted everything so that the police believed *he* had been threatened and was just defending himself with the pepper spray."

In early September 2007, Hilton's anger at Tabor, who he believed had cheated him out of thousands of dollars in commissions, erupted like a volcano. Hilton had not seen Tabor in a few months because he had been on one of his extended treks into the woods. He telephoned Tabor in a rage and wanted five thousand dollars in what he said were unpaid commissions. He was so angry that Tabor could barely understand him.

"He would just shout out at me, incoherent, just crazy stuff, accusing me of cheating him out of thousands of dollars," Tabor said.

On September 9, 2007, Tabor told the GBI, he went to

Fulton County's Northeast Precinct and filed a "harassing communication problem that may lead to serious safety issues for himself and his family."

In this formal complaint Tabor said how Gary Hilton, a former employee who had become homeless, had made threatening telephone calls to him over the past two years. *The victim advised that he has received numerous phone calls trying to extort money from him,* the complaint read.

Tabor said Hilton complained that he was hungry and that he needed money to feed his dog and demanded that Tabor pay him anywhere from five hundred dollars to $25,000. Tabor remembered what Hilton said on the telephone, which he recorded.

"Do what is right," he told Tabor. "Do not think I'm afraid of you."

He told Tabor to leave a check for $25,000 at his front door and he would come by the next day, Wednesday, to pick it up. "I will never make an unlawful threat to you," he continued. "I will whup your ass. If that's a threat, so be it. I will fuck you up."

Tabor wasn't sure what to do. Reporting Hilton's actions to the police might result in nothing more than a charge involving harassing telephone calls. That would make Hilton even angrier and more dangerous than he already was.

Tabor said he had decided that the best way to get rid of Hilton was just to pay him. He wrote Hilton a check for $2,500, but he couldn't resist placing a note inside an envelope with *RANSOM* written in big red letters with a marking pen. The note Tabor included was typed in large upper case letters and showed Tabor's disgust and resentment. Tabor wrote that Hilton was a tough guy who made threats to get money that was not owed. So far as he was concerned, they were more than fair and square, with Hilton getting the better of the deal. Tabor called Hilton an unappreciative piece of garbage; and if it had not been for Tabor, Hilton would either be spending his life behind bars or six feet under the ground.

I HAVE DONE MORE FOR YOU THAN ANYONE ELSE IN YOU [*sic*] MISERABLE FUCKING LIFE, Tabor wrote.

Tabor's letter claimed that Hilton was homeless, with no means of support, and that Tabor took pity on him by employing him and taking in his dog and giving them a place to stay. Tabor noted that when Hilton's van broke down, it was he who came to his rescue and even bought him a new van. Tabor said he had paid Hilton every penny due to him and $18,000 more by Hilton's own count. Tabor said the $18,000 figure didn't even include the $70,000 Hilton received from him in the form of free rent and utilities. Who else would have done so much for him? Tabor asked Hilton.

SO FUCK YOU, Tabor concluded. *HERE IS YOUR $2,500 RANSOM.*

There was no way that Tabor had wanted to come face-to-face with Hilton. He left the envelope for him, but Hilton didn't appear to retrieve it. Tabor told the agents he believed that Hilton thought Tabor might be setting a trap for him. Tabor stayed away from the house the next day but drove to the location on September 6, at about ten o'clock at night. He saw Hilton standing on his driveway with his dog.

"I had to drive right past him in my driveway to park my vehicle," Tabor said.

According to Tabor, Hilton began heckling him, but keeping his distance. Both men held packages or a bag in front of themselves so that it was impossible for either one to tell if the other had a gun. Still facing Hilton, Tabor said, he had backed over to a different door and gone inside his house. Tabor got his Glock 17 nine-millimeter handgun and went out the front door to confront Hilton. When Hilton saw the Glock, Tabor said, he ran to the end of the cul-de-sac and then disappeared into the woods. Tabor said he assumed Hilton had parked his van there.

After Hilton left, Tabor saw that he had ripped the check to shreds and left it, along with the note Tabor had written. Tabor believed that he had done nothing more than stoke the rage inside of Hilton and was very much afraid for his wife and five-year-old daughter, who were in the house the night Hilton confronted him. He had reported the incident to the Forsyth County Sheriff's Office the next day.

The GBI special agents had already seen the complaint that Tabor had filed. He had told the deputy that his wife and daughter had arrived approximately twenty minutes before he did and didn't see Hilton on the property.

According to the police report, Tabor said that Hilton must have hidden in the woods behind his house and didn't step back on his property until his wife and children went into the house. Hilton wore camping clothes and a webbed belt around his waist, and attached to the belt were an ASP baton and cans of pepper spray. Tabor said that he owned a house in Chamblee and that Hilton might be using it to make camp with his van. According to the report, Hilton had lived in the residence during the time he worked for Tabor, and Tabor believed that he might have retained keys to the house. Tabor was told to save all of his telephone messages.

Victim advised that his wife and he are afraid of what the offender might do next, the report read. Tabor said he would send his family to stay with relatives in Lawrenceville, but he would remain at the house.

Even as Tabor filed the complaint at the police station, Hilton called and yelled at him over the telephone in such a rage that he was incomprehensible. When Tabor told the GBI agents that he had been paying for the telephone that Hilton used then—and over the past few years—they could hardly believe it. Tabor explained that he kept Hilton on as a "consultant" after he closed the siding business and let him keep the telephone. He said it would be a way for him to keep track of Hilton by getting a bill showing from where calls on the telephone were made. Unfortunately, he could only track Hilton after receiving a bill, not in real time when the calls were made.

Hilton called him again on January 3 and demanded money again. This time he claimed that Tabor owed him $10,000 and went into another rant, and warned him not to try and set a trap for him with the police. Tabor played a portion of the conversation, which was recorded on his voice mail for the GBI agents.

"Don't do anything stupid," Hilton said. "If the heat's on me, I'll know where it came from, and I know where the hammer will fall."

Tabor told the GBI that he had been afraid of Hilton since January 2007. "He started to say he had multiple sclerosis and couldn't work," Tabor said. "He started to say he had MS without ever getting a clinical diagnosis. I only talked with him a couple of times a week. He found someone who prescribed Ritalin and something else that he injected into his leg."

When Tabor saw Hilton in September, he said there was a marked change in him both physically and mentally. "He'd speak so fast you could hardly tell what he was saying," Tabor told the GBI. "You could tell he was really juiced up. He was taking more than one hundred milligrams of Ritalin a day. He smoked pot."

Tabor noted that Hilton's appearance had also changed. His eyes were wild, he was scruffier, and he had lost his front teeth. "He told me that he pulled some of them himself with a pair of pliers," Tabor said. "He became increasingly odd."

Howard asked Tabor if he and Hilton ever had any "guy talk" about women, and Tabor said no and that he had only seen Hilton with Brenda Porter a few times. "He had a general loathing of women, particularly lesbians," Tabor said. "He thought they were the meanest people on earth. But he had been married several times for short periods.

"He never looked at chicks," Tabor continued. "The only thing he seemed to have genuine affection for was his dog, Ranger. That dog was the only thing he seemed to care about. Both dogs (Ranger and Dandy) were the only things that were important to him."

When Ranger died, Tabor said, Hilton was depressed for weeks and he carried Ranger's body all the way to the other side of Big Stone Mountain. Hilton selected a site he liked, buried Ranger, and lugged fifty- to one-hundred-pound stones all day to build a monument to the dog.

That was the last question of the interview, but the GBI would find gaping holes in Tabor's answers, which would bring them back to question him once again about Gary Hilton.

Chapter 7

The devils had come to Hilton during the night, driving him half crazy with their taunts and visions of terror. There was Gary Hilton, aged four, looking at his hand and realizing that he would die and that he would someday be nothing more than a skeleton. There was death awaiting him in a pit filled with thrashing alligators as his step-father held him over it, high in the air, and threatened to drop him in.

Hilton had come back angry to the hidden campsite in Dawson Forest. He was furious with the world and with John Tabor, in particular. That Tabor had expected him to settle for $2,500 after all the thousands he had been cheated out of was beyond belief. He had worked his ass off and it wasn't his fault that Tabor was a lousy closer.

Then there was Brenda, whom he had treated like a princess, never hitting her, educating her. She was only fifteen or sixteen when they met and he had taught her so much. She had appreciated his brilliance and the practical knowledge he had accumulated by being almost thirty years older than she was. Used him up and dumped him. Now, in the time of his greatest need, she had turned her back on him over a few lousy bucks for gas money.

And there was Meredith Emerson, the woman he had abducted, the one who pulled his strings like he was a puppet. All he wanted was her damn PIN numbers so he could get some money from one of her ATM accounts. But would she help? No. All she did was run him around in circles—lying to him, when he had been so solicitous of her well-being.

Now there was this god-awful noise of a motor revving and the high whining of wheels spinning not far in the distance. Some idiot had managed to get stuck. The cold snap had broken and the dirt road was muddy as the ice and snow melted.

Hilton was parked in the woods, but Michael Andrews, the truck driver, was stuck and his tanker truck blocking the road. Hilton believed that the man had been pumping or dumping water from Shoal Creek. He started walking toward the truck.

"Got stuck," Andrews said, getting out. "Can you give me a hand?"

"No, you can get out your own self," Hilton told him. "I've got stuck lots of times and got out by myself."

Andrews noticed that the man kept his distance; and when Andrews moved, the man seemed to move into a defensive position between him and the dirty white Astro parked farther on into the woods.

"I don't know," Andrews said. "It's stuck good. The GPS said the road was open."

"I could've told you it was closed," said Hilton, who knew the road was cut off long before the GPS did. "Did you call the police for help?"

Andrews told him that he had dialed 911.

Hilton cursed, turned, and hurried back to his van. On the far side of the van, and several yards away, Emerson was tied to a tree with Ella beside her. Camping equipment was scattered around the ground.

"We got to get out of here," he said as he freed her. "This place is gonna be crawlin' with cops."

Emerson began to gather up equipment in neat stacks. She had become very compliant, thanks to his professional behavior, Hilton told himself. Now she was being too compliant.

"We ain't got time to be neat, hon," he said. "Just throw stuff in the truck so we can get out of here. There's gonna be cops any minute."

Within minutes the space had been cleaned up and Hilton went screeching out of the forest with the rear tires throwing up a rooster's tail of mud. First he had secured Emerson, and then he went flying like a bat out of hell, thinking that the old clunker might fall apart any minute.

Dawson County Sheriff's Office deputy Chester received a call from dispatch at 10:24 A.M. about a large truck broken down on Sweetwater Church Road on the dirt portion and that it was blocking the road. Dispatch connected again with the truck driver, Michael Andrews, via GPS and sent Chester the coordinates from him to type into his mapping system. The map showed that the truck was stranded on Shoal Creek Road inside Dawson Forest Wildlife Management Area, just a few feet north of the River Ford.

The deputy arrived at the stranded truck at 11:24 A.M. with Ranger Jason Robertson. The vehicle was a large white landscape truck bearing the name *Top Turf Lawn Care* on its side and was wedged between both banks of the roadway, completely blocking the road.

Robertson's GPS indicated that the road was passable, as did Chester's system. Unfortunately for Robertson, the water had risen in the creek and the narrow road was muddy. When he came to the ford, the water was so high and swift that he was afraid to cross it.

The deputy and ranger had both left the scene by eleven twenty-eight. They had missed Hilton and his captive by fifteen minutes.

Hilton drove on automatic pilot, thinking of the hardship in his life, his MS, how hard it was to get a few bucks ahead. Maybe he should give up and try a different line of work. But what had he ever done except be a professional criminal? Not much. He, among all men, knew that he could not lead an ordinary life. He had known it since he decided to go homeless and live mostly in the mountains away from people. It had dawned on him that he was a professional soldier on an eternal combat alert.

It wasn't much of a life, but what the hell, it was a life. It was *his* life.

After a while, Hilton found another secluded spot to pull over and hide the van. He led Emerson about one hundred yards into the woods and tied her to a tree. He felt that the MS made him shaky. After he chained Emerson, Hilton grabbed coffee, a cup, and the coffeepot and walked back to the far side of the van. He checked to make certain that Emerson couldn't be seen from the road, and then he made a small campfire to brew the coffee.

Being in the woods usually relaxed him, but everything seemed to be crashing around him. He reminded himself that he was a professional soldier, like one of those badass Navy SEALs who were the baddest of the badasses. He had a book about them in the van that he read and told himself he was like them, able to push himself to do ten times more than he thought he could. When he met that limit, he could force himself to withstand ten times more, again and again.

Hilton often tested himself by running through the forest, flashing through light and shadow like an old-fashioned flickering movie. Muscles burning, lungs aching, he kept running, pushing himself more and more, like a Navy SEAL. Overcoming the pain, outrunning the thrashing alligators in the pit below, running harder and harder, he was running from death. Ten years ago, he was younger and buff, and ran with his shirt off, showing off his rippling muscles beneath his mahogany tan, a smooth-operating machine that women couldn't resist. The female park rangers would make it a point to drive slowly beside him, hooting and hollering, giving him catcalls, reaffirming his life, leaving the fear behind.

Gary Hilton was running all of his life—running from death; staying ahead but never losing his fear; being tough; scaring people with his arsenal of bayonets, knives, and pepper sprays, beating them with his collapsible baton; being tough to stay ahead of the dark fear of becoming nothing more than a skeleton.

As he squatted by the small fire, he had one of his intense monologues that played frequently inside his head:

People who try to fuck with me are relatively rare, but I put myself in a position where I have a high exposure to that type of people. That was in dog situations. It's people with dogs. The average dog owner doesn't know jack shit about dogs. The average animal control officer doesn't know shit about them. They assign human qualities to dogs; and what that means is that they want dogs to be like humans, which is be nice and get along.

Well, that's not the way it is in the dog world, because when dogs talk to each other, they quite often revert to the wolf world; and the wolf world is more incredibly savage and brutal than you can ever imagine. Wolves are one of the only animals that I know of, other than human beings, that will run down, and run down, and run down, and run down, and go, and go, and go, after another member of their own species and kill it.

Just for the sake of killing?

No. It's if they get in their territory rather than just run them out, if they can . . . they'll go and go. . . . Other animals, it's just [protecting their territory], but a wolf pack, if they detect another wolf from outside their pack in their territory, they'll run it, and they'll run it, and they'll run it. They'll kill it. You've got your alpha male and alpha female within a pack. Leaders of the pack, okay? They're studying them out in Yellowstone now, so they're really getting good data on wolves in the last ten years. I heard a wildlife biologist on video say an alpha female may get up in the morning and kill her mother and run her sister off.

That's how savage and brutal the wolf world is, and that's what dogs can revert to when they're talking to each other. These humans don't understand that in the dog world or the wolf world, there are no assault and battery laws. There are no murder laws, and quite often, there is no fear. Imagine such a world where there is no murder laws, and there is no fear, which is why you see little Chihuahuas getting killed all the time. They won't back down, right? You grab them, one shake, and they're gone, man. Y'all have seen little dogs get killed that way, you know? They won't back down, you know? No murder laws. No aggravated assault. No assault and battery laws, and quite often no fear. That's what the dog world is, and you've got to understand that and be appropriately cautious.

Humans don't understand that. Not only that, they are aware that their dogs may fight and have fought. They're aware of that, but on the other hand they can't control the dog. The dog isn't trained. No one has enough time to spend with their dogs, to begin with, to get them properly trained. So that means the dog is going to have to lead his life at the end of a leash, and—and *he's jerking around, and what they want to do is—is let their dog run loose, and every-everyone that the dog confronts they want to say it's okay. He's friendly. You know? And they know it. I had people . . . I've had people let their dog confront me, and fight . . . and me fight the dogs. Have them call the police on me, and then in the succeeding year have seen that same person and that same dog get in two or three more incidents of the same.*

A woman at Stone Mountain had two dogs, one hundred fifty yards from me. I spotted them, and you're at a loss. You're kind of conflicted as whether to call her and warn [her] or not. The fact is, as soon as they hear you call, the dogs are coming after you. You know you don't really know what to do. I called to her, "Yo, got a dog here. Dog under control." Dogs come right at me, from a long way's away. A hundred fifty yards away. Dogs split up, so I'm—I'm doing stick (baton) work on one; and when they split up, then you're going to have to use pepper spray if they split up. You're going to have to spray one with pepper.

But you had to be careful with the pepper. It's hard to actually disable a dog with pepper, but conversely, dogs sense the pepper immediately, and it will turn them. It will turn them momentarily. If the dog is determined, it will come back; so you know, you just take a shot at it, and do a little stick work. The thing about the stick or the baton is that it can be used in a graduated manner, and that it does command respect in most dogs. The beauty of the whole thing is the graduated manner, as opposed to pepper or opposed to a bullet.

In other words, in fighting a dog or a human with a stick, my goal is to shape the situation. My goal in a stick fight with a human or a dog is not to make contact with the dog. A successful stick fight is preventative. To me, it's shaping it with a stick and not making contact because it takes it to a whole new level, especially with a human being. You hit a human being with a stick—regardless of the situation—it's probably going to ruin your day, buddy. It may not go your way, either, even though it always has. I've had the police called on me thirty times at the least— and no exaggeration—in seventeen years. No exaggeration at all. At least thirty times.

I've had them called five times in Murphey Candler Park. I've had them called three times at Stone Mountain alone. That's eight times right there. At least thirty times. And in every single time that the police were called on me, the police have confirmed that I did not act unlawfully, and there's been a couple of times that police have written me a letter saying that I could press charges if I want. The one time it didn't go my way was not with a police officer. It was with animal control. Animal control are not police officers, and matter of fact . . . in uniform is all they are.

Police officers, the good ones, and most of them are good ones these days . . . police work, of course, has become highly professionalized, and I'm talking DeKalb North, in particular. . . . DeKalb North has seen a lot of me. Police officers are trained to interrogate people and to arrive at the truth. I found that police officers may not be able to tell if you're lying; but if you're telling the truth, they can tell generally. And in every thirty times, with the exception of that animal control, it went my way; and if it had not gone my way, I was going to jail with assault with a deadly weapon.

That can be up to twenty-thousand-dollar bond in some places. Like this instance I had to spray the dogs. Stick work in a graduated manner raises from merely presenting the stick, to all the way to contact. The feinting with the stick, faking with a stick, you know? One thing I learned about faking with a human being . . . dogs are real good with movement. They pick up movement like that, but humans, no.

I learned with humans that if you're going to feint at a human, don't do it at combat speed, because I'm too fast for them to see, and it doesn't make an impression on them.

I did that one time to a human. We were in the middle of a confrontation. He had a big loose male and there was a female. It was a real melee. This was one of the few times that the guy wasn't bigger than me. Usually, if you have a stick, the guys always try to be bigger than you. Well, this time the kid wasn't. He was only my size, boring right in on me, so I did my thing. You know, I did like that real quick. So what happens is the tip of the stick is going right at you, and then coming back so you don't get the traversing motion. You don't get the impression of that traversing motion; and as a result, it was so quick that he didn't even see it.

But the point is that I goofed up and I just touched him. He didn't even see it, but he felt it. He said, "I don't believe you did that. I don't believe you did that. Did you see him do that?" I look behind and his buddy was coming up behind me, which was another thing. Keep your focus light when you're fighting. That's a critique that you can always make no matter how good of a fighter you are. Stick fighter or a street fighter. You do these post after-action critiques, and you break it down and try to analyze what you did wrong, what you did right, so you can learn from it.

You can always make a critique; I didn't keep my focus wide. You tend to fixate on the target. You've got to keep your focus wide. Not only to look for other threats, but to look for witnesses. Witnesses, of course, are a whole different thing. If you have witnesses, you act in some way; and if you don't, you may act another way.

Typically, you want witnesses 'cause they always lie, naturally. But again, the police can tell when I'm telling the *truth. They come, and I tell them the truth, and it makes sense to them; and the other people are—are not telling the truth and they're giving a lot of excuses and rationale why they assaulted me, basically. But anyway, what I learned from that, in addition to keeping your focus wide, which is always what you're learning, is that when you do a feint— number one, when you feint against a human, don't do it at combat speed. Make your feint real broad, okay? Don't do it at combat speed. And number two, don't feint to the head area. That's so if you goof up, you won't have a head strike, you know, which you never hit a person in the head or neck unless it is a fatal-force scenario.*

In other words, you never hurt them unless you're willing . . . unless you want to kill or seriously injure them. A fatal-force scenario is where you got a big guy, and he's got you. No hope at all of escape. That's a fatal-force scenario. But up to that, it's going to be a . . . Knee is my favorite place. That works pretty good.

Hilton enjoyed telling about his prowess in fighting and of the people he had beaten in hand-to-hand combat. With his oldest acquaintance, Walter Goddard, Hilton acted out his moves with the baton, performing what he envisioned as a graceful ballet of martial arts, with himself as the hero.

He had telephoned Goddard a day or so ago and left a long rant on Goddard's answering machine after John Tabor had refused to give him the $25,000 he demanded. Anything bad that happened to the girl now was Tabor's fault; it was on Tabor's head, not his own. His white-hot anger at Tabor was bubbling like the lava inside a volcano preparing to erupt.

Hilton poured the remainder of the coffee in his cup into the campfire. It hissed and blew a cloud of steam as he stood up. He stretched his body to prepare for the long day he knew lay ahead and picked fresh clothes from the van for Emerson. She would never wear them; they were for show, to keep her calm. He fished around in the tool well in the van until his fingers found and gripped the handle of a heavy, rusty steel jack. He tested its heft in his right hand and covered it from view with Emerson's fresh clothing before he walked back to where he had tied her.

Emerson's eyes grew wide and frightened when she saw him.

"Nothin' to be worried about, hon," he said. "You're going home today."

Emerson gave him a look that told him she doubted him and that she was afraid.

"Look, I even brought fresh clothes for you," he said.

Emerson appeared to be relieved. She thanked him and asked if he would be sure to leave her cell phone with her because the addresses and phone numbers of her friends were stored in its memory. Hilton told her that he had the phone, but he didn't inform Emerson that he had taken out the battery and thrown it away.

Hilton stepped slightly behind her and tossed the clothing he held onto the ground. Emerson was looking away. Taking a handful of her hair, he tugged it gently back.

"I need you to put your head back so I can untie these knots better," he said.

Emerson complied and turned her head slightly toward him as she did so. She saw the tire tool in his fist, raised high, already coming down toward her in a blur. "No," she whispered a fraction of a second before the heavy tool crushed into her skull.

Hilton struck Emerson's skull again and again with the tool, since he was the consummate professional combat soldier going about the final phases of his mission. He struck her until he was sure she was dead; then he sagged, with his back against a tree, exhausted, panting, arms hanging at his side. Before he completed the remainder of his duty at the site, he had several tasks to perform.

When he felt rested, Hilton freed Emerson's body from the tree and laid it on the ground. He walked back to the van and retrieved a cheap kitchen butcher knife with serrated teeth on a thirteen-inch blade. Back at the body, he stripped off the clothing and put it aside and started to remove the head. He sawed and sawed, thinking that he and Emerson had had several good days in the woods together—even going on a long hike with their dogs—before it ended like this.

Once the head was separated from the body, Hilton placed it inside a plastic garbage bag and filled another bag with Emerson's bloody clothing. He used a larger black trash bag to hold her body and dragged it into a tangled area of vegetation and dropped it on the ground and removed the bag before concealing it with fallen branches. Hilton didn't want the body to be buried because it decomposed faster when exposed to the elements, and then it took law enforcement longer to identify. After finishing this task, Hilton carried the bag with the head and bloody clothes to a spot about thirty yards from where he had placed the body and covered it the same way. He walked by both sites several times and was satisfied that everything was hidden even at close range.

Hilton rested again and washed his hands and arms with bleach from one of the buckets he had purchased from a Dollar Store to remove any trace of Emerson's blood. Bleach was one of the few chemicals that washed blood away; but even when it was thoroughly cleaned, there were still traces. Blood, which was unseen by a forensic scientist, could be detected by spraying an area with luminol, darkening the room, and then illuminating it with ultraviolet light. Blood spatters previously unseen popped out in brilliant blue. A new way to find blood

DNA that is even more sensitive than luminol is now being used by some forensic investigators. Hilton's attempt to destroy the blood evidence was absolutely futile.

When he had finished, Hilton telephoned Brenda to beg for money to buy enough gasoline to get out of Georgia. He was surprised and furious when Brenda broke the telephone connection after she recognized his voice. He dialed again and got a busy signal. Around four o'clock in the afternoon, he dialed John Tabor's telephone and Tabor broke the connection. Furious, Hilton called Tabor back, around six o'clock, and was transferred to voice mail, where he unleashed a lengthy verbal onslaught against his former boss.

Hilton drove to Cumming, where he looked for a suitable location to turn Ella loose. He just couldn't find it in himself to kill the dog, and now he didn't want it to wander into traffic and get hit by a car. He found a busy shopping area with a Kroger grocery store and a pizza shop and released Ella. There were food smells and pizza deliverymen milled around outside. Sooner or later, he believed, Ella would make her way over to someone and be recognized as Emerson's dog from television news or a photograph in a newspaper.

Emerson had told him that there was a microchip implanted under Ella's skin and it would not be difficult to identify the dog. At the very least, Ella would smell the pizza and walk over to where the delivery boys were smoking and joking with one another. Hilton had not asked, but Emerson voluntarily told him about Ella's microchip. The dog would be associated with him when he set it free, Hilton knew, but he just couldn't kill Ella— even though he had not given a second thought to brutally killing the dog's owner.

As Ella trotted away, Hilton drove off to find a place where he could dispose of all the bloody evidence that littered the floor of his van.

Chapter 8

Hilton pulled into a gas station/convenience store near Cambridge Square Shopping Center, at the corner of Johnson Ferry and Ashford Dunwoody, and parked near one of the large green Dumpsters not far from an air pressure pump. He walked inside the Chevron gas station and received permission from the clerk to throw some things out of his van into the Dumpster. Hilton turned his van so that its rear door faced the Dumpster and began carrying large trash bags and other items from the back of the vehicle. Dandy stayed near him.

Hilton seemed unconcerned. He didn't realize that there were people watching him and recognizing him as the man suspected of having kidnapped Meredith Emerson. His photograph had been plastered all over the newspapers and on television throughout Georgia and Florida, and Dandy's description had also appeared. Hilton had become what he thought of as "famous," the very thing he believed would lead to his downfall.

One alarmed person watching Hilton unload his van was Diane Clohessy. She immediately dialed 911, and a dispatcher asked for the location of her emergency.

Clohessy: Hi, I'm from Cambridge Square Shopping Center and I'm calling about that person, Gary Hilton, in connection with the woman who's missing, the hiker. . . . I'm walking my dog, and at the gas station up here, there's a white van and a red dog wandering around, like his red dog.

Dispatcher: Okay, what's the location you're at, ma'am?

Clohessy: Cambridge Square Shopping Plaza, and I didn't want to get close enough, but I sent one of the workers out to get the license plate off the van. And it's, ah, not the license that's been published, but it's a North Carolina plate, so . . .

Dispatcher: Okay, Cambridge Square. Where's that located? What street is that on?

Clohessy: Actually, it's Ashford Dunwoody, where the Starbucks is, and McDonald's and the Chevron station. He's at the Chevron station. He's got a whole bunch of stuff he's pulling out, like he's living out of his van, pulling out and organizing stuff in his van.

Dispatcher: Okay, Ashford Dunwoody. What's the nearest cross street?

Clohessy: Johnson Ferry. Right on the corner of Johnson Ferry and Ashford Dunwoody.

Dispatcher: Okay, so the white van in front of . . . where?

Clohessy: It's in the gas station, you know, in front
              of the car-cleaning place. He's going to
              be gone in a few minutes. If you got a
              car, just send a car over.

Dispatcher: Okay, well, ma'am. I'll try to get some
              information so we have someone to look
              for when we get there.

Clohessy: It's a white van. He's got a red dog. He's
              unpacking it. He's packing it up. It's got
              North Carolina plates on it.

Dispatcher: Can you see the plates?

Clohessy: WW28113. They're not the ones that are
              published but, you know, they're North
              Carolina plates and he's got a red dog
              there. He's going to be gone if somebody
              doesn't get here. The whole state is
              looking for him.

Dispatcher: I understand, ma'am, but if he leaves
              you can give us the direction of his travel,
              okay? What's your cell phone number
              you're calling from, ma'am?

Clohessy: I don't know. I borrowed this cell phone.

Dispatcher: And what's the name of the gas station
              again? You said . . .

Clohessy gave him the information and hung up
without knowing that another dispatcher was taking information from another concerned citizen parked near
her. Paul Craine had recognized Hilton and the dog the
instant he pulled into the Chevron station. He immediately called 911 and said: "The person of interest in that

missing woman case is at this Chevron gas station at Ashford Dunwoody."

Dispatcher: Chevron Gas Station at Ashford Dun-woody?

Craine: It's right across from . . . What's it called?

Dispatcher: Give me two intersecting cross streets, sir. Ashford Dunwoody and what?

Craine: It's right by the corner of Ashford Dun-woody and . . . What road is that, Jenny? Shit. It's definitely him. The van is there. The dog is there. I saw his face.

Dispatcher: Is he still there now?

Craine: He's in the store right now.

Dispatcher: Okay, I need two intersecting cross streets, sir. Or an exact address.

Craine: Okay, I'm going to get that for you. Hold on one second . . . 3500 Ashford Dunwoody.

Dispatcher: Okay, and that's at the Chevron?

Craine: Yes, and it's definitely him. Definitely.

Dispatcher: Do you have the tag number of the van?

Craine: No. I can . . .

Dispatcher: Is the dog . . . You said the van is there?

Craine: The van is here. The dog is here—the red dog, and I saw the man's face. And I've been watching the news and I know it's him. I know it's him.

Dispatcher: Can you get the tag, sir?

Craine: Yep. Stay on the line. . . . He's throwing stuff in the Dumpster here. Okay, I'm going to drive past them right now. Trying to get the tag for you guys. I'm absolutely positive it's him. He's got the red dog with him and everything. WNZ8113, and it's a North Carolina tag.

Dispatcher: And that's a tan van?

Craine: No, it's a white Astro van with North Carolina plates. I've no doubt in my mind that it's him. We were just a foot away from him. . . . Johnson Ferry is the crossroad. I've got him in my sight.

Dispatcher: Okay, give me a description of him.

Craine: He looks like he's in his sixties . . . ah . . . disheveled. He's got the red dog with him . . . and he's got white hair . . . a beard . . . reddish eyebrows . . . like a four-day growth of a beard.

Dispatcher: What does he have on?

Craine: He's got on a green long-sleeved sweat-shirt and he's wearing a hat. He's empty-ing all of his stuff out of his van. Ah, dark pants. I can't really tell.

Dispatcher: And he's got a beard?

Craine: He's got, like, a stubbly growth. It's not, like, a full beard, but . . . he's making multiple trips back to his van. Getting stuff out and taking it to the Dumpster. Pillows and a blanket. And it looks like he's got a sleeping bag right now. Taking it all to the trash. It's definitely him.

Dispatcher: And the Dumpster . . .

Craine: And he's looking around like he's as guilty as sin.

Dispatcher: Sir, and it's at the rear of the location?

Craine: Yeah, the Dumpster's right by the car wash. He's still unloading stuff. He looks like he's taking his time. I thought he looked at us, but I guess not.

Dispatcher: And you seen the sleeping bag?

Craine: Yeah, he just threw his sleeping bag in the Dumpster and now he's taking a backpack and throwing it in the Dumpster. I can go take him down, if you want.

Dispatcher: No, sir, stay right there. And he threw a sleeping bag and a backpack into the Dumpster?

Craine: He took his sleeping bag there and threw it in and now he just took a big hiker's backpack and threw it in the Dumpster.

Dispatcher: Can you stay on the line with me, sir?

Craine: Yes, ma'am. Now he's got something that looks like a jacket or bedroll and a purse . . . taking it to the Dumpster. It looks like a green jacket.

Dispatcher: And . . . a purse?

Craine: It looks like a purse. He looks like he's finishing up. You guys gotta hurry.

Dispatcher: Okay, stay on the line, sir.

Craine: Okay. And he's holding all the stuff at arm's length–like. I don't know what that means, but . . .

Dispatcher: Okay, stay on the line with me, sir. And where's the dog?

Craine: The dog is following him around. It's loose. But, like, it stays with him, like, two yards from him at all times. It's a red, looks kind of Lab-ish, or golden retriever. Definitely the dog I saw on the news. He's got one of those spelunking lights, a caving light on his head.

Dispatcher: On his head?

Craine: Yeah, like he's wearing, like, a light. Just trip after trip, taking stuff to the Dumpster.

Dispatcher: And you're in your vehicle watching him?

Craine: I'm in my vehicle just fifteen feet away from him. Watching him. I've no doubt in my mind that it's him. Somebody else walked by that I knew from high school when we were trying to get the license plate and heard me talking to you . . . and he recognized him as the guy on TV, too, and he said that we better get out of here.

Dispatcher: Okay . . . okay.

Craine: He's got stuff in bags that he's emptied on the ground that he's taking load by load to the Dumpster by the car wash.

Dispatcher: You were describing, like, a flashlight that is attached to his hat or something?

Craine: It's kinda like those people were going to use if they were going to go caving or something. It's just, like, one light on a strap you wear around your head. He's closing the door of his van now. There's still lots more of the stuff he's got way down by the side. So I don't think he's done yet. But it looks like he's gathering up, so just . . . He's got another backpack. He's taking another backpack to the Dumpster. Another . . . this is the third backpack that we've seen him take to the Dumpster. I'm just shaking. We were just using the ATM and I saw the old man and the red dog and that Astro van. And I said, "Oh my God." Is there somebody en route?

Dispatcher: Yes, sir.

Craine: Okay, because he looks like he's going. . . . He's finishing up.

Dispatcher: Yes, sir, somebody's coming.

Craine: Fantastic, because, I mean, the way he's look . . . Here we go. Here come the cops. Yes, yes.

Dispatcher: Wait, are you still there?

Craine: Yes. They got him. I mean, they don't have him yet, but they're getting out. They got him now. Two cruisers pulled up on him. Two of DeKalb's finest. Oh my . . .

Dispatcher: Yeah, they've got more comin', sir.

Craine: Awesome.

* * *

Two DeKalb County police officers were the first to arrive on the scene. Lieutenant D. L. Tracy was the first. He had pulled his car into the Chevron station and saw Hilton squatting in the grass near a white Astro van. Hilton had been unloading garbage bags from the vehicle and placing them on the ground. Tracy leaped out of the vehicle with his gun drawn and identified himself as a police officer.

"Get down on the ground and place your hands behind your back!" Tracy said.

Hilton looked surprised to see a policeman with a gun pointed at him. He did what he was told to do. Within a minute, another officer, who was also with the DeKalb County Police Department, arrived and quickly hand-cuffed Hilton's wrists as police officers from several jurisdictions pulled up to offer assistance.

After being convinced that Hilton had been squeezed into that area by his pursuers, John Cagle, the GBI's special agent in charge (SAC), had saturated the DeKalb County with officers from several jurisdictions. Among the police units to arrive were the Georgia Highway Patrol (GHP) and the U.S. Marshal's Office. The marshals wanted to arrest Hilton on a warrant for failure to appear, while the GBI and the Union County Sheriff's Office wanted to question him about the disappearance of Meredith Emerson.

Hilton had laid "numerous" items on the ground by the van, including clothing, and a large stack of plastic trash bags filled with other items. Numerous things had been thrown into the Dumpster, but the van still contained a welter of gear, including more filled trash bags, sleeping bags, clothing, and a portable stove. The license tag on the van was for North Carolina: WWZ8113. Both callers had failed to report the tag number accurately.

Police officers taped off the crime scene and forensic investigators arrived to start the laborious process of searching for evidence. Their job of retrieving and marking items from the Dumpster was not as glamorous as is the work of CSI detectives on television. It is tedious and takes close attention to detail, but forensic evidence is vital in putting together a criminal case in this high-tech age.

The police secured search warrants for the van, Dandy, and a warrant to search Hilton and to get samples of his hair, fibers, and DNA. They were careful to do everything by the book, and were careful in their documentation and identification of evidence.

Special Agent Jeff D. Branyon, of the GBI, took hundreds of photos at the crime scene, in and around the van; and Hilton was taken to the GBI Region 8 office by the DeKalb police, where he would be interviewed. When samples of hair and fibers were taken from Dandy, the dog was turned over to DeKalb Animal Control.

Special Agent Dustin Hamby helped Branyon sort through, itemize, and bag evidence from the Dumpster and from the bags Hilton had piled in the parking lot. Some of the clothing, sleeping bags, and other items were still wet with blood. This fact alone gave nightmares to most of the law enforcement officers who were involved in the hectic race against time to find Meredith Emerson alive. They had probably missed catching Hilton and saving the murdered hiker by just thirty minutes.

Special Agent B. D. McElwee contacted Branyon from GBI district headquarters and told him that Hilton was complaining that he needed some medicine that was located in a "fanny pack" on the Astro's dashboard. The fanny pack contained odds and ends, such

as tweezers and a whistle. There was a medicine bottle
from Dixie City Pharmacy in Gainesville, Georgia, for
twenty-milligram tablets of Methylin, prescribed by Dr.
Harry Delcher, an Atlanta endocrinologist. Hilton paid
in cash, as he always did, and there was a receipt for
ninety dollars from the doctor's office. Methylin is used
primarily for attention-deficit/hyperactivity disorder
and narcolepsy. ADHD is a disorder that can cause hy-
peractivity, inability to sit still, and inability to concen-
trate. Narcolepsy is a sleep disorder that can cause a
person to fall asleep without warning during normal
daytime activities. Delcher had diagnosed Hilton previously with MS, fibromyalgia, chronic fatigue syndrome, and autoimmune disease. Hilton paid $185 in
cash for the diagnostic visit.

Hundreds of items were bagged and marked for evidence. Significantly, backpacks, envelopes, jackets, and
pillows were found with rust-colored stains, which tested
positive for blood. Field testing determined that some of
the blood found among the evidence was human, but it
could not be associated with either Emerson or Hilton.
Hilton had been trying to discard all items with blood
spatter—except the floor's van, which he had attempted
to scrub with bleach.

"Forensically, this guy knew what he was doing,"
Bridges said later. "This (Emerson's murder) wasn't the
first time the guy did this."

The search for evidence led to additional backpacks,
clothing, and blankets that were stained to various degrees by a rust-colored spatter. Branyon tested the stains
with phenolphthalein and determined that the stains were
made by human blood. All of the evidence was bagged
and identified for further testing at the GBI forensic
laboratory.

Most of the outdoor gear was from top-of-the-line

producers with standings in their specialties that equal Prada and Ralph Lauren for high fashion. What's more, much of the expensive gear seemed to be so new it had not been used. Some of the brand names were North Face Gore-Tex, JanSport, REI, and Columbia Sportswear Company. There were rolls of duct tape, bloodstained rags and paper towels, several different kinds of outdoor ropes and cords, chains, padlocks, and pornographic magazines. In the cargo area Branyon found an insert inside packaging for a Monadnock expandable police baton.

U.S. Marshals found Emerson's credit cards. The GBI had previously checked with four banks to determine whether any attempts had been made to use Emerson's cards and PINs. The banks told the GBI there had been none. But when the U.S. Marshals offered to help in the search, they found that attempts had been made on January 1, 2, and 3 on two of the cards. The private companies that provided security for the banks apologized and blamed faulty computers. Had the banks' security reported correctly, it would have given the police a better idea of Hilton's movement pattern and could have saved Emerson's life.

As the investigation progressed, the GBI was able to isolate several instances where Meredith Emerson could have been helped and wasn't. None of these instances were the fault of the GBI or others in law enforcement, who all worked like swarms of bees in northern Florida, Georgia, and South Carolina, exhausting every lead, every hint of Hilton's life and habits. In the two days since Emerson was reported missing, police had quickly discovered the unidentified suspect's name, and had come within a hairsbreadth of catching him before he killed Emerson.

GBI special agent Mitchell Posey discovered a small library of videotapes of commercially broadcast shows.

All of them had a similar motif: crime. There was a tape of *60 Minutes* documenting the case of Dalton Prejean, who was on death row for murdering Louisiana State trooper Donald Cleveland on July 2, 1977. When he was fourteen, Prejean had previously killed a taxi driver and had served time in a juvenile facility. At a hearing near his execution date, a psychologist said that Prejean had suffered from brain damage caused by abuse when he was a child and was unable to think of another solution besides shooting the trooper when he slammed Prejean's brother's head on the hood of the car.

The parole board recommended that the death sentence be commuted, but the governor refused it. Although the U.S. Supreme Court issued a state of execution on the date Prejean was sentenced to die, the *60 Minutes* broadcast ended without revealing Prejean's ultimate fate. (Prejean was executed in the electric chair on May 18, 1990, when he was thirty years old.)

The same videotape included a report on a convicted con artist named Noel Jay Calise, who rented cars and paid in cash to make it harder for police to track him. There was a tape containing recorded broadcasts of *Cops*. Also included was an episode from *America's Most Wanted* that reported on how Patrick Mitchell was arrested for bank robbery in Little Rock, Arkansas. Mitchell went to what he thought of as a safe haven and tried to rob a bank in South Haven, Mississippi. While he robbed the bank, two customers telephoned the police to report a suspicious character. Police were waiting to arrest Mitchell when he left the bank. There were several other tapes whose themes centered on child pornography, kidnapping, and murder.

While investigators gathered evidence at the Chevron station, Gary Hilton had been transported to the GBI Region 8 headquarters. The normally loquacious Hilton, who ordinarily spoke in bizarre and nonstop sentences, did a complete turnabout. As he and his police escorts arrived at the outside steps leading inside the building, Hilton went limp, and would have fallen flat on his face if the detectives had not caught him. They had to carry him inside to the interview room, where he sprawled facedown on the floor, with his eyes wide open. He clammed up. Mum. Not a peep out of him for the next few hours, except to say he needed medication.

Hilton was sprawled on the floor, facedown, when Bridges entered the room and spoke the few words he would utter for what seemed an eternity. Bridges said Hilton turned his eyes on him, but he felt as if the suspect was looking right through him. The GBI agent felt a cold chill and felt as if he had been hit by a hammer, so strong was the anger and hatred emanating from the man on the floor.

"I'm Special Agent Clay Bridges," he said. "You have the right—"

"I'm not saying anything to you," Hilton snarled. "I'm not saying anything without an attorney present. I'm making no statements. I'm waiving no rights."

"I want to make sure you know what your rights are," Bridges said, and read them to Hilton. Hilton didn't look at him and showed no emotion. The GBI special agent felt as if Hilton could see right through him and was looking at the wall on the other side of the room through him, with a scowl on his face that seemed set in stone.

Hilton lay on the floor. He blamed everyone but himself for Emerson's death.

If John Tabor had been square with me, it *never would have happened. What if I tell the GBI agent,* you *tell*

Tabor that I killed the girl, but you tell him that girl is dead because he is a fucking smart-ass girl.

And instead of . . . instead of telling me, Gary, the jig's up, you know . . . I don't know what the fuck was going through his mind that . . . he didn't know the girl was dead. The girl wasn't. She was alive. I had the girl. You know, shit's gone down that the girl's missing and apparently been abducted by me. What the fuck was in his mind trying to lure me to . . . You think you're going to rescue the girl that way?

Like I'm going to bring the girl there . . . What the fuck was going through his mind? You tell Tabor if he had just told me . . . and it makes sense. You're . . . It's intuitive. If he had told me, "Gary, they know it's you. They're looking for you, and if you've got that girl" . . . just like you told me. The first thing you said to me is "Gary, if there's any way that that girl is still alive, please"—words to that effect—"please tell us." You were exploring that possibility right from the get-go. Not Tabor. He's too busy being a yuppie, smart-ass girl. Okay? And trying to lay his coy little trap, and . . .

. . . Well, I couldn't pick it up that night or the next day, but I might be there the next day. And the girl was still a-fucking-live. I still had that. Now, I got to go off . . . you know, and I was just, you know, I came unraveled, arrested. I slept almost twenty-four hours a day for . . .

Oh, yeah, he's kind of weird. Mostly he's afraid of me, and it—it just may be that his wife doesn't know he's . . . I doubt that. The last night that I was telling him, "John, you're working an agenda that's not working for either of us. It's not working for me because I'm not getting paid. It's not working for you because it's not going to happen, and that is . . . I will never unlawfully threaten you, John."

I said, "Now, I can understand there's two reasons why

you might think you could go at me into unlawfully threatening you. One is that if you had done to anyone what you have to me, they would be so mad and so outraged that they may well utter an unlawful threat. Secondly is the fact that, well, I'm a stud and the training I've received and the fighting I've done is a matter of public record. The training I received is a matter of public record, and the police have been called on me thirty times. The fighting I've done is a matter of public record.

"But, John, you're forgetting something. In all those instances I acted lawfully. I keep my actions lawful. Now, as far as blackmailing you goes, he had never broached that subject, but I—I wanted to throw this in. . . . I said as far as blackmailing you goes, what John Tabor . . . What am I going to do? Tell your wife you're a lousy faggot that lies about everything? Man, I'm sure she's known that for several years." I told him . . . and it's my feeling, you know, Jan is dumb, you know.

Again, when you love someone, you have this dreamboat of a guy. . . . He's a dreamboat for the average, you know . . . He's forty-four . . . was born in '64, man. Okay? He's in his midforties. Your average schmuck in his forties is a sack of fucking shit, man. You know, he's done spread out. Man, Tabor's a stroking dude, man. I mean, he's tall and good-looking, and he handles himself beautifully. He's so impeccably mannered. Of course, they pose and they're precious, and that's the way they do it. And so I can understand his wife being blinded by that for several years; but again, she's an attorney. She was first in her class. She's not stupid.

But he never came on to me or shared his experiences with me. Never. Because if you're friends with a faggot— if it becomes an open thing between you that he's a fag, then you're hanging around with a faggot; and in my experience, if you're hanging around with a faggot that's acknowledged to be a faggot . . . I shouldn't use those words. I think the world of gay guys, by the way. Gay guys, as a group, are more handsome, more talented, more smart, more everything than straight men. They are. They're beautiful, and talented, and everything. Good-looking, too, you know, but one of the ways you tell a guy is a homosexual if he's just too good-looking and dressed too damn well, like Rock Hudson.

Tabor's always known that . . . for many years . . . that I knew because he—he knows me better than anyone, and he understands how sophisticated I am. By sophisticated, I mean a sophisticated person understands what they're seeing, and sees almost everything. That's what I mean by sophistication. In other words, I've been to New York City. So, Tabor knows I'm an extremely sophisticated guy, you know, and the only reason I'm not rich is because I'm crazy.

There's a downside to everything. You know what I mean? Yeah. I mean . . . you know, but even at this point, I wouldn't trade it for being the average, incognizant schmuck that's going and plodding along doing a job, career, family, going to church, doing all those dumb-ass, mindless, brain-dead, fucking things, man. I wouldn't trade it even now to be incognizant as the average person. People have the capacity to deny truths that are as big as the nose on their faces. This whole dimming of awareness is a human psychological phenomenon that, number one, reduces tension, and number two, facilitates social inter-action. It's a psychologically proven phenomenon that can be demonstrated in the laboratory that we dim out awareness of situations.

It's almost like the guy's got a big wart on his nose, but you don't look at it. That kind of thing? And that's what drives cops mad because cops understand that every-

body's got an asshole. All you got to do is look for it, and it can drive you nuts. You know, it's seeing the dark side of things. And I saw the crime scene guy. He had forest mud on his knees and the toes of his boots, and that meant he had been down on his knees in the mud in front of a dead body that used to be a young girl.

Hey, you're authorized, dude, because you know Michael Moore? The guy . . . that filmmaker, you know? He has referred to Americans as grinning idiots, and no truer words were ever spoken, you know. Especially since 1996, they all have the teeth whitening. You know, prior to 1996, if you would go to a dentist, the dentist would be wearing a lab coat that white right there.

If you went to a dentist and said, "Doc, I want you to make my teeth as white as your lab coat there." The Doc would say, "Well, I'll do it, but don't tell anyone it was me that did it, because it looks so unnatural." You know what I mean? Now everybody's that way. They're grinning fucking idiots. I call it a dental display. It's like you took chimpanzees and they do a genital display. You see a chimpanzee in the zoo, they'll go like that. That's a genital display.

Humans do a dental display. That's why I love my teeth. These are the artistic, philosophical statements, and they're practical, too. If someone is fucking with me, I'll go, "Aaarrgh!" It'll scare the shit out of them because they know I'm for fucking real. I ain't no dummy. I ain't posing a bit. I got my hot teeth in. Can I help you? How you going to help me? Do I look like I need some help? You're too ugly to help me.

Special Agent Clay Bridges paced around the room. He squatted beside Hilton. He tried to flatter him and tried to make him angry. Nothing seemed to penetrate the consciousness of the man on the floor. Scowling, eyes unblinking. Bridges would never forget those cold, unblinking eyes. And when he thought of Meredith having to look at them—while helpless to escape—it about broke his heart.

When he was assigned to the case, Bridges talked to everyone he could who knew Hilton and Emerson. He figured the better he knew the perpetrator and the victim, the better chance he would have of finding Emerson alive. In the nearly eight hours that he had been in the room with Hilton, Bridges had not seen the slightest expression on Hilton's face except the scowl.

The man *must* care about something, Bridges thought. There had to be some way to get through to him. Once he cracked the dam that blocked Hilton's emotions, Bridges hoped the pressure would create a flood of information. How did he find that chink in Hilton's armor?

And then he remembered Ranger, the dog that Hilton had before Dandy. People had told him that Hilton loved that dog more than anything. Hilton had wept for days when Ranger died. Ranger was his best friend, and even a psychopath needed a friend, and it was Ranger he talked to and with whom he discussed things.

Such was his love for Ranger that Hilton had carried him high up on Big Stone Mountain to one of his favorite views. There he buried Ranger and spent most of the day lugging huge rocks to build a monument to his friend. Hilton visited the monument regularly to remember his dead dog.

Bridges knelt on the floor next to Hilton and put his lips close to his ear. "I want you to think about her family," he whispered. "I know that probably doesn't mean anything to somebody like you, because you are obviously deranged. How about this? Do you remember how much you loved Ranger? How about I go to Stone Mountain and I take Ranger's body and I put it someplace where you'll never know where it's at? That's how the family of this girl feels. They don't even know where her body is. How would you feel if you didn't know where Ranger's body was? How much would that hurt?"

Hilton's eyes filled with tears and he turned toward Bridges with a look of pure hatred. "Why don't you just go ahead and stick the needle in my arm now, bitch?"

"Okay," Bridges said.

Those eyes, the special agent thought. He would never forget those eyes.

But the dam had cracked and, after resisting all night long, Hilton was ready to talk.

Chapter 9

Once Hilton allowed himself to be moved off the floor, he was escorted to the Atlanta Detention Infirmary, where he was treated for broken fingers on his right hand. Hilton had noticed when he first met Hilton that his right hand was swollen to twice the size as his other hand. Hilton had refused to have treatment except to complain about needing medicine for his MS.

Hilton had decided to talk—on his conditions—but he continued to be surly and growled at the doctor and the nurse in the dispensary.

"What happened?" the doctor asked.

"You haven't been keeping up with the news," Hilton growled. "It's from punching that missing girl hiker. You know, bone against bone."

The doctor looked surprised. "Fist against cranium," Hilton said. "Don't worry. It hurt me a lot more than it hurt her."

Following treatment, police asked the doctor if he had noticed anything symptomatic of multiple sclerosis.

The doctor replied, "No. I'd be much more likely to diagnose him with psychopathic bipolar disorder."

Based on the interview and what Bridges said was

"significant" DNA evidence, the possibility of a plea bargain was almost immediately started. The plea bargain would call for Georgia to take a possible death sentence off the table and substitute it for a plea of guilty—with Hilton being sentenced to life in prison. Under such an arrangement Hilton would almost certainly never breathe free air again. He would be ninety-one years old when he became eligible for parole, if he beat the odds and was still alive at that time.

The GBI was under the impression that the murder had been committed on Blood Mountain, which would have been in Blairsville. Special Agents Matthew Howard and Dustin Hamby loaded Hilton into a police car for the two-hour trip from the Atlanta Police Department (APD). Hilton was handcuffed and shackled, according to GBI policy, and his seat belt fastened. They left Saturday, January 5, 2008, at 6:30 P.M. for the Union County Jail in Blairsville.

Hilton had reverted to his motormouthed persona and talked incessantly during the two-hour drive. His pleasantries began with a dark scowl and angry voice: "You guys are pissed at me. Eye fucking me. That Atlanta jail is just torture. I'm just waiting to die. You want to torture me in the meantime? Good, we torture lots of people."

Howard said they weren't going to torture him; they were just taking him back to the mountains. Hilton had expressed disdain for urban environments, and Howard thought this might have a calming effect. Hilton said he thought Blood Mountain was in Lumpkin County.

"That's good," Hilton said. "The Union County Jail would be mostly white. They're going with state charges? They want to turn me over to the state so they can execute me.

"I'm fucked, totally fucked. I was just trying to figure

out who I was going to give my dog to before I was going to turn myself in." He looked at Howard. "Why don't you take my dog, man? If I sign a release form? Hey, I ain't going nowhere. I'll never breathe free air again, pal."

The police officers had their digital recorders on and were recording every word. Through some convoluted feat of reasoning, Hilton started to talk about himself, which seemed to be his favorite subject.

"Son, I'm telling you, I'm an observer," Hilton said. "I'm a philosopher. I'm a man of vast . . . I've been a professional beggar for twenty years, and I'm going to tell you who has the biggest heart is going to be men."

"Really?" Howard asked.

"You're fooled by a woman's nurturing instincts and her softness, but a woman isn't soft. It's the difference in our personalities. Men tend to be more confrontational and grab the whole thing, while women affect an air of softness and get it a bit at a time."

"In other words, manipulative, you mean?"

"Much more. And always remember, they got the pussy. We're fucked. We're totally. But hey, that's okay. Don't worry about it. Be a Republican. Have a party. Your world is kaput. Your world is over, pal. It's gone. Your children will never, never . . . You want your kid to grow up to be a lawyer? Forget about it. There is no future for your kids. There is none."

Hilton continued nonstop with his bizarre, nihilistic rampage: "The Muslims got us by the gasoline. Before, they had to come across oceans to get at them, and once they came across oceans, they had this huge country that, even if they could get at it, they couldn't invade us and occupy us. Napoleon was over half-a-million men. The Germans were three-and-a-half-million men. Okay, these were huge armies. Napoleon, in 1812, over half a million . . . half a million. Okay, the Russians just soaked them up. Just the vastness of it. They couldn't get at us. Now they don't have to.

"Again, I'm going to tell you . . . I've told you before, and I'm going to tell you again, we have this huge, vast, interconnected, socioeconomic structure. You're embedded in a matrix, in a world that isn't real. That has been constructed totally for you, and is all interconnected. It's built on values [that] are virtual, okay? But it's built upon the harsh reality of cheap gasoline. It's a house of cards, and, son, once that starts, the ripple effects are going to be unimaginable. But, just to give you guys an idea of what ripple and the interconnectedness of everything, we have a bunch of people here with subprime mortgages that don't pay their mortgage. Okay. A bunch of African Americans and other low-rent people that don't pay their mortgages, and what does it end up?

"Now that's child play," Hilton said.

"But you see?" Hilton continued. "You see the interconnectedness of this? Now, what's going to happen when that . . . What's going to happen if gasoline . . . If nothing goes bad—I told you—I told you before, I've handled atomic bombs. Okay? I was in special weapons, and I've handled atomic bombs that damn big that weigh seventy-nine pounds, and what's going . . . That's assuming nothing like that happens.

"That's assuming nobody gets weaponized anthrax and shuts down our postal system. All it would take is a few anthrax letters to shut down our postal system. Everybody's forgotten that. Okay. But if nothing bad happens, what's going to happen if gasoline goes up a buck a year for ten years, and in ten years it's thirteen dollars a gallon? Son, it's going to bring you down. It's going to bring you down. That's why they can bring the fucking death penalty on me. Okay? Go ahead. Try me. Bring it on, okay? Because it's going to take three or four years to

come to trial. It's going to—even at the federal level—
they'll be able to knock a little time off."

Hilton stopped talking long enough to make a quick
calculation. "It's going to take an average of about twelve
years to—to impose it," he said. "Maybe even longer,
really. And—and—and by then, you know, now we're
talking seventeen years, this society . . .

"You were a little rough on me the first night," Hilton
said, "but I don't blame you. You might have had a live
girl on your hands, for all you knew, but you treated me
fairly. You've been a man of your word. You're cops, of
course. I understand that, and we're never going to be
friends, but you've been a man of your word, and in the
end you lived up to your deal, and in the end you treated
me professionally, so I'm—I'm giving you something.
I've given you cooperation. I promised you cooperation
that night. I gave it to you. The only question I didn't
answer was on the advice of my attorney, and I would
have answered that.

"You asked whether she was doomed from the beginning."

The agents wanted to know why.

"Because I just told you, once you've done it, you're
either going to kill her or get caught. There's no other solution. If that sounds cold and cruel, yeah, it was. It's the
soldier in me. A soldier just does or dies. Okay?"

A moment of hesitation, and then Hilton continued
speaking. "Yeah. And I'm trying to impress on you,
though, there was nothing sexual or pleasurable . . ."

"You talk about being a pro."

"It was dreadful. It was dreadful," Hilton said. "You
asked me what was it like to cut someone's head off."

"Okay. It was dreadful," Hilton said. "It was so dreadful that the only thing you could do is go on autopilot. I
told you it wasn't real. Yeah. It's so fucking dreadful that

all you can do is do your duty or go on autopilot. It's the same as combat soldiers that told me from Vietnam . . . they told me the same thing. They'd see bodies, you know, with guts, you know, roped all over the place, heads blown off, and it didn't. . . . It wasn't real. It just didn't look real.

"But it's dreadful. There was no pleasure or anything else, and when they say, well, you're the one that chose to make money by killing. There's other ways to make money. There's bank robbery, and so forth. Well, you know, in retrospect I regret not attempting a bank robbery. I really do. 'Cause all of this shit got me nowhere but caught. Okay? And so, I might have been caught robbing a bank, but if I had scored . . . if I had got five grand . . . I could—I could live off that for over half a year or worse, you know, and so, yeah, yeah. . . . But as to why I chose to kill for money, part of that was rage against society. Sociopathic rage against society. Against all those people that are now coming forward and so forth. How did you find Walter Goddard? He must have called you, or did you get him off my cell phone?

"Anyway, I . . . we did a deal. I promised you cooperation, and by all rights, I shouldn't be talking to you," Hilton said. "My attorney has warned me a million times don't talk to no one without an attorney, but I'm not telling you nothing, you know what I mean? We're talking about history, and I was going to save the history for the profilers, but there will be psychologists and psychiatrists, so they'll want to go over that. I'm telling you right now, I'm going—I'm going to dig my heels in. I don't want federal custody. They're going to send me to supermax. I just know they are. What about it?

"They sent Ted Kaczynski there (*Editor's note: Commonly known as the Unabomber*). All the notorious people. Listen, Rudolph went there and he only killed one person, and indirectly two. (*Editor's note: Eric Rudolph killed two people, and one person indirectly, in 1996 and 1998 when he exploded pipe bombs near Olympic venues in Atlanta and at abortion clinics near Birmingham, Alabama.*) Okay? He killed one woman with a bomb, and another guy had a heart attack. Okay? He only killed one person. Oh, no, he killed two. The police officer. He only killed two people and they—they sent Kaczynski there and he only killed two people, but it was the Unabomber.

"And he's in supermax," Hilton said. "So it's where they send the notorious, infamous people. Okay, they're sending my ass to supermax—"

"It's debatable on who calls you notorious and who calls you, you know, just a . . . a mad guy. You know what I mean?" Howard said.

"You know, Jack the Ripper, whatever you want to put it. Okay?" Hilton said. "But, of course, first, they've got to convict me. And if they want to spend a million dollars, two million to convict me, and then . . . and then another two million to get death, and then another eight million to defend the death penalty and get around . . . and get around to executing me seventeen years from now, when I'm seventy-eight years old and I'm decrepit and everything. Hey, they can do it."

"Who is going to be the one that has to call you notorious, though?"

"Me."

"You are?"

"I'm infamous," Hilton said. "My God. I mean I've read a little of the news. My lawyer's brought me a little bit, but I don't really want to read it. . . . It's really a fucking . . . you know . . . a drifter with a mean streak. That's what the *AJC* (*Atlanta Journal-Constitution*) article was. 'Drifter with a Mean Streak.' Or no, *misfit*. 'Misfit with a Mean Streak.' Yeah. Well, misfit I am. Well, maybe it's true. I do have a mean streak.

"They don't understand there's something a little more than that, though.

"They don't understand that, except for this rampage, I was the injured party," Hilton said. "I kid you not. They have screwed, blued, and tattooed me every which way, society has. They've called the police on me thirty times when they were the transgressor trying to get—"

"Those people in the park?" asked Howard, meaning parks where Hilton walked his dogs.

"Yeah. And all of society trying to get me in trouble. If they had their way, they would tell lies to the cop. The cop would arrest me and send me to the penitentiary, take my dog away, and ruin my life just because they don't want to be wrong. Okay? It's as simple as that. You talk about cruel and heartless, man. You talk about, you know, killing motherfuckers. You start getting that thing, you know. You're just raging at society."

"You're getting . . . You're getting a little bit into the . . . in the . . . You're, you know . . . more than what we're trying to discuss here," the GBI agent said, warning Hilton that he might be exceeding the parameters of the plea bargain.

"What are you trying to get at, except a biography? You're not going to give this to the press?"

"No."

"I'm saving this for a book, man. Hey, I've got to keep some money on the books," Hilton said. "No one's called you up and said, 'Hey, I got some money for Gary Hilton.' I got to get some money on the books. And my coverage, you know, I deliberately kept coverage of me limited. You notice when they try to do the perp walk, I insist that we run? I got the vest on and everything, and the sooner they can get me into that car, the better—although they don't even have to get me in the car. They can walk me right through, and I'm the one that insists on running to the car, you know. Did you see the way we . . . Did you see it on TV?

". . . Oh, yeah, running. I'm the one that wants to do that. I was going . . . I was leading them, and they opened that door, and another one opened that door, and I'm the one that just dives in headfirst, you know," Hilton continued. "Kind of like a Hollywood celebrity that's been bad, and now . . . you see what I mean? The more you limit it, the bigger demand it makes. If I had come walking out like Eric Rudolph, they'd have said, 'Oh, he's so fucking smug is all he is.' But when I come . . . you know, when I come running out and dive into the car wearing the vest, it's a mystique, you know."

Howard said, "You got a style about you, Mr. Hilton."

"It's the style now, yeah, so—so no one's got pictures of me, either, but I got them. I got five thousand pictures of me. Yeah, five thousand pictures from 1990 on documenting everything on my daily life. Nothing unlawful. Nothing unlawful. Yeah, I've got it. I've got it. No one has a damn picture of me as far as I know, except mug shots, and no one has a single picture of me not under arrest. No one. Nobody."

Howard burst Hilton's bubble. "I think actually Goddard has some."

"Have you found some? Oh, yeah, yeah, yeah. I'm sorry. North Carolina had two of me that a woman took, yeah. That a woman took in . . . in Transylvania County. Oh, you've come across some more? Well, I wouldn't be . . . I wouldn't be surprised because people are . . ." Hilton's thoughts tripped over each other. ". . . I'm like the Lone Ranger. What other pictures have you come up with?"

Howard said, "We got some pictures of you from . . . Is it out West somewhere?"

"Out West?"

"Rainier, I think."

"You mean Mount St. Helens more than likely," Hilton said. "I was at St. Helens, but I was at Rainier, too. I only spent an hour or two there."

"You talked about wanting to be a guide or wanting to be a . . . teacher."

"Someone just took a—a picture of me, huh? I'm not surprised. Someone took a picture of me, and I know who it was. It was another fucking woman. Women are just . . . There was a guy in *New York Times* Sunday magazine. He was of Iranian descent. American born and everything, but he was Iranian, and he was . . . decided he was a photographer and decided to do a project traveling to each state capitol taking pictures of it, and making a montage, and this and that.

"Well, he was taking an airplane to pick up his van for the first leg of his trip, and he explained what he was doing to a woman. She took pictures of him while he was asleep and snitched on him," Hilton said. "At each capitol, security gets harder and harder. Security was waiting for him. They got him on the terrorist list. He was arrested several times and detained. Finally had to stop it because this woman took his picture while he was asleep and snitched on him. Okay?

"And so there's a woman in North Carolina at a picnic area," Hilton continued. "She drove up. She's just a piece of white trash and her boyfriend apparently was driving, and I think she was drunk, too. She was acting like she was drunk. She was being very forward and everything. No real inhibitions. They drove up there, and she said out the window . . . I had, you know, my technical clothing on, as usual. Presenting my typical spectacle, you know, as, you know, I was being a spectacle . . . you know, doing my shtick, and she said, 'And what is your costume supposed to be?' You know? She had a smart mouth, basically, and I said, 'I am the prophet of microfiber.' But, you see, it never caught on. You can't even get this stuff anymore. It just fucking blew her mind. She didn't know what to fucking say."

Howard said, "I was fixing to say you probably got her pretty good."

"I'm almost sure the photograph was taken from where she was sitting, and I'm almost sure it was her, a piece of white trash. She takes this photo. She saved it for four months or whatever. She ain't nothing but a piece of drunk white trash herself. Okay? So I guess there's actually a lot of pictures."

"This is what I'd like to know from you. One thing I'd like to know . . . where all have you hiked? Where all have you been all over the United States as far as—" Howard asked, but was promptly interrupted.

"Oh, I know what you're getting at, the unsolved murders."

"I'm not talking about any *unsolveds*. What I'd like to know is how accomplished of a hiker are you?"

"I'm going to tell you something," Hilton said. "I have never met anyone ever, anywhere, anyway, that has the time in the woods and the time on the trail that I have. I've never worked—full-time, anyway—in my life, except for the U.S. Army and for the six months I went straight [that] I worked full-time. Okay? In '79, '80, I worked six months. Other than that, I have never worked full-time. I was a criminal, okay? I was a career criminal, unlawful charity from '73 to '93. Okay? For twenty years. Okay? And so I've never worked full-time. I've been a criminal. I couldn't get up and go to work every morning, and I've just been a soldier.

"It took me until the '90s to really realize what I was doing. I was just replicating what I did in the army. I was doing field maneuvers. I was replicating what I did in the army. And I came to understand that I was just on perpetual field maneuvers is what I was. That's good enough, so I'll just do it as a career," Hilton said. "Nobody, but nobody—and I've had the dogs, too, which means I always have a hiking companion. One thing that holds a lot of people back from getting a lot of time in the woods, again, is an activity is not valid unless you are with someone else. That's human nature.

"So, of course, it's hard. You ask ten people, 'Oh, do you hike?' 'Oh yeah.' 'Hiking?' 'Yeah. I hike.' 'Well, let's go next Saturday.' 'I got a wine tasting next Saturday, you know.' That kind of stuff, right?

"In other words, when the pavement ends, they get nervous. But I had the dogs . . . man, the worse the weather is—the more cold and nasty, wet, dreary, bitter, and windy the weather is—the better they like it. They're duck dogs. They're game dogs. They're bird dogs. And so I always had a hiking buddy. That was the revelation in our lives.

"That was the time I ceased to become the poor tortured sociopath that was trying to fit in but couldn't. That I never could, and would never be accepted, anyway. . . . I went from that to—to never being alone and understanding my place and purpose in life and the true nature of my personality, and what my fate was, which was to be alone. I came to understand that was my fate . . . to be alone. That was me. And to try to be something else would be to ensure unhappiness. Okay? And that really picked up in '91, when I started dog running, but it—it got going in the '80s, from '84 on. Ask Walter Goddard. He'll tell you, man—all the stuff I . . . Walter Goddard. . . . I'd go out into the woods every weekend and just . . . even around here is Gwinnett County, [and it] wasn't developed like it is now in '84.

"Oh my God, man, huge tracts of woods along the Yellow River and so forth. They're all subdivisions now, but you could just go hiking in Gwinnett County. Hell, they had a deer season in Gwinnett County, you know. And so I'd just been driven—like you're desperately . . . You guys are desperately running from it—your existential awareness. Well, in a sense I am, too, and I was a hobby runner before. . . . I started hobby running in '78, I told you, you know. That's how I met my wife. Long distances and everything. And I did that, and starting in '84, I discovered the North Georgia Mountains, and by then I had been pavement running for six years, and so the field maneuvers in the mountains was just replicating what I did as a paratrooper, and it was a new form of exercise. I'm telling you, when you're in shape, there's just something to a certain personality. . . . It's just something totally addictive to going like the Ever Ready bunny."

One of the GBI agents tried to interrupt, but Hilton was on a roll, and kept talking, thoughts tripping and stumbling over themselves, drunk and falling, but occasionally giving a glimpse of himself to the agents.

"And entering the state that I call hyperfatigue," Hilton continued. "When you enter hyperfatigue, it's sort of like a runner's high. When you enter hyperfatigue, the world is a different place. You're like a god. The very fabric of space and time is altered. You can do it, running real easy. Run over ten miles on a hot day. A vision quest. Yeah. The American Indians when they were young, the men, as a rite of passage, they would go without food, water, and sleep for a couple of hundred hours. Trust me, if you go one hundred ten hours without sleep, you'll hallucinate."

"Been there?" Howard asked.

"Yeah."

"We were talking earlier and you described yourself

as a pro," Howard said. "I mean, in talking about the eye of a police officer, when you and I encounter one another, I'm going to know you?"

"I'm a pro in that I'm not just styling," Hilton said. "You see, the average civilian, their entire life is a style. Nothing is real. They're rock climbers. Yeah. Hiker. Oh, well, twice they've driven up to Neel's Gap and done the little last part of Blood Mountain and they climbed Blood Mountain. We're all different in that we even . . . Everything is virtual. We even virtually grieve. We even have virtual grief. We see the candlelight marches for Meredith Emerson and people show up. People that don't even know the girl. Most of them don't, and they carry the things and they . . . Hey, son, if they want to grieve . . . What about if they want to grieve, I mean, thirty-five thousand people a year get shredded, maimed, and beaten to death in car wrecks. Okay? What I'm talking about is a virtual grief."

"You're saying it's like a 'Support the Troops' sticker on the back of your Toyota?"

"Yeah. It's a virtual thing. It's a style. They're talking the talk and they're not walking the walk, and they're styling and that's why you see posers. That's my word. That's what yuppies are. They talk instead of do. They pose instead of act, because they're perfectly precious. Right?"

"Okay," Howard said.

"I really started seeing that they were standing around perfectly precious and posing. They won't talk to you because they're afraid to. The yuppies work on the philosophy of 'it's better not to say anything and let them think you're a fool than say something and let them know you're a fool.'"

"A little bit wiser," Howard said.

"A police officer can see that I'm not just styling. All

the hikers you see . . . they're dressed as depicted in TV commercials of what a hiker is supposed to wear. They're wearing all cotton. Only just now are you starting to see a little technical clothing. You'll see some hikers with a technical shirt on. In other words, a not cotton shirt. Okay. Or microfiber this and microfiber that. Just now. I was stunned. In 1990, when I got into the microfibers, I predicted the demise of cotton. I said jeans are finished. Jeans are just nothing but lousy, stinking rags. They're wet. God. I mean, they're heavy, anyway."

"Soak up water," Howard said.

"Oh my, they're never dry. They're heavy as can be. Uncomfortable compared to microfiber. Jeans? Jeans are out. Was I wrong?"

Howard said, "Everything old is new."

"Man, it's a uniform. No one . . . ever . . ."

Howard guided the conversation back to Hilton's meaning about being a professional. "What's the attitude you take about your professionalism? Is it just extended to lifestyle?"

"I tend to try to systematize everything and break it down."

"You're saying discipline?"

"No. Understanding. Whatever activity you do. Just like a police officer does. He just learns. Everything for a police officer, every kind of situation, everything, is systematized for him and he does it by the numbers," Hilton said. "Except a police officer's training is just awesome. It's so varied. They're taught every kind of situation. The shoot/don't shoot training that police officers do these days. They use their own service weapons and actual sets. Constructed bank lobbies or parking lots and they use their own weapons. They wear armor, full-body armor similar to paintball armor, and they shoot each other at close range with their own nine-millimeter service weapons using a reduced power load and bullet. It's so awesome to see them do that.

"They'll shoot it out at ranges like that, man. It's just totally awesome, and they do it over and over and over again. So, as a result, you see some pudgy fuck police officer that, man, can handle a piece. Just fucking awesome, man. And they're trained all the way by the numbers, and that's what I'm talking about."

"And as far as your own training or your attitude toward summiting a mountain or whatever?" Howard asked.

"It's all systematized. Even my walking is systematized. I have a block of instructions I can give you on how to walk. If I'm teaching someone about backpacking, I'm going to teach them how to hike. I'm going to teach them how to walk. I'm going to teach them how to dress, get dressed, and I'm going to teach them how to piss. You'd be surprised how easy it is if you're pissing to piss on your equipment. Your clothes or your equipment. You know, you got this . . . I'm going to teach you how to take a shit. Right?"

"Like, when you're planning to summit a mountain or whatever, do you come up with contingency plans, like 'not making it by this certain time, then I'm going to go down to base camp.' That type of thing?" Howard asked.

"Yeah. And you do for purposes of equipment. You do the worst-case scenario planning," Hilton said. "In other words, what if I fall and break a femur? What if the dog goes down? Hundred-pound dog. What if your dog comes up lame? What if you've got an old dog and he comes up lame? What you going to do? You can't leave the dog. 'Stay here. I'll go get the sheriff and come back. Here's a flashlight. Here's a whistle. Here's a sleeping bag. Here's some food. Here's some water. Cool out.

Listen for my whistle. Blow your whistle I'll have the sheriff with me.' You can't tell the dog that.

"The dog weighs a hundred pounds. What you going to do? What if you—you know—and you're not on the AT (Appalachian Trail). I only use the AT generally as a connector. I'll climb the mountain to the AT, take the AT along the ridge, and then come back down another way. Then you're really, truly mountain climbing. So you're cross-country. What you going to do if the dog goes down? What you going to do if the dog gets its foot sliced up? As I said, what you going to do if the dog gets a thorn? What you . . . and what else? Your glasses. Reading glasses, if you wear glasses. Okay? That kind of thing. It goes on and on and on. . . ."

And so did Hilton. On and on. Howard tried to guide Hilton back to what he meant by calling himself "a professional."

"You read ahead and knew the law, that sort of thing," Howard said. "That professionalism is kind of permeated throughout—"

"When you get desperate, you ignore it," Hilton said. "In other words, when you're going out to kill somebody. If you're seen by a single, other person on the trail, then that day is screwed. But when you procrastinate because you don't want to get up and kill somebody and you let it go and you say, 'Oh, I won't kill anyone today. I'll just go hiking with my dog and have fun. We're doomed, anyway.' So you get down to the point where, well, with like Meredith, I had forty dollars and several days' food. So I had to kill somebody in that period of time. When you get down to the bitter end, you ignore all the rules you set, which I did, which got me caught."

"You strayed outside your own criteria."

"In other words, Blood Mountain is a good place to hunt because it's the most used day-hiking trail in the state of Georgia. I mean, this is a three-and-a-half-mile hike up, fourteen-hundred-foot climb and return, so it's a seven-mile walk with fourteen-hundred-foot elevation gain. I'm amazed at the number of people that do it. I've seen people in the bitter weather that Meredith was taken in—eleven degrees at night. I saw the sun setting behind my shoulder and three boys going up, not carrying a single thing, and one of them wearing shorts. They're betting their life, literally, that they don't stumble and hurt themselves, and it's amazing not more people get in serious trouble up there. It's a good place to hunt in that you have a huge selection, but it's a bad place because you—"

"Too many witnesses?" Howard asked.

"So the way you would do it would be to lurk in a blind, so to speak. Off the trail. Observe with binoculars and lurk. But I didn't do that, either, because . . . and a bunch of people saw me, and then it was a mistake to pick Meredith. Because she almost whipped my ass. She damn sure did. I lost control of both weapons, both the knife and the bat. Showed her the knife, she grabbed the fucker. It was a bayonet, so dull as shit. All it is, is a spike to stick with. It's not a knife. Grabbed the bayonet, and somehow I lost control of the bayonet and lost it period. It went down.

"I pulled the bat and deployed it. Grabbed that. I mean, I'm better than that. I am, but I found out she was a fucking black belt, which don't mean shit. Again, they're styling. These black belts, they're styling. They're not fighters. On the other hand, doing that kind of thing does increase your coordination, your hand eye, et cetera. . . . It gets you more used to hand-to-hand combat as opposed to an untrained person, even though they're not really fighters and she really . . . She was real quick with her hands and had no hesitation about grabbing weapons and everything. Not only that, she was hard to subdue. She fought like hell, man. Fought, and fought, and fought. Then once I gained control of her and got her ten, fifteen feet away from the trail, on the little side trail I told you about, she started fighting again, and I had to fight her again for several minutes, and her doing that is what got me caught because, if I had been back to the crime scene just a few minutes sooner, just several minutes sooner, I would have beat those people that found the bat and I would have picked it up. But I had to fight her twice, bring her all the way around the corner of the mountain and then secure her to a tree. She fought me fair and square."

Chapter 10

Walter Goddard told the GBI that he was startled to answer the phone on January 2, 2008, and find a message from Gary Hilton. Goddard said he had met Hilton more than twenty years ago and that he knew him better than anyone, but he had not heard from him in several weeks. Goddard immediately called the GBI when Hilton left a message and the telephone number to a cell phone that John Tabor had given him to make calls for Tabor's siding business.

"I'm concerned about this girl and her parents," Goddard said. "I hope he has done nothing. I know him. I read about the couple up in Ducktown (John and Irene Bryant), but I don't think he's capable of doing something like that—although he has recently gone through some bad times with this Tabor guy."

Goddard said he knew quite a bit about Hilton. He met Hilton when Goddard was in his early twenties and they were both telephone sales solicitors for a defunct chemical company in Tucker called KEM Manufacturing.

"I'm fifty-two and I've known him since I was twenty-three or twenty-five," Goddard said.

Hilton always struck Goddard as "a kind of a homeless

guy. I've seen the dog and I've seen the van. He's not a friend, but more of an acquaintance, but I've seen him for sure within the past three to four weeks."

When Goddard saw a photo of Hilton and Dandy on television, he turned to his wife and said, "I think that's Gary. It looks like his dog and his van."

Basically, what it boiled down to was that he's a con man, Hilton told the GBI special agents. He was a nice guy, but he was a con man. He was not honest and had spent a little time in jail for telephone solicitation, Goddard said.

During the last telephone call, Goddard said, Hilton ranted and raved almost incoherently on their voice mail, until it could store no more information. Then he telephoned a second time and did the same thing again. Goddard's wife was having a good time entertaining people by having them come over to listen to the rant. Goddard described it as "a long, expansive message about how he got screwed by Tabor."

Goddard described Hilton as "pretty athletic and a big-time runner. I just kind of stayed in touch with him somewhat distantly. Quite honestly, I kind of feel a little sorry for him in a way. He got some raw deals, but he brought a lot of it on himself.

"He might have had a pretty bad temper if you really crossed him, but I just don't see him doing some of the things they're talking about," Goddard said. "He's lonely, a loner. He pretty much told everybody he was going to live in mountains. He had telephone books and got paid a percentage for siding jobs."

The agents wanted to know if Hilton was charismatic. The answer from Goddard was an unequivocal yes.

Goddard remembered that Hilton told him that he had some military background and that he was "somewhat of a survivalist. He can take care of himself. He told me recently he was diagnosed with MS and he was under the belief that he was dying. He told me that about the late [part of] this past summer."

Goddard said that Hilton talked "a little bit" about his military background and that, at one point, he was a pilot. Hilton liked guns and loved to talk, using aviation terminology.

"He craved a gun," Goddard said, "but he couldn't get one after he got arrested, so he used air guns and a police baton." He and Hilton used to go into the woods and shoot air guns on occasional weekends, Goddard said.

Hilton liked to explain and act out maneuvers that highlighted his fighting skills. These were long monologues:

"The old Flying Boxcar—the instructor said the hardest thing about jumping a Fairchild C-119 is getting up to twelve hundred feet. You talk about fear. I've never been so afraid in my life after that first jump. Ever. A gut-wrenching, knee-knocking fear.

"Usually, it's the first. After that, they get progressively easy. The courage fades over time, just like combat. After you're out of it for a while, and you got to go back, you're real scared at first. I'll tell you, I just didn't know what to expect that first time, so it was just a wild ride for the first trip to the door. But after that, I got used to it, but at the same time that's something you always think about.

"Everybody visualizes what a parachute jump would be. I did, too, before I made one. What everyone fails to realize or visualize is the noise.

"It's just the noise and the wind. Most people, they think of parachute jumping, they think they're just jumping out because you see it. It's not a sound picture. It doesn't have that C-130 drop speed of one hundred twenty-five knots, you know, and so you're one hundred thirty-five miles an hour—that's about a class—every piece of nylon goes waving.

"Just turned seventeen when I joined the army. . . . Got my first adult arrest. I was seventeen in late November, and I got my first adult arrest. The judge nol-prossed it when I told him I was going in the army. That's what the army was like back then.

"They waived my felony rules. They may have waived even a high-school diploma. They're going right back where they were in the '60s. A bunch of kill-crazy psychos, man. Cheap-paid killers, man. That's what we all were.

"Oh, man, I'm telling you. My—my right . . . I was in Bravo. A Bravo company for a year before I went into special weapons, and the great majority of the guys in there were not high-school graduates. One enlisted man had some college. He had two years of college, and he was actually a U.S Reserve—that is volunteer airborne. And then re-upped and became RA (regular army). Yeah, so he was a draftee. He was the one draftee in the company, and he was the one that had any college at all.

"That's what it was like back then. It was like a French Foreign Legion, you know. You get out of going to court by saying you're going into the army, you know. So, yeah, I got a vagrancy arrest, childish stunt. Me and another guy was going in the back of Royal Castle, which is like Krystal. That was in Florida, Miami-Dade County, where I lived, and the Krystal of, like, Florida. You knock and use the bathroom. We were going in the back and stealing food out of the back of it, and then throwing it at cars. Seventeen years old, acting like a child. You know, we . . . you know, a gross of eggs, which is only about that big. A gross of eggs is one hundred forty-four eggs.

"Oh, chocolate custard pie. Just walk out in the . . . I'm a sociopath, man. I'm what they call an antisocial.

That's the new name for it, an antisocial personality. In my day it was called a 'sociopath character disorder,' is what it was known as.

"Yeah. You just walk out in the middle of a street, stand on the yellow line, four lanes, you know. Some people come along, you're standing right there in the middle on the yellow line, center line, and they're looking at you, and you're looking at them. . . . They're thinking, 'He's not going to throw that thing, is he?' And then run like hell. Oh, I mean, tons of fun, man. Idle youth, you know what I mean?"

Hilton also told Goddard about how he became a pilot who never flew again after obtaining his licenses:

"I entered Miami-Dade Junior College, going pilot, a career pilot program using my GI Bill. It paid ninety percent. Back then, a private pilot license cost nine hundred bucks. You can get a Cessna C-150S for eleven bucks an hour. Dual, with an instructor, for fourteen an hour. The VA would pay ninety percent of your flight costs.

"Oh yeah, and the tuition was one hundred fifty a semester because it was a community college. So I got the degree and the commercial ticket with a multinational engine and instrumental reading, and I got a Certificate of Flight Instructor Instrument also.

"CMII, CFL license, Certificate of Flight Instructor Instrument. Yeah, yeah. The instrument reading then was an additional forty hours, as much as it takes to get a private ticket. Private ticket was forty hours approved."

Goddard had asked if Hilton got a commercial license, too.

"Oh yeah, commercial, with a multi and instrument, and then the instrument instructor. I've never flown since."

Hilton gave demonstrations and lectures on how to fight:

"If you know how to use it, it's a whole lot different than not knowing how to use it. You don't do it this way, like this. You should sling it out. If backed up against a wall, I can take care of myself."

"Once we were out on a trail and a guy approached him," Goddard said. "Gary got mad and said he was going to take him out. I thought he was kidding. He came across as a very gentle person."

Goddard wasn't sure about Hilton's sexual orientation, but he thought that he "might go both ways." He mentioned that Hilton had stalked a "girlfriend" for years. When he described the object of Hilton's attention, it seemed to the GBI agents that he was describing Brenda, the sixteen-year-old girl he had sex with and then stalked at her college basketball games.

Goddard said he couldn't put his finger on anything specific to make him think that Hilton had homosexual tendencies. He reached the conclusion through a number of things. First, there was where Hilton had lived back in those days, on Eleventh Street, near a notorious hangout for gay men looking for companionship. Hilton used to spend many of his evenings, and late into the night, cruising through the park, according to Goddard's recollection. He thought he saw a hint of the feminine in the way Hilton dressed.

Back in those days Hilton loved the sport of bodybuilding, and Goddard said that he was "very strong for a little guy. The pictures in the newspapers, they make him look like a stooped old man, but I tell you, that guy is strong as an ox. When he got into bodybuilding, he thought he was Superman. He thought he could beat up on somebody. What happened is he approached someone on Eleventh Street and that guy just beat the absolute crap out of him down there. But he kept hanging around the gay guys' park."

On the other hand, there were signs that Hilton had what Goddard considered ordinary sexual habits. "I will tell you that if you pull him over and look in his van, you'll find a bunch of pornography books. Old ones. Nothing you'd see on the shelf. Not *Penthouse* or *Hustler.* He carried porn. He was very peculiar in a lot of ways, and I don't know anything about his family or even if he has one."

He's pretty much a loner, Goddard said. He was in the hospital having stents put into his coronary arteries following a heart attack when he saw him on TV. "I couldn't believe it. It almost gave me another heart attack."

Hilton was involved in illegal telephone solicitations much of the time that Goddard knew him. Hilton would make the calls to prospects that he selected by driving in neighborhoods and getting the addresses of people who needed siding. He would match the address with a name and telephone number and call to make his pitch for siding. If not actually working for someone, Goddard said, Hilton simply made up a product or charitable organization and made a telephone call.

Goddard said Hilton ran newspaper ads to find people to pick up the checks. It amounted to chump change, ten or fifteen dollars. But it was flimflam. He wasn't getting rich off it. Goddard was quick to note that he didn't stick around long enough to get details on how Hilton went about it. The agents told him they would come back later if they needed more information.

The agents asked Goddard if Hilton had any particular fetish in pornography.

"Maybe, but nothing really kinky," Goddard said. "I'd say it wasn't even true hard-core. Old stuff, which was surprising."

Any girlfriends? the GBI asked again.

Goddard shrugged as if that wasn't much of a possibility.

"He was kind of ugly, too," he said. "Last time I saw

him, he had a front tooth that had rotted out. He looked awful. He couldn't drink, or at least he couldn't handle it. He might have been on some medication."

Hilton lived with a guy that Goddard didn't know. He thought the roommate might have been a lawyer, but he wasn't sure.

"He didn't really have a home. He paid for his residence on Eleventh Street, paid by the week."

Goddard said Hilton was always prepared to protect himself in the woods. He had three to five pepper spray canisters, the collapsible baton, and an air pistol. But he wanted a real handgun badly, Goddard said. He said that Hilton was "quite knowledgeable" about guns. He said that Hilton once told him, "If you looked at my military records, you would find that I'm a sharpshooter with rifle and pistol, either hand, and an expert in knife and bayonet fighting."

The GBI checked this information and found it to be true. The weapons that Hilton said he "handled" were not conventional bombs and bullets: they were nuclear weapons designed for tactical battlefield use.

Goddard said that Hilton was intimately familiar with all of the hiking areas in the Appalachian Mountains and would be anywhere. He knew that Hilton traveled from one part of the country to another and was almost always on the move. The Atlanta Tract of the Dawson Forest Wildlife Management Area was one of the places he liked best. Goddard said that Hilton knew Atlanta's parks well and had even traveled to the western United States to hike.

"The harder and colder it is, the better he likes it. He was into power hiking in a big way," Goddard said. "He loved to go to the mountains. He went to St. Helens. He liked to do things to the extreme. If it was snowing up there, he was right up there. That was right up his alley. He liked it hard. I've seen him running in snow at Stone Mountain."

Goddard told the GBI agents the same thing that Brenda had said: Hilton had changed a great deal for the worse in the past few months. Just as Brenda hadn't recognized Hilton three months ago, neither had Goddard.

"He had lost a lot of weight," Goddard said. "He was quirkier and he had pulled his front teeth out. He looked awful." Goddard thought that Hilton might have said something about having gone to a VA hospital, but he wasn't certain. Hilton had not asked him for money, as he had asked Brenda.

Goddard seemed surprised by the question. "Did I loan him money? No, but he always had money. He had bogus accounts set up, but he always had money with him in an envelope, sometimes two thousand dollars."

The GBI agent asked, "Did he ever say anything about people he doesn't like? Did he say anything about having a list of people he needed to kill?"

"No, but it wouldn't surprise me to know that," Goddard said. "If you turned on him, it wasn't a good thing. He never let things go. He never liked his father or anybody. I hate to say this, but if she (Meredith Emerson) had turned on him, telling him to leave her alone, he would take that as a personal rejection. He probably would have approached nicely—he's a nice guy, he really is—but if he felt rejected, it would go from bad to worse. He might have gotten a little pissed," Goddard said. "I'm saying he's capable of that. He would take a rejection personally. I don't, in general, think of him being the type who would harm somebody. I really don't."

"If it was a guy, could he do it?"

"If it was a guy, maybe, but I don't know. I really don't know."

The GBI concluded the interview, but they would have

more questions for Goddard later. Goddard's father had sold Hilton a car, and Goddard remembered in the years that he knew Hilton, he had owned a black Mazda pickup and a dark-colored Camaro. Since the GBI opened its tip line, it had received scores of calls about encounters with a man resembling Hilton. Some of them described him as having a black Mazda; others, as having a car similar to a Camaro in different years.

There were already suspicions that Hilton might be responsible for at least one other death. Law enforcement officers in the North Carolina State Bureau of Investigation, GBI, FBI, and FDLE had already noted some similarities in the deaths of Irene and John Bryant in North Carolina, Cheryl Dunlap in Florida, and Meredith Emerson in Georgia.

"I hope you guys get him," Goddard said. "I feel sorry for this girl's parents."

As the agents were leaving, Goddard recalled something.

"I just remembered. He went by the name of Mack. He thought Gary was too feminine."

Chapter 11

The group of men had gathered on Monday under close security to form a secret caravan to Dawson Forest that cool evening of January 7 at about 5:30 P.M. The center of attention was Gary Hilton, whose inflated sense of self basked in its warmth like a cat lying in a sunbeam. The GBI was represented by Special Agents Clay Bridges and John Cagle; Union County by Sheriff Scott Stephens; Todd Dawson, investigator with the public defender's office; Neil Smith represented Hilton; and last, but not least, Enotah Judicial Circuit district attorney (DA) Stanley "Stan" Gunter.

The meeting and its purpose had been kept secret because none of them, with the possible exception of Hilton, wanted to have a huge contingent of news media representatives to be present at such a critical junction.

Gary Hilton had agreed to tell where Meredith Emerson's remains were in exchange for a plea of guilty to murder and a sentence to life in prison. The man who had been running from death all of his life was still running.

There were two police vehicles in the caravan. Other police units had already been dispatched to the general area where the caravan would go. Hilton sat in the back-seat of the lead car with Bridges, who would record an interview with Hilton as they drove to the crime scene in Dawson Forest. Smith and Gunter accompanied them and Stephens drove. The others followed behind them in a separate car.

Dawson Forest was so big—and the area they were heading to was so remote—that no one except Hilton knew precisely how to get there. They discussed the best way to go.

"I'm sitting here trying to rack my brain on how to get down there," the sheriff said to the others. "We could take those back roads. . . ."

Cagle agreed and they started off.

"You need anything to eat?" Hilton asked, as though hosting a friendly social gathering.

No one was hungry.

"I've got to keep you alert now," Hilton said, expressing concern for everyone's blood sugar levels. "Sheriff, could you take your police radio down just a notch? Or off. Or whatever you want to do?" Hilton asked. He nodded toward Bridges. "I'm gonna talk to him on the way down there."

Stephens switched the radio off and Bridges asked him for clearer directions on how to get to where they needed to be. Hilton rattled off instructions and looked pleased at his knowledge of the backwoods areas.

"Cut loose with a cigarette, Sheriff," he said. "If you got any."

Bridges told Hilton they would get on down the road and then get out of the car for a cigarette.

"Forget it," Hilton snapped. "I don't have any."

"Did you know Meredith Emerson before . . . ?" Bridges asked.

Hilton answered that he had not. Under questioning

by Bridges, Hilton told his version of how the events had occurred. He said he had gone to Blood Mountain because there were always a lot of people there and "it was a good place to hunt." He wasn't sure, but he thought he had been camping illegally at Vogel Park for two or three days before he saw Emerson. He mentioned that he had stalked another woman the day before he saw Emerson, but he had abandoned the hunt because he discovered she had family just a short distance behind them.

When he first saw Meredith Emerson, Hilton said, he approached her while she ate trail mix and fed her dog. He started to chat, and then kept walking with her as they headed toward the summit. Hilton said he let Emerson go on ahead of him because his multiple sclerosis made it too hard for him to keep up. Instead, he intended to attack her when she descended.

"Did you form an opinion at that point, or did you form an idea at that point that you wanted to abduct her?" Bridges asked.

"Yeah. This was driven really by nothing but the desire to obtain her cards and PIN number," Hilton said. "Rather than pick a couple and the guy fights back and you gotta kill him. Well, where are you at?

"So I felt it would be easier to establish control over a female than a male. Not that I couldn't whup a male, but once you whip 'em, you might be left holding the bag, so to speak."

Hilton was getting revved up; and the more he talked, the faster the words came out of his mouth. The answers were sometimes to the point or followed a tortuous route of disjointed and bizarre ideas. Bridges would then have to stop him frequently to get him back on the subject or to answer the specific question.

"Then you had decided to specifically abduct her on the trail to get her cards and PIN number?" Bridges asked.

"Well, I should say, potentially. If nothing better came along."

Hilton told how he had waited off the trail and stepped out when Emerson came back. He had a knife in his hand and demanded her cards and PIN numbers. Instead, she surprised him by knocking the knife away and disarmed him again when he pulled out his bayonet. They went tumbling down a ravine, along with Emerson's water bottles, and chew food for her dog.

"And then I produced the baton. She fought that and I lost control of the baton," Hilton said. "And I'm good, too. This little girl, hundred-some-pound girl, was whupping my ass."

Hilton said they wrestled and went tumbling down a ravine. "I had to hand fight her. That's where I got multiple fractures in my right hand. I could not get control of her. She would pretend that I was in control and then start fighting again. So I had to hit her a number of times."

Bridges asked if he had used only his right hand, and Hilton answered yes. "Straight punches in the face or the head." He claimed that Emerson was in no pain when the fight was over, after he had clubbed her with a heavy branch, and only suffered a broken nose and two black eyes.

"Hold on a second," Bridges said. "Once you hit her in the head and the face, how many times would you estimate that happened?"

"Hard to say. She wouldn't stop fighting. And then she'd stop and she'd start fighting again. And yelling. I needed to control her and silence her."

Bridges asked Hilton what happened after he gained control. Hilton said that he took her on a switchback trail that couldn't be seen from the Byron Herbert Reece Trail, tied her to a tree, and then went back to "clean up the crime scene." He wanted to retrieve his baton, knife, bayonet, and anything that might have shown that a struggle took place. Three hikers were already there, Hilton said. While hiding behind a boulder, he saw that these items already had been found and that the hikers were heading down the trail. Hilton lay flat on his stomach for a while as he tried not to be seen.

Hilton next told Bridges that he returned to Emerson, untied her, and removed the duct tape he had used to help secure her to the tree. He put a noose around her neck with a three-hundred-pound test line, and he marched her off the trail to an area not too far from where their vehicles were parked in a lot at Vogel Park.

"Were her hands free?" Bridges asked. "You didn't have those zip tied?"

"No. Just had the noose around her neck. I told her I had a pistol, which I didn't. By that time she was totally compliant."

That made him "very solicitous of her condition and comfort." He added, "My intent was not torture. I understood the situation."

The two police cars were driving on steep, winding mountain roads, and Bridges had to stop the interview for a few minutes. He said he was getting dizzy and needed a short break. Once they got on a smoother, more level stretch of the highway, he continued the interview. Hilton told how he had tied Emerson to a tree in the woods that was close to the parking lot but couldn't be seen because the shrubbery was so thick.

It was just before sunset, Hilton said, when he brought Emerson out of the woods and secured her inside with chains and a rope. They were both getting cold, Hilton said, and he was worried that the law would show up any second, because he thought the hikers who found his weapons and Emerson's water bottles and dog stuff would have notified the cops.

"It was cold, and as soon as the sun goes down, the heat radiates right out and the temperature drops like a rock," Hilton said. "I was concerned that someone might have heard her yelling, because sound carries forever in cold air."

After he got Emerson in the car, Hilton said, he made sure she couldn't get away.

"I had two lengths of chain padlocked to the seat mounting. The front-seat mounting. One chain padlocked to a seat attached to the car. The shortest one was four or five feet long. The other was about nine feet long. It was a link chain."

"How did you chain her?" Bridges asked.

Hilton told how he had used chains and padlocks to chain up her body. He used the short chain, about four feet long, to wrap around her neck and pulled it so tight that Emerson could not possibly have gotten her head free. Hilton claimed that he didn't secure her feet or hands and that Emerson was never gagged, or had her mouth taped shut, even though he said he had taken duct tape with him when he abducted her.

"She could have grabbed something, smacked me up the side of the head while I was driving," he said. "She could have reached around and got a stranglehold. It was just to keep her from jumping out. I put a childproof latch on the sliding door so it could not be opened from the inside."

He told Bridges how he had put the dog in Emerson's car and headed toward Blairsville. Emerson, he said, was worried about her dog and she continued to express her concern to him, even after he was several miles away on Highway 129 North. To keep her calm, more than out of concern for Ella, Hilton went back for Emerson's dog.

"Did she ever give you her PIN number while you were asking for it on the mountain?"

"After I got control of her, she gave me a PIN number. It was incorrect. She never gave me a correct number. Sorry if my breath is bad. I been drinking coffee."

"You had her cards and PIN number and took her just to make sure it was the right PIN number?"

"Correct."

"Is that something that you had planned to do, anyway?"

"Yeah."

This was critical information and Bridges wanted to make certain he wasn't going outside the limits of the plea agreement. He turned to Hilton's lawyer, Neil Smith.

"Neil, everything with you okay so far?"

It was. Then without prompting, and in the most casual conversational voice, Hilton said:

"I'm gonna tell you right now. There was never any plan to let her go. I knew if I let her go, I would be identified. I knew that she couldn't be let go."

"So you . . ."

"I knew she was doomed."

The law enforcement officers in the car felt the information settle down on them like a dark fog. Hilton had just confessed to premeditation to murder. They were being civil, acting friendly, to keep Hilton talking freely. Not showing their anger and disgust took a great deal of effort, but they were able to maintain their professional detachment, at least on the surface. Bridges had never felt such disgust for a person and he said later that being near Hilton caused him to feel waves of evil washing over him, something he had never felt before.

He asked if Hilton was telling him that he decided to kill Emerson while they were on the Reece and Appalachian Trails, and Hilton said that wasn't what he meant.

"I can't . . . I'm not telling you that," Hilton said.

"On advice of counsel?"

"You already told him, I think," Smith told Hilton.

Hilton continued with his story, telling how he had driven to the Appalachian Community Bank in Blairsville. Emerson kept him running back and forth to the ATM, which was across the street from where he had parked, and none of them would work. After several attempts he drove to a bank in Canton and went through the same futile motions, holding a towel over his face. He warned Emerson that she had better stop dancing him around.

"She said, 'Well, I think I just changed it, and I'm not sure of this, and blah, blah, blah. Go try it again.'"

Hilton said he tried again—with the same results. "So she's telling me, 'It's gonna work. Must be a wrong bank. Maybe a Wachovia?' Just a whole bunch of stuff she said, and—"

"So you went to Gainesville to attempt it?"

"Yeah, I needed a larger metropolitan area because I'm walking up to ATMs with my face covered. Late at night with my face covered. You gotta be kinda careful about what ATM you use. If anyone sees you on a cold, late night on foot at a drive-in ATM and covering your face with a towel—you know some police officer just passing by . . ."

Hilton explained that he liked to try ATM cards after dark, but not too late. The temperature had dropped and it was also cold, which was something that worked against him.

"On a bitterly cold night, a police officer passing by would have been curious as to why is this guy walking around at an ATM holding something over his face?" Hilton said.

"Gainesville was pushing the envelope. It's a fairly large metropolitan area, still active by the time I got there. But on such a bitterly cold night, it's effectively late early, because people clear off—"

"You're telling me it needs to be dark, but there needs to be enough people so that you don't stand out," Bridges said.

"Exactly. Any police officer is curious and inquisitive if he's any good," Hilton said. "Anytime he sees anything that's inappropriate to any situation, he asks himself, 'Why is that guy here?'"

Even though conditions were okay in Gainesville, Hilton said, Emerson sent him to the ATM machines at least five times with incorrect PINs. He started to get worried about being there so long and "throwing up a red flag" to a policeman who might pass by. Throughout all of this, he claimed that Emerson was in the van, secured only by a loose chain, and that she could have yelled for help.

"Could she have slipped it over her head?" Bridges asked.

"No. What I mean, loosely is—"

"She wasn't choking?"

"No. It was just so she couldn't slip. . . . She had freedom of movement around in the van."

"And her dog was with her, so you think she felt comfortable . . . not making any noise?"

"She wasn't going nowhere," Hilton said, "and I told her if she made any noise, it was curtains."

"How did you put that to her?"

"You go messing around and I'll shoot your ass."

"Four or five times she kept trying to convince you [the PIN] would work?"

"Oh, she convinced me. She ran me back and forth like an idiot." Hilton laughed. "I mean, really. You know. Some eternal optimist."

Hilton said that Emerson kept making up different stories about why the cards weren't working and continually convinced him that she had finally told him the right one.

"She kept me running." He laughed. "She sent me running back and forth to that thing holding a damn towel in front of me."

Finally, he said, it was becoming too late to keep trying without arousing undue suspicion. "I'm like . . . some days with the MS I can't get out of bed. Some days I get to this point I can't even remember anything. By this time I'd had it."

He drove toward Dahlonega and up into the higher elevations. It started to snow. He wanted to go higher up, Hilton said, but by then he was shot, couldn't think straight, looking for a place to camp. For some reason he went into downtown Dahlonega, but he didn't remember why. He wasn't mentally functioning by then. He was starting to "flag out" and couldn't think or focus.

"The snow was coming and it was accumulating rapidly, and there was probably two inches on the ground," he said. "I was losing traction and control and I came around a curve, and a car had sort of slid off the road and there was a sheriff's deputy there—car, with its blue lights. And I was struggling uphill. I knew it was just gonna get worse."

Hilton told how he worried about the deputy stopping him, or that Emerson might cry out for help, and he knew the deputy was going to block off the road to keep people from driving higher up the mountain. He turned around and drove back. The deputy was busy assisting a motorist who had run off the road and gotten stuck.

Driving on, Hilton told how he found a place to camp on private property in a remote area off Nimblewill Creek Road, where he made camp for the night. According to him, Emerson helped unload the van. They spent the night outside in sleeping bags. Hilton did not mention that he raped his captive, as he had told the police in a previous interview.

At this point Hilton asked, "Sheriff, could someone spring for a cup of coffee for me at a drive-in so that I can keep going on this thing? I'm sorry. There's McDonald's."

Bridges told him that they would keep talking for now and get coffee later. Hilton said there was a McDonald's they could go to when they made a turn at Dawson Creek Road. Hilton apologized and reassured the others in the car that he wasn't going to back out of his deal to show them where to find Emerson's body.

Returning to the business at hand, Hilton told how Emerson had run him around with false PINs at Regions Bank in Canton and he got no money. Remembering, Hilton broke out laughing and shook his head. He said that after he found a campsite, they spent two nights there, and they went for a long hike in the woods the next day when the temperature reached a record low of eleven degrees.

"She had a good time," Hilton said.

"How did you keep her from running off while you were hiking?"

"Even though she's been kidnapped, she's having a good time. I told her I'd shoot her ass down if she tried to run. No, she commented on how beautiful it was. She was enjoying herself. I could tell."

Bridges asked how long they had hiked and if Emerson ever tried to get away.

"We hiked for hours," Hilton answered. "She never tried to get away. She was very compliant. They always become compliant."

It was as if a jolt of electricity had struck the law officers in the car. Hilton had said *they* become compliant, not that *she* had. Was it a slip of the tongue, or had he done this kind of thing before? At this point there was no connection made between the Cheryl Dunlap murder in Florida, Irene Bryant in South Carolina, and her husband, John, who was missing and presumed dead.

"I don't know exactly why that I didn't try to run the cards or do the end result." (By this, Hilton meant why he wasn't trying the ATM cards or killing Meredith Emerson, the young woman he said was having such a good time.)

By now, they were getting near the crime scene and the police were having difficulty finding their way around. Hilton gave them directions from memory, as if he knew every stone and fallen branch in the deep forest. As he gave directions, Hilton described how he had seen a tanker truck drawing water near his campsite and had driven off in a hurry after he and Emerson packed the camping gear.

Bridges interrupted the interview when he saw other vehicles on the road when they were about a mile from Shoal Creek.

"That's not the media, is it?" he asked. "How the hell did they—"

"You want my boys to take care of it?" the sheriff asked.

"Yeah. What can we tell 'em? Tell 'em to get out of here?"

There were several trucks from television stations and cars filled with reporters who had somehow not only gotten word that Hilton was taking police to Emerson's body, they had also managed to find the remote area without Hilton's help. The police officers who had driven ahead of the van carrying Hilton herded reporters and vehicles behind the police cavalcade. They wouldn't let them follow any farther.

Hilton described the short, but complicated, route he took to drive Emerson to where he said he told her she was going home. A fast talker by nature, Hilton was speaking with such rat-a-tat-tat excitement that Bridges had to remind him several times to talk slower.

". . . She just laid down in the back and relaxed," Hilton said to the special agent. "She was always at ease. . . ."

The sheriff had missed a turn and was lost, but Hilton knew exactly where they were. He steered them back on course, scolding them for being so inept. "We goofed up. I told you the first road. This is not it," he said. "We got to go to the next road."

After the cars were on track again, Hilton continued telling Bridges how they had driven to the site in the deep woods, secured her to a tree with line and a chain. He made several trips to the van, which he had parked several yards away, and brought Emerson's clothing and cell phone. He said he made a big show of putting the gear where she could see it. After that, he went back to the van, made a campfire, and brewed coffee.

"I'm staggering around by now," he said. "I have just, I have had it. I can't even think straight. I'm, you know, I'm just staggering—just staggering—multiple sclerosis."

Hilton said he drank a cup of coffee and tried to pull himself together. When he felt calmer, he took a tire iron from the van, held it by his side to conceal it from Emerson, and walked back to where she was tied and chained. She looked nervously at him.

"I was afraid you weren't coming back."

At this point, Hilton laughed. "You glad to see me?" he asked.

"I gave her a book to read and walked up and made as if to unsecure the chain, uh, struck her with the . . . jack handle. Just a straight jack handle. The solid iron bar. Struck her with that. She said, 'No. Let me go.' She put her hands up. . . . I kept striking her and she . . . You'll see

some defensive wounds to her hands. She lost consciousness and . . . I kept striking her to ensure she was dead.

"I unsecured her, removed her clothing, for forensic
evidence, you know. . . . That blue jacket you have, uh,
that's soaked with blood, that's mine. The pile pullover,
the fleece pullover that's soaked with blood . . . that's
mine. The pile pants that she wore—she had a pair of
sweatpants on over that—that's mine. She was wearing
a lot of my clothes 'cause I kept her dressed warmly."

It appeared that most of the clothing Hilton removed
from Emerson's body belonged to him; the blood, however, was from the brutally beaten body of the young
woman.

Bridges asked where they would find the tire iron,
which had not been found. Hilton said it should be on the
grass near the air pressure pump at the Chevron station,
because he had intended to throw it in the Dumpster with
the blood-soaked clothing.

Hilton continued, "Okay, removed her head with a serrated knife. Which you probably have in the Dumpster."

"A serrated knife?" Bridges asked.

"Yeah, like a butcher knife . . . just like it would come
in a set of serrated knives. One sharpened edge . . . it was
just your standard, cheap, twelve-inch. You would call it
a butcher knife."

"Is that difficult to do? To take somebody's head off?
I'm not asking for—"

"It didn't seem real. It doesn't seem real—looking
back on it."

"I can't imagine a kitchen knife being able to do that,
is what I'm getting at," Bridges said.

Hilton held his hands about a foot apart. "This is a knife
with a blade this long that's serrated. And so it's a saw.

"It's just sawing," Hilton said. "All you gotta do is keep
sawing, sawing . . ."

"Right."

". . . Sawing, sawing. Then you get through the joint. . . . That's what it's made for. . . . A little bigger than you would use to cut up a chicken . . . but you'd cut up a leg of lamb or anything else."

"I—I . . ." Bridges couldn't get his words out.

"Simple as can be," Hilton said. "Just a cheap knife."

"Did you conceal her head in anything, or did you . . . ?" Bridges asked.

"No. I bagged her head, in a white bag, and took it with me. Took that and the two sleeping bags she was using—and the mattress and the book she was reading—back to the van and drove up to whatever it is to the next place we'll be going. And took some of her bloody clothes . . . Actually, the bloody clothes I discarded at the head were her clothes and the bloody clothes I discarded in the Dumpster were my clothes."

"Right."

"That I wanted to keep and wash because they are nice clothes."

Hilton described his grisly activities with the calm detachment of an accountant reading a routine financial report. He was careful to accentuate every detail to emphasize that he was a "professional," who would leave nothing to chance. He told Bridges that he had poured bleach all over Emerson's head and body after he had removed all of her clothing and bagged it. He was hoping to remove fibers from his clothing and his DNA, he said.

Hilton took the head and clothing to one location, removed the head from the bag, and loosely covered it with branches and leaves and other forest debris, leaving openings so that the elements would cause it to deteriorate faster. He said he did the same with the bagged clothes at another site, about twenty feet west of where he placed the head.

"And so I poured liquid bleach over her and, again, this is not to . . . done to preclude identification or for any other reasons," Hilton said. "I knew the body would be found sooner or later. These bodies, the body in here sooner or later is gonna come to light. It is."

The next sentence caused the hair on Bridges's neck to prickle.

"And this is not the first body that's been discarded here," Hilton said.

The sheriff's police radio crackled.

"They got the body," Stan Gunter announced.

Cagle replied, "Go where the head is. We got the body."

The sheriff was having trouble finding the spot where the body was, even though other law officers were already there. Hilton knew exactly where they were, even deep in a remote area of Dawson Forest. He described what he had done to hide the body while he gave directions to what he called "the kill site."

He directed the sheriff over a series of ridges, then to find a small road and go down a steep hollow. When he first went to the site, Hilton told them, he saw what he thought was a lost camper in a pickup truck.

"I saw a pickup there, but I stopped, backed in, and turned around to the kill location," Hilton said. "As he drove by, I waved at him. It was law enforcement."

"Really?" Bridges asked.

"Yeah. It was that close. It was that close. She wasn't even secured, either."

After a while the law enforcement officers were deep into the woods and could go no farther in the car. They got out and walked among trees, and boulders, across rock and leaf-strewn ground and found the bloody clothing and body. The law enforcement officers had been working around the clock for weeks; their red-rimmed eyes were bloodshot in sockets darkened by fatigue. Tears welled in those eyes and lumps formed in stomachs and throats.

"Was this difficult for you at all?" Bridges asked. "As far as to take her life? Do you have feelings one way or the other about it, or was . . . You just needed her for a necessity for you?"

"No, but it was like an—an out-of-body experience. Of course it's surrealistic. Removing a head is just unreal," Hilton said. "You look back on it and you say, 'That wasn't even real.' I don't know what it was. You might say an altered state? I—I just don't know. It was hard. You gotta remember we had, uh, spent several good days together, actually."

"Right. Right," Bridges said.

"Actually, she did not have an unpleasant time . . . consistent with being kidnapped. We did all the camping activities together."

"Is this the first time you ever done anything like this before?" Bridges asked.

Hilton referred the question to his attorney, who told Bridges that the plea agreement stated that he would only be asked about the murder of Meredith Emerson. Neither Hilton nor his attorney answered the question.

The crime scenes were secured and Hilton was taken back to jail. Dozens of forensic technicians worked all day and late into the night, gathering and tagging evidence.

When they were finished and the cars had left, one by one, Bridges remained behind. He walked to where the body had been found and felt an ache in his heart as he thought of the victim chained, frightened, and doomed, listening to Hilton's warped ideas spilling out of his mouth in an incessant torrent of words. He shuddered, closed his eyes, and prayed for Meredith Emerson.

Chapter 12

During the course of a law enforcement juggernaut that had covered hundreds of miles and used hundreds of man hours, Lee Darragh, district attorney for the Georgia Northeastern Judicial Circuit, seemed to have been inadvertently left out of the loop. Like a giant earthquake or a volcano that causes a tsunami, the tips to police officers throughout the region had the mountains trembling as the investigation changed minute by minute. When Hilton had decided to start talking, the first words the GBI thought about were "plea bargain." Dawson Forest was huge and their chances of finding Emerson's body were remote.

Federal officers involved in the case weren't anxious for Hilton to be convicted and sentenced to death. They believed he had more than a few killings under his belt. As the chief law enforcement officer in the county where Emerson was killed, Darragh should have been the one calling the shots for adjudicating the case. This chase had covered so much territory—so fast—that their heads were spinning. Who had jurisdiction?

Emerson had been reported missing in Gwinnett

County, and Blood Mountain, where she was kidnapped, was near Blairsville, near Enotah County. The law officers brought in Enotah County public defenders Ines Suber and Steven Been, who were appointed to represent Gary Hilton in plea bargain talks. The most serious choice against Hilton at the moment was kidnapping with intent to do bodily harm. There was no doubt, even in Hilton's mind, that he had been caught with a smoking gun in his hand. That would be murder with the maximum penalty of death—the thing that had terrified Hilton since he was four years old.

Hilton was taken into custody by the DeKalb County Sheriff's Office in Atlanta and was taken to Union County, where he was being held pending his appearance in magistrate court, similar to a grand jury, to decide whether or not he would be brought to trial. Emerson had been murdered in Dawson County.

The plea bargain had already been agreed to by Hilton and the state by the time Darragh was notified that it was even in the works.

"I have no involvement," Darragh told the press. "I have had no discussions with the defendant nor any representative of the defendant concerning any plea negotiations in the case."

The only thing he knew about a plea deal, he said, was that federal prosecutors had urged the state to take the death penalty out of play.

GBI special agent Clay Bridges said there had been significant evidential discoveries in Hilton's Astro van. When a federal agent talked with Bridges about the death penalty, he said, "Somebody's going to get him on the death penalty."

When Hilton was to appear in magistrate court, Darragh reiterated that he was not part of the plea bargaining.

"I have no involvement," he said at a press conference. "No involvements in any discussions between the defendant and DA Stan Gunter. I have had no discussions with the defendant nor any representatives of the defendant concerning any plea negotiations in this case." (Gunter was the DA for Enotah County circuit.)

"I was made aware of the discovery of the body and the possibility that she was killed in Dawson County," Darragh continued. "Neither I nor any member of my staff was made aware of, or was involved in, or invited to, any part of any discussions between the U.S. Attorney, DA Stan Gunter, of Enotah Judicial Circuit, nor any attorneys for the defendant."

Law enforcement officers in North Carolina, where Irene and John Bryant were killed, and in Leon County, Florida, where Cheryl Dunlap was beaten to death, said there was evidence in the van that linked Hilton directly to all three of these murders. Irene Bryant and Cheryl Dunlap were both beaten to death with a blunt instrument, just as Meredith Emerson had been killed. Emerson and Dunlap were both decapitated after death, but Bryant was not. John Bryant's body had not been discovered by the time Hilton faced magistrate court, although he was reported missing in September 2007.

On the morning of January 6, 2009, Hilton was brought to magistrate court under heavy security. People in the area had developed a deep hatred for Hilton based solely on news reports. He wore an orange jumpsuit over body armor that protected him from his neck down to his hips. A SWAT team had been called on duty to protect Hilton, and there was at least one SWAT sharpshooter on the roof of a tall building.

Hilton entered the magistrate court in handcuffs, leg irons, and shackles, and his face glowered. When Dawson County chief magistrate Johnny Holtzclaw asked how

Hilton pleaded to the charges, the prisoner boomed out, "Not guilty!" A motion for bail was promptly denied and Hilton was taken to Dawson County Detention Center. There he was arrested on a warrant for the malicious murder of Meredith Emerson.

Waiting in the wings with his own warrant for the first-degree murder of Cheryl Dunlap was Leon County sheriff Larry Campbell in Tallahassee, Florida. The on-going investigation by the GBI to wrap up the Emerson case was yielding strange finds. A criminal lawyer, who also produced DVD movies for retail sale, stepped forward to say that Hilton had developed the story line in 1995 for a movie called *Deadly Run*.

Samuel Rael said that Hilton came up with an idea about a serial killer who takes people to his cabin in the woods, and then hunts and kills them. The killer kills men and women alike, and is not limited to a club as his weapon choice. He uses a pistol to murder two girls close-up after he picks them up in a bar and flies them in his pontoon-fitted airplane to his remote mountain cabin. Minutes later he kills with a rifle, and also kills a group of pursuing police officers with a hand-carried rocket. The bodies in *Deadly Run* drop like flies, until the serial killer finally takes a bullet.

Killing people in the remote woods seemed to be a theme of which Hilton was quite fond.

"I knew he was a sociopath, but I thought he had a very creative imagination," Rael said. "He was very enthused about that. He helped me outline the plot, the concept, and the ideas behind it. He had ideas of how we could do what we did, having people let loose in the woods and hunted down like prey."

Rael said that Hilton helped write the script, shoot

locations, and gave the lead actor lessons on killing. Hilton was "very enthused," the lawyer-producer said, about the project.

Hilton attempted to fight extradition to Florida, where he faced the death penalty if found guilty of Dunlap's murder. In April, he screamed at a Lamar County Superior Court judge, Thomas "Tommy" Wilson, that he would fight extradition to Florida from Georgia. He also demanded a court-appointed attorney. Since extradition is a civil matter, Wilson did not grant Hilton's request for legal help, but he gave him twenty days to file a habeas petition to challenge his arrest.

For this appearance Hilton wore white coveralls with blue trim and a strap on his arm that contained an electronic control device. A state corrections employee stood by to shock Hilton, should he start causing trouble. Following the hearing Hilton was taken to the Georgia Diagnostic and Classification Prison (GDCP) in Butts County. There he lived what was a high life by his standards. He was separated from the other inmates in what is called "administrative control," where he has a small private cell, a toilet, hot and cold running water, sink, desk, built-in bed, and "three square meals a day." He claimed to be content and that the other inmates had a nickname for him—"the stud hiker."

On April 17, 2008, Captain Dewey Smith, of the Pickens County Sheriff's Office (PCSO), South Carolina, interviewed Hilton at the Georgia Corrections Center. Jason Knapp, who was a sophomore at Clemson University, had disappeared while hiking in South Carolina in the Table Rock area. The case was cold and there had never been any strong suspects. No remains were ever found. There were three other unsolved murders in the general area; and since Hilton had surfaced, he immediately became a "person of interest." Smith was hoping that Hilton might provide answers to solve the cases, once and for all.

But Smith had misjudged this man by thinking he might appeal to the compassionate side of Hilton's nature by stressing how much pain the unsolved cases caused their friends and family.

Hilton stuck out his hand when Smith and his deputy walked into the interview room.

"Hi, everybody!" he said cheerfully. "I'm Gary Hilton."

The two police officers introduced themselves.

"Hey, great, man! I didn't think y'all looked like attorneys, y'know?"

"No, we're not attorneys."

"I thought these guys are just too tough, man. You know, attorneys are pussies. Half of 'em are metrosexuals." He laughed heartily. "You got a look on you that you could be in Hollywood, I'll tell you." He laughed again.

"By the way," Hilton smiled. "Today is Friday, isn't it?"

"Today is Thursday, the seventeenth."

"By God!" Hilton laughed. "Time flies by here. No one messes with me. They treat me real good. I'll be glad to talk with you, all you want," Hilton said. "I would love nothing else but to clear up only things that I have been involved in, for the family."

Hilton said anything he told them would be a "professional recitation."

"I have remorse for what I have done," Hilton said. "But once you get past the initial embarrassment of talking about it, which is only right at first, it just became a professional recitation." Hilton said he was giving up no information to the state of Florida or anyone else "for free." He said he just wanted to be left alone to live his life in peace.

He said he would give one piece of information for free: that he had committed no felonies in September 2007. Following that, Hilton presented a rambling recitation that produced nothing relevant to anything being discussed. He went on for half an hour.

The police officers showed him a picture of Knapp and said it was a photo of the young man who was missing. They asked him if he recognized the face.

"Yeah, I seen this type of face a million times," he said. "This is almost a generic young yuppie face living in a virtual la-la world. I always ran down those loose male dogs I'm afraid of. Don't let your dog confront me. I got a bad attitude. Better keep this dog away from me. Gonna rip his head off, always bigger than me. They come up to me, and the next thing they know, they'll be running for their lives." Hilton howled with laughter.

Hilton made a sarcastic apology in which he poked fun at the police officers for being emotional about the case and the families for seeking any kind of closure.

"Oh, let me tell you directly, I'm sorry about your loss, and I see victims' families crying in court—my victims' families crying in court. I know what you're missing. I know what you would be missing if you knew your son was gone. And so I know what you're going through, not knowing what happened to him, where he is. And I want to assure you, ma'am, that if I knew anything that had happened to your son, I would not refuse to answer. I want to assure you that there is absolutely no light I am going to shed on the matter of your son. I say that, realizing that it certainly fits in with the modus operandi that I am assumed to have used in several crimes that I am suspected of. And in this case it is coincidence, and, ma'am, you gotta always leave room for coincidence. So I'm sorry I can't bring you any closure ultimately."

Hilton mentioned that he was suspected of two

murders in North Carolina and another in Florida. "I am not going to tell you I did those, but I am telling you is, I'm not telling anybody I didn't do them, okay?" he said. "I'm not saying I didn't do them, but what I'm saying is there's nothing outside those three murders, no nothing."

The interview continued with Hilton giving his opinions on the police, yuppies, society, doomsday, and other subjects close to him, and how glad he was to be a sociopath. And then he gave a horrible description of killing someone and said that only his cold, calculating, sociopathic paratrooper experiences could have prepared him for this.

"It's hard to beat someone to death," he said. "What I mean, it's hard emotionally, and it's hard physically. You take an iron bar this long and you think, 'Solid iron bar,' you can hit one time and crush their skull, and it doesn't happen that way. That thing bounces the fuck off, just like smashing a concrete block with a rubber cover—don't smash like eggshell. They don't go unconscious. They start screaming! Man, you gotta beat 'em and beat 'em and beat 'em and beat 'em. And finally you get the skull fractured enough, until blood starts coming and starts splattering everywhere—in your face, blood spurts, and blood gets mist in your eyes—and it just puts a red film over everything. It's tough as hell, okay? And I was able to do it."

The two detectives left the interview without having learned anything useful that might help them solve the mystery of Jason Knapp's disappearance.

A hunter stumbled upon the skeletal remains of Jack Bryant on February 2, 2008. The remains were in Macon County, just off a Forest Service Road, not far from Standing Indian Campground, in northwestern North

Carolina. It was almost two hundred miles away from where the Bryants' vehicle had been found. Transylvania sheriff David Mahoney said there was "no question" that Hilton was responsible for the two murders. Mahoney said there was more than enough evidence to meet North Carolina's "minimum" standard for the death penalty.

At first, there was a question of whether the state or the federal government would have jurisdiction over the case. The murders were committed on federal land. The U.S. Attorney General's Office had taken over the case and was going about gathering evidence for a trial. Mahoney said that Gary Hilton was the one single suspect and that the evidence against him was overwhelming. Public defenders representing Hilton were wildly successful in enforcing a gag order that put an iron curtain around information surrounding the Hilton case. Not a glimmer of information was released since the gag order was put in effect, although it was known that there were over four hundred witnesses expected to testify for the state, including Samuel Rael, the producer of *Deadly Run*. Reportedly, two vans loaded with evidence were shipped from Georgia to Florida.

There were dozens of unanswered questions remaining in the murder of Meredith Emerson, especially concerning Hilton's relationship with John Tabor, which the GBI found confusing. Why did Tabor buy Hilton an Astro van, which he drove into a rut and smashed the oil pan? Why did Hilton call him for help? Why did Tabor rent a vehicle to pick up Hilton and his belongings from the ruined van? Why did Tabor pay for a new van? Furthermore, why didn't Tabor mention that two additional guns were missing from his house, including a MAC-10 automatic assault rifle and a handgun of the same caliber that was used to kill Jack Bryant?

The police also hoped for additional clarification as

to why Tabor didn't call them on January 4, 2009, about an hour before Emerson was murdered. The GBI said he had promised to do so if Hilton telephoned again. In fact, the GBI said Tabor never contacted the police, but waited for the police to contact him.

These questions might or might not be answered when Hilton was tried in Florida, depending on what evidence from previous cases was allowed to be heard. In the meantime Hilton held the reputation of being a vicious, sociopathic killer, even in the unlikely event that he was exonerated in Florida and in North Carolina.

Hilton was also named as a suspect in at least two other unsolved murders:

A fisherman made a grim discovery on December 6, 2007, in Ormond Beach, near Daytona Beach, while fishing from the Tomoka River Bridge. He found several plastic trash bags containing a dismembered human body. The victim of this grisly murder was Michael Scot Louis, a twenty-seven-year-old man from nearby South Daytona. Police believe the case bears a strong resemblance to Hilton's other crimes.

Rossana Miliani telephoned her father in Miami from a Cherokee Ramada Inn, near Bryson City, North Carolina, on December 6, 2005. That was the last time he saw or heard from her. Miliani was on a hiking trip from Miami when she disappeared. She was seen in the company of a man around sixty and seemed to be exceptionally nervous. A sketch of the man, drawn by an FBI-trained artist, bore a striking resemblance to Hilton.

Police in Bryson City listed Hilton as a person of interest.

Chapter 13

For a man who had been involved in so much petty theft, the police record for Gary Hilton was skimpy. Hilton had more than fifty run-ins with the police in the past thirty years, not counting those that were scrubbed from his juvenile record. The police knew very little about the man who had become so notorious. Was he a longtime serial killer who had managed not to attract attention, or had he simply gone on a rampage, as he claimed? The GBI and FBI were attempting to gather as much information as they could to develop a profile.

Hilton was interviewed frequently, and after his initial freeze on communication, he had thawed and information flowed from him in torrents—some of which helped develop the murder case against him in Florida, and some which simply showed how his mind worked. Bridges and Howard let Hilton talk as much as he wanted, because his revelations were sometimes surprising.

Bridges: I understand the FBI came and talked to you the other day.

Hilton: On Thursday.

Bridges: We're not with them on anything. We just basically want to get a background on Gary Hilton, just to finish up our case.

Hilton: Yeah.

Bridges: It's our policy that we go ahead and make sure that you still understand what your rights are.

Bridges read Hilton's rights to him again and continued the interview.

Bridges: I understand that you met your first wife in the military?

Hilton: Yeah.

Bridges: What was her name?

Hilton: Ursula.

Bridges: And you met her in Germany?

Hilton: Uh-huh.

Bridges: How long were you guys married?

Hilton: Just married in . . . married in '68 and divorced in '71. I'd been going with her since '65. She was sixteen when I met her.

Bridges: Really?

Hilton: Yeah. Yeah, that was the worst mistake I ever made was running her off.

Bridges: Really?

Hilton: Gorgeous girl. I mean, truly gorgeous. I'm telling you, the best body I've ever seen. She had a body so good she'd be at the swimming pool. She'd be going to the ladies' room, and I—I walked along behind and seen the little boys in a trance walk behind and follow her right into the ladies' room. I mean, she was stunning. Stunning, and not only that, she was a good German hausfrau. Her father was a police First Sergeant.

Bridges: That's like a chief, right?

Hilton: He was enlisted, though, not an officer. That would be the highest enlisted rank. . . . He was a police officer. She had an older sister that had already married a GI, an E-5, so that kind of smoothed the way for me. But, at any rate, she was gorgeous, a fine girl brought up by a police officer, a fine German hausfrau. Kept a spotless house, meals ready, only wanted to do what I wanted to do. And not only that, she had . . . Her training was as a draftsman. In Germany, they start them at about fifteen into an apprenticeship program where they go to high school half a day and learn a trade, or a vocation the other half. Whether you're going to be a waitress or whatever you're going to be. It's called learner, an apprentice. So her apprenticeship was as a draftsman. It was no computer-assisted drafting back then. None, no CAD.

Howard: Those women hand-drew everything, didn't they?

Hilton: Everything, hand-lettered everything.

Howard: Even on the symbol.

Hilton: Yeah. It's what a draftsman was, so it was a high-paying trade, and it was hard to learn, very demanding and difficult. And, of course, right up a German's alley because it demanded precision.

Howard: I was just thinking that.

Hilton: She came over after I married her. She immediately proceeded to get a job. Leslie Lumber Company. My mother worked there, so that was her in. She got a job working in the Truss Company, drawing trusses. They made trusses to order for buildings, and every one had to be drawn. That kind of thing.

Bridges: So you actually brought her back to—

Hilton: Yeah. I married her after I'd been going with her a couple of years. I married her shortly before I left for the States so that would put her in line for a visa. American visas were hard to get. Now she was my spouse, you know, an advantage. I left, and she stayed briefly with my parents. Rented a guesthouse, on a property on the Biscayne River. A hundred twenty-five a month. Sort of catty-cornered across by my mother and stepfather's house, and about two to three months later she came over. I worked another couple of months until December and quit.

          What got me off of that is that I worked fifteen hours a week as a student assistant at the college in the audiovisual department.

Bridges: Right.

Hilton: At that time, mind you, the campus was the largest in the nation. Twenty-seven thousand students in one campus. Their audiovisual department wasn't just a bunch of old sixteen-millimeter projectors. We're talking about production studios, TVs, movie production studios, on-staff artists, on-staff announcers. We could make our own slide presentations and everything with our artists. Announcers could narrate them. We had a closed-circuit TV system in '67.

Howard: Really?

Hilton: Yeah, using the old one of the two-inch tape. We had what we called a "film tray," where we could project movies into a TV camera and show them over closed circuit. Nobody had that. There was no such thing as a VCR or VTR, then videotape recorder, back then. Totally cutting-edge, and so it was a big operation. Their distribution center, which did every kind of presentation, handled every kind of in-class presentation, from slides to putting a TV set in for closed circuit to actually a movie. We did over two hundred runs a day out of our distribution center. It was a real operation. They'd have about thirty student assistants per shift just working in the distribution center, with two staff members supervising them. I worked as a student assistant for fifteen hours a week. When I graduated, they offered me a staff job, good pay. Good pay, $3.25 an hour. That's like UPS drivers started back then, which is the equivalent of fifteen an hour now.

Bridges: So you went to work there?

Hilton: I worked there in 1970 until late 1971, and they fired me.

Bridges: Why did they fire you?

Meredith Emerson's driver's license with her photo was among the evidence found in Hilton's van. *(Photo courtesy of GBI)*

Emerson left this note for her roommate on a chalk board to tell her she had gone hiking. *(Photo courtesy of GBI)*

One of the many missing posters used during the massive search of more than 64,000 acres of Dawson Forest in an attempt to find the missing hiker. *(Photo courtesy of GBI)*

Emerson's abandoned car at Vogel Park, where Hilton imprisoned the young woman in his own vehicle. *(Photo courtesy of GBI)*

A Post-it note was placed on Emerson's car after her boyfriend found the abandoned vehicle on January 2, the day after Emerson was kidnapped. *(Photo courtesy of GBI)*

The bayonet Hilton used when he attacked Emerson. She fought back and knocked the bayonet from Hilton's grip. *(Photo courtesy of GBI)*

The collapsible baton Emerson forced from Hilton during their struggle was bagged as evidence in as many as three murder investigations.
(Photo courtesy of GBI)

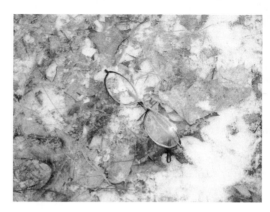

Eyeglasses belonging to Emerson were found off the trail where she fought Hilton. *(Photo courtesy of GBI)*

Hilton chose a remote, blocked road to drive to the campsite where he murdered Emerson after three nights of holding her captive. *(Photo courtesy of GBI)*

The site where Emerson's body was found in the deep woods after evidence was gathered. *(Photo courtesy of GBI)*

Wearing a homemade mask, Hilton tried to use Emerson's ATM card five times but she gave him false PIN numbers. *(Photo courtesy of GBI)*

Emerson was held captive most of the time in heavy, rusty chains that were padlocked and welded to the van's steel floor. *(Photo courtesy of GBI)*

Hilton was arrested at a convenience store as he desperately tried to remove all traces of blood and forensic evidence from his van. *(Photo courtesy of GBI)*

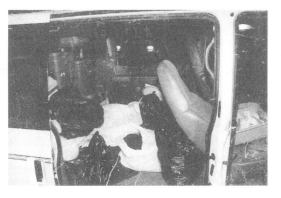

Hilton washed the van's insides with bleach after emptying it. *(Photo courtesy of GBI)*

Several witnesses, who were in touch with Emergency Dispatch simultaneously, watched as Hilton bagged and unloaded evidence from his van. *(Photo courtesy of GBI)*

Investigators discovered fresh and older forensic evidence in bags that Hilton had disposed of in a Dumpster. *(Photo courtesy of GBI)*

Police found several large bags filled with bloody clothes, sacks, and other gear. *(Photo courtesy of GBI)*

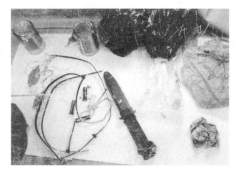

Hilton carried this knife, bayonet, and collapsible baton all the time. They were tagged for evidence, as were the bags of bloody clothes from Hilton's van. *(Photo courtesy of GBI)*

Emerson's personal items, including her ATM cards, were found in Hilton's van. *(Photo courtesy of GBI)*

Some of Emerson's hair was found on a piece of duct tape inside Hilton's van. *(Photo courtesy of GBI)*

Hilton tried to dispose of Emerson's jacket, which was still wet with her blood. *(Photo courtesy of GBI)*

The bloody clothing that Hilton tried to get rid of before his arrest was in several different sizes. *(Photo courtesy of GBI)*

After being taken to a police interview room, Hilton lowered himself to the floor and refused to speak, move, or acknowledge the law officers who were present. Hilton remained like this for hours. *(Photo courtesy of GBI)*

Hilton seemed to put himself in a near comatose state after he was taken into custody. *(Photo courtesy of GBI)*

Hilton's right hand was swollen because he broke four fingers in his struggle to abduct Emerson. *(Photo courtesy of GBI)*

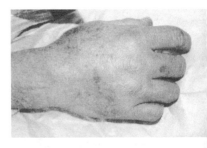

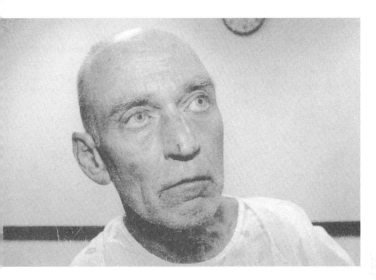

Hilton was arraigned for kidnapping with bodily injury shortly after his arrest. *(Photo courtesy of GBI)*

Hilton was cleaned up and his beard shaved several hours after his arrest. *(Photo courtesy of GBI)*

Dawson/Hall County DA Lee Darragh represented the State at Hilton's sentencing. A plea bargain took the death penalty out of consideration after Hilton agreed to show police where he had left Emerson's body. *(Photo courtesy of Dawson/Hall District Attorney)*

Superior Court Judge Bonnie Oliver accepted Hilton's confession and guilty plea, pronounced him guilty of murder, and sentenced him to life in prison without parole. *(Photo courtesy of AP World Wide Images)*

Hilton, in body armor, is escorted from the court after sentencing. He was extradited to Florida and arrested for the kidnapping and murder of missionary nurse Cheryl Dunlap. *(Photo courtesy of AP World Wide Images)*

MISSING PERSON

CHERYL DUNLAP – 46 YRS OLD
Wakulla County, FL

Name:	Cheryl Dunlap
Date Missing:	December 1, 2007
Missing From:	Wakulla County, Florida
DOB:	11/18/1961
Age:	46 yrs old
Hair Color:	Brown
Height:	5'4
Weight:	120 lbs
Eye Color:	Brown
Sex:	Female
Race:	White
Complexion:	Fair
Police/Sheriff:	Wakulla County Sheriff
Officer/Deputy Name:	Officer Scott Delbeato
Officer's Phone #:	850/926-0878
Officer's Case #:	
TES Case #:	07-826

Cheryl Dunlap, age 46, was last seen on Saturday, December 1, 2007 at the Wakulla County WalMart and has not been seen or heard from since. Cheryl was last seen wearing a white or light colored shirt and blue jeans. Her white 2006 Toyota Camry was located on Hwy 319 south of Tallahassee.

Call: 281/309-9500
Toll free 877/270-9500
info@TexasEquuSearch.org
www.txeq.org

Photos and posters were distributed nationwide during the search for Cheryl Dunlap. Like Emerson's, Dunlap's body had also been decapitated.

(Photo courtesy of Texas Equus Search Organization)

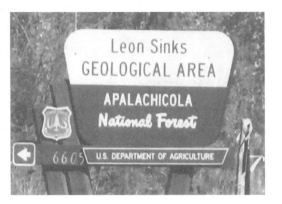

The entrance to the Leon Sinks Geological Area, where Cheryl Dunlap was kidnapped by Gary Hilton. *(Photo courtesy of Linda Watts)*

Glenda's Store, where a number of witnesses spotted Hilton while he camped in the Apalachicola National Forest. *(Photo courtesy of Linda Watts)*

The pay phone outside Glenda's Store, where several witnesses testified they spoke with Hilton. *(Photo courtesy of Linda Watts)*

Lead defense attorney Ines Suber sits with Hilton at the start of his trial for the murder of Cheryl Dunlap. (Photo courtesy of WCTV)

Prosecutor Georgia Cappelman examines a printout of Hilton's brain scan during a recess in the trial. (Photo courtesy of WCTV)

Hilton smiled as he left the courtroom after the first day of his trial for Cheryl Dunlap's murder. (Photo courtesy of WCTV)

Hilton gave the WCTV camera a hostile stare as the court prepared to reconvene after a recess. *(Photo courtesy of WCTV)*

Hilton stared into the WCTV camera just minutes before receiving the death sentence for the murder of Cheryl Dunlap. *(Photo courtesy of WCTV)*

Hilton: Absenteeism. Taking quaaludes. Like I said, I ran that girl off. You know why?

Bridges: Is that about the time you and her split?

Hilton: Yeah. Within four months after we divorced, I ran her off. I decided here we are, beautiful girl. Made even at that time twenty-five, thirty percent more money than I did even on my good-paying staff job. In other words, she made the equivalent of twenty dollars an hour, okay? Good grief. Well, perfect house, squeaky clean—you could eat off the damn floor—meals ready, worked to boot, gorgeous girl, and, really, only wanted to do what I wanted to do.

And if I didn't want to do anything, she'd, you know . . . didn't like it, but she would do it. If I wanted to sit around and smoke pot or something, you know, she didn't do any drugs, didn't drink. I was a pothead, of course, by then, and we smoked. . . . We used to smoke on campus. The staff would go into the air-conditioning room and take some student assistants there, and we would go in and smoke. We had a film society where we showed avant-garde films every Thursday night, that kind of thing. The auditorium would be lit. Finally the cops would get wind of it, came in, and busted twenty-seven people. That was the end of the film society. Drugs back than had not been demonized. They were demonized very effectively under Reagan.

Bridges: Right.

Hilton: And he finally got that federal Anti-Drug
          Abuse Act of 1986 in, which did it for drugs.
          That was in '86. So you end up with a Ja-
          maican housewife importing a kilo of coke
          with two other people, and one of them
          had a firearm in their house, and they was
          arrested. They add that up . . . Macon house-
          wife got thirty years, no parole, and is serv-
          ing it right now. Yeah, yeah, yeah. That's
          your demon facing drugs right there.

Bridges: You say you got fired from that job for
          absenteeism because you were taking quaa-
          ludes? How many years were you married
          to her?

Hilton: Summer of '68 to summer of '71.

Bridges: So three years?

Hilton: Uh-huh.

Howard: Did you break it off with her or did—

Hilton: I ran her off. You know why I ran her off?
          You know, I'm telling you all these qualities
          she had. . . . Well, remember this is the cul-
          tural revolution. It's really hitting home. By
          1970, everyone was, in effect, doing the
          '60s. You know what I'm—

Howard: Caught up to everyone?

Hilton: Yeah, you know, it really hit people in
          California who were doing the '60s in the
          early '60s. They were taking acid while it
          was still legal, you know. In '63, '62, '61,
          you know, and so they were really doing the
          '60s. The real hippies, and by 1970, now, you
          know, the masses, including me, were doing
          the '60s. So I was doing the '60s in the '70s.

Howard: Well, the army took away from that, too, I imagine.

Hilton: Oh yeah. I did a flip from being gung ho to being a liberal. You know, down with the establishment. Anyway, we had the cultural revolution going on, and I was in college, and even though I wasn't on the teaching staff, it was almost as being on staff. Air-conditioning, blue-collar job. Nothing else. It's white shirt and tie, and running a learning center or running a distribution center or this and that, supervising thirty student assistants, that kind of thing. Air-conditioned, intellectual, that kind of academic atmosphere. Right?

Howard: Yeah.

Hilton: And my gripe against her was that she was just empty-headed and didn't have a thought in the world. She was not sophisticated enough and not intellectual enough. You talk about stupid. Women today have too many thoughts. You know what I mean? If you could find a woman that's just simple and plain or "Whatever *you* want, honey, and here's your food, and I got the house clean. I'm good-looking to boot, and I make more money than you." Well, my God, you see how stupid I am? I'm an idiot. There's a pattern throughout my life of taking good things and just squashing it.

Bridges: Did you ever run around on her while she was working at the college? I mean, all the—

Hilton: No, I didn't, except at the end.

Bridges: After college, or after your—

Hilton: Well, I fell into the clutches of this woman who was eight years older than me. She was from a New York Jewish diamond family. That Fifty-fourth Street diamond family. Diamond folks. That dude has done million-dollar deals with a handshake. They wrap the diamonds in paper. Everyone's got their particular fold, and they hand each other a million bucks in diamonds and shake hands, and that's it. You can't get into it. You got to be born into it and Jewish. Okay?

Howard: What was her name?

Hilton: Paulette. Her maiden name is Paulette Goldman.

Bridges: Paulette Goldman? And she was four years older than you?

Hilton: Eight.

Bridges: Eight years older than you? Okay?

Howard: And it was the Greenwich Village of Florida?

Hilton: Yeah. All that stuff has probably been torn down now and big condos probably put on it. Back then, it was a village. Like Buckhead Village used to be, but only much, much bigger. All kinds of cool, hip people lived there. And, of course, Coral Gables was a very rich place—and this was right on the boundary—so they bought her a house, and she'd come to the university by majoring in sociology. She managed to graduate with a bachelor's degree in sociology. I moved in with her. And, boy, you know, that was not a good influence.

Bridges: Really?

Hilton: She's the one that got me started on the downs. I never had a down. We called them downs. Central nervous system depressants. Put it that way. Depress the functioning of your central nervous system.

Bridges: Right.

Hilton: Back then, it was the hypnotics in the form of hydrochloride, which is a quaalude, high risk. And, of course, the barbiturates. Barbiturates were still widely prescribed at that time, just for sleeping pills. We're talking about Amytal, Seconal, Nembutal, and the combination of Seconal and Amytal was Tuinal. It was blue and red. Cats liked that, and they were considered the king. They were very narcotic. Your opium derivative.

Bridges: What was the street name for them back then?

Hilton: Downs.

Bridges: Just downs?

Hilton: Tuinols, or tummies, and then others were called by the colors they were. Reds, blues, and yellows. I wouldn't be surprised if it's impossible to get ahold of a barbiturate these days.

Bridges: Right.

Hilton: Then there were classes of antidepressant and sleeping pills, you know. That was what people said. "Oh, go take a sleeping pill." That's what they were talking about.

Bridges: Did you classify yourself as a hippie back then?

Hilton: You know, by then, you know what the hippies were? It was just every kind of outlaw street person in the world. Kind of counter-culture.

Bridges: Right.

Hilton: Misfits. And the whole country was awash in them. It was just awash in them.

Howard: That was the thing to be back then. That was the movement coming.

Hilton: Yeah, of course, they, themselves, were wearing a uniform and doing the stuff. Piedmont Park and Peachtree in Atlanta was just awash in them. The whole country was full of just raggedy-ass young people hitchhiking and doing not much of anything. At that time we thought drugs were going to be legal within a few years. The amazing thing to me that I'm always shaking my head over is this great big, huge cultural revolution that we had in the '60s and '70s has almost utterly vanished. It's back to the '50s now. Back in the '60s, that would be a bad thing.

"Get into business and take care of business, Mr. Businessman." That would be a bad thing to say about someone. And now what does every young person want to do? They're all just, you know, little geeks on, you know, keyboards pecking away, you know. The

Bible said, "The meek shall inherit the earth." Well, I know what he meant, just a fat fuck behind the keyboard. Right? Got ten times more power than me and I'm a stud. I can whip ass left and right. More powerful than me. Fat fuck sitting at a keyboard.

Howard: Sitting at a keyboard.

Hilton: Yeah. I learned to type in the '60s in the army when almost nobody could type unless you were a reporter or a writer, but I won't type now. Shows that I'd never make it on the outside, which is why I'm sitting here doing like and realizing this is the only place for me. I've said it before, and I'll say it again. You could take me to the front door of this jail and say, "Go forth and sin no more." I would literally have to turn back around and walk back in here. There is nothing out there for me, and you see what my relationship with society as a whole is. I mean, it's only five percent of people that will come forward to knock me, but the other ninety-five percent are going to speak up. . . . "Oh, I know Gary Hilton. He's a great guy." "I know Hannibal Lecter, you know Hannibal the Cannibal? I know Hannibal Lecter. He's a great guy." No, they're not going to say a damn thing.

Howard: You'd be surprised—people who come forward and talk pretty good about you, actually.

Hilton: Oh, really?

Howard: Yeah.

Bridges: Getting back on track to the '70s. How long did you stay with . . . What was her name?

Hilton: Paulette.

Bridges: And what did you do at that point?

Hilton: We broke up, and by then I was destroyed. Totally destroyed. I mean, here I am now. I'm deep into downs now. Barbiturates are physiologically addicting. Well, so are quaaludes for that matter. But quaaludes are psychologically addicting. The hypnotic class of drugs. And now I've been taking those for years, heavily, through her. A lot of them and I had lost my job. My good job. Got fired from that. My hair had grown long. I was homeless.

Bridges: So what did you do?

Hilton: Started working in what would now be called telemarketing, but it was no such thing back then. Back then, there was no telemarketing. Telephone sales really consisted of people in phone rooms—boiler rooms they were known as—impersonating police officers, labor union officials, civic leaders, and firefighters is what it was. You would be working in a FOP (Fraternal Order of Police) phone room and there would be detectives in there with their guns and the phone gang would be sitting around going, "Hey, Joe McGuire, National Police Officers' Association. I think you know an officer can't give you a license to go ninety miles an hour down the expressway or beat your wife, but I think you understand we'd appreciate donation."

You'd never directly tell them you were a police officer. You just imply that you were. Same with a firefighter. Same with labor union officials. You know, you'd say, "Hey, I'm Phil, CIO, we're putting together a book for our convention. Supporting the kids at the same time. Going to have the governor in. Going to have a nice event. I think you understand that any support you give to organized labor will never hurt you."

At this point Hilton started an angry rant about the history of unions in America and how his father got his head "busted in"—he never knew his father—and how he would send people to different industrial complexes and shut them down, "turn them into parking lots." Bridges let him go on for a while and then asked: Had you moved to Georgia at that point?

Hilton: Yeah. I moved to Atlanta.

Bridges: About what time frame are we talking about you moved to Atlanta? Seventy-three?

Hilton: Yeah, it was several months after we had broken up and I was just homeless. I was working phone deals down in Miami-Dade, and getting my teeth cut. You know Dade County was really a hotbed of this type of phone fraud. So was Atlanta. A lot was going on in Atlanta, but the reason I came up to Atlanta was I'd been born here, but yet it was the only place I hadn't been to, 'cause I grew up on racetracks all around the country. I left Atlanta when I was six years old.

My mother moved us to Tampa, and then a year later she married my stepfather.

Howard: How old were you when she got remarried?

Hilton: Seven. And so Atlanta . . . hadn't been . . . There was a lot of phone jobs here then of that type. Junior Chamber of Commerce, police, all kinds of police organizations.

Bridges: You said phone fraud? Did you actually—

Hilton: Here's the difference between phone fraud and legal phone work. In legal phone work, they took your money from you and passed it around and split it. I'm not going to lie, guys, okay? The phone fraud, I'd take the money and keep it all myself. That's the difference. Can you dig it? Two for ten would go to the cause, and then it would be split among the telemarketers, the laborers, and sponsors. So they'd take that basket of money and pass it around. Everybody would take some. That made it legal. If you took the basket of money and just kept it all yourself, that was fraud. That's the difference. I know very few charities these days that are truly what people think they are.

Howard: What attracted you to getting involved in that?

Hilton: Oh, because you could work fucked up, with long hair. It wasn't a job.

Howard: Appearance wasn't a big deal and all that.

Hilton: No. If you sat there with a glass of beer or a bottle of whiskey in your coat jacket, or a wine cooler in a glass, yeah, you could be fucked up on that stuff. I mean, the promoter would often advertise the job and say, "Habits are okay, if you can afford them." If he was real strict, he would say "no habits," and these jobs would be advertised in a billboard publication known as the *Amusement Bulletin*. That was a newspaper for outdoor expositions, state fairs, arenas, that kind of thing. Quite often the calls that you were pitching was going to be a benefit show or a state fair or something like that. So you would be calling a million of them, and you would be bringing in a country-and-western show. We want to bring in a bunch of underprivileged kids to it, just a dollar a kid, and all the proceeds are going to the boys' farm. You know, the boys' ranch.

Bridges: Did you ever get back on your feet in Atlanta or just continue to do that?

Hilton: I never did, because I'd been deep into downs, and now reality is setting in. I can't get any more downs and for a person that has an addictive personality toward downs, what the problem is . . . What makes a lot of alcoholics alcoholic and so forth is that they have a high level of anxiety within them.

Bridges: Uh-huh.

Hilton: You see this in heroin addicts, too. Same thing. I mean, white, intellectual heroin addicts that manage their habit or the habit manages them. You have a high anxiety level. They can't turn the motor off. They can't relax and the thing about what makes alcohol and all these central nervous system depressants so addictive is that here you have a person that has a hard time relaxing, who has a hard time partying, you might say, has a hard time being loose, is always anxious and worried. In my case it was just a high level of what they call existential anxiety, which is the awareness of your future. You know you're going to die and there's a psychiatric school of thought that says existential anxiety is responsible for most of human neurosis.

Bridges: Did that bother you back then?

Hilton: Since I was four years old, my earliest thoughts were of death and that I was going to die.

Bridges: Really?

Hilton: At four years old I could place it because of a situation I was in when I thought of it, and when I was four years old, I was pondering the fact that this hand one day will be a skeleton. Yeah, when I was four years old.

Howard: What was the situation, if you don't mind me asking?

Hilton: It was an intellectual thought. It was the awareness that my future . . .

Howard: Oh, okay.

Hilton: The humans are the only animal that I know of that really has to cope with it, although it's really hard to tell. Hard to tell. It's a tremendous psychic load and the knowledge of our future nonbeing, or of the inevitability of our death, is the thing that shapes our entire life. Your life, my life, and everybody else. It's the thing that is responsible for the activities you do which came from the thought.

Howard: Or don't do.

Hilton: Okay, you're so busy. You have your family.
You have your activities. You have your
work. You have your church. What you're
doing is running from existential anxiety. If
you stop for one second and there's nothing
to distract you, like your kids and everything else, or that are "the most important
thing in the world to you," and if that was
just emptied out of your mind, the existential anxiety will catch up to you and it's just
hell without the comfort of believing in an
afterlife.

Believing in supernatural ghost stories,
you see. I mean, we have the president of the
United States, the most sophisticated and
powerful country in the world, standing up
there telling the world that he believes in a
ghost story, which is what Jesus Christ is,
and that kind of thing. Talking about Jesus
and that—that's a ghost story. That is one of
the supernatural, you know, and—and here
we are, the most advanced people ever, and
we're talking about ghost stories. They all
do it.

You see how stupid they are? They're
total fucking idiots, but they're just being
human beings, you see. They're just being
human beings. They're running from their
existential anxiety. That's what's responsible
for being so busy. Why are you wearing that
tie? Why are you devoting yourself to work
for the betterment of society? Hey, son,
forget it. Any good anthropologist can tell

you. Hey, don't you know that there [is a] supervolcano under Yellowstone? There's over seventy supervolcanoes. The supervolcano that is the Yellowstone Plateau. These things are so big that they're hundreds of square miles in size. They may have magma chambers that can take a million years to fill. The supervolcano under Yellowstone has erupted three times in the last two million years. It has an average cycle of six hundred thousand years. When it erupts, it basically wipes out, downwind, the eastern part of the U.S. If you're looking at a map of the U.S., Yellowstone is here and projects to come like that, and it basically, you know, it will cover the whole eastern seaboard in several feet of ash and just destroy any civilization in that area. Well, it's erupted three times in the last almost two million years, and guess what? It's got a cycle of six hundred thousand years, and guess what? It's been 630,000 years since it last erupted. That thing could pop off any minute, pal. Okay. They know the power of that.

Howard: Meteor—I'm always talking about.

Bridges: Matt's always talking about that.

Hilton: Well, that's another thing. That is more unpredictable. It's going to happen, but when? We don't know. We know this is going to happen. We know the time scale. Hey, checking out the Olympic plate up there in the northwest, okay? In 1967, they had a mega, and a super . . . a superearthquake in Alaska, over nine points on the Richter scale. It's only the third one ever known to human beings, and in this case, they were able to observe the effects. Relatively few people were killed because at that time Alaska was sparsely populated. But geologists had an idea of what a mega over-point-nine earthquake would do, geologically speaking.

But they were only theories, and they were able to study the effects of this to confirm it, and they had found that the Olympic plate has, in the last twenty thousand years, shook itself out with a plus-point-nine earthquake eighteen times. Okay? And not only have they confirmed it, they have geological evidence by studying the continental shelf under the ocean and then it goes down to the depths of the ocean, and in that were kind of like ravines, sort of, or canyons.

The GBI agents let Hilton continue without interrupting him because his free association of thoughts often led to something important to the case.

Hilton: Geologists had a theory that a megaquake was made under the sea and it would leave a record. They were able to study the effects of the Alaska earthquake and see that that was so. So they drilled off, like, Washington State, okay, into these ravines right at the edge of the continental shelf. That's how they found it had shook itself out, plus nine earthquakes eighteen times. It was right there in the layers, pal. Okay? Now, at an average of about five hundred and something years between shakeouts . . .

Bridges: Uh-huh.

Hilton: Guess. You know when the last one was?

Howard: About seven hundred years ago?

Hilton: Well, we got a little ways to go. We're in the zone, though. It was Christmas Day, 1700 or 1699. We can dig up the redwoods that were buried in the tsunami tidal wave now. And, of course, they're dated, and now that we know what we're looking for, that, in fact, is what happened. Okay? Hey, I'll tell you about Rainier. You've got to see Mount St. Helens. That's the most awesome sight you have seen. Okay? They say it erupted with the power equivalent of four hundred atom bombs. You'll believe it when you see that. Oh, I hiked up into the blast zone, where the road ends, and right up there, where the blast came right out, where you see—

Howard: How close to the earthquake was it?

Hilton: Oh, that was in '95.

Howard: Grown back by then?

Hilton: No.

Howard: In '95?

Hilton: Fifteen years after it. No, it still looked like the moon. You would still see a few sprigs. All on west, unless you were on the east side of the Olympic Mountains, which is only a coastal strip about a hundred miles. The rest of Washington and Oregon are deserts. They grow a lot of stuff because they're just irrigated heavily, and all those states are just basically volcano deserts. If you drive through western Colorado, Utah, Idaho, Oregon, and Washington State, except for that coastal strip, you'll come to realize that this place is all volcanic. Everything there is volcanic. All the rocks are volcanic. There's no dirt out there, so it's kind of volcanic.

You carry a duffel bag down there and you realize this place is going to blow the fuck up one of these days. What about Mount Rainier, man? I mean, Mount Rainier just looms over Seattle, okay? The western face of Mount Rainier is just rock. It's just really mud and rocks glued together with ice. All that has to do is be heated and you'll have these huge mud flows. That mud flow that killed forty or fifty thousand people down in South America, about fifteen years ago, you remember that little girl was trapped in it and they tried to get her out?

Howard: Guatemala or Venezuela.

Bridges: You're obviously well-traveled. You've been . . . you've been to several places.

Hilton: Anyway, the point is *listen.* Again, I'm not judging you because I understand. You're doing the best you can to handle your psychic load. You're doing . . .

Within that rambling dissertation on geology, seismology, and agriculture were some nuggets of valuable information. The investigators had now heard from Gary Hilton's own lips that he had traveled in the western part of the United States, and they had been given an approximate time period. Any unsolved murders in those areas and time periods that fit Hilton's modus

operandi might be a step closer to being solved. Howard
steered Hilton back to something else they were trying
to pin down: what kinds of vehicles Hilton had owned
and when he had owned them.

Howard: I know you had a Camaro for a little bit.
         Was that in the '70s?

Hilton: It was 1980. Brand-new Camaro.

Howard: Was it a *Smokey and the Bandit* type or . . . ?

Hilton: It looked like it, although it was just a six-
         cylinder. But it was a California Camaro in
         the Van Nuys, California, Assembly types.
         Light, clean, black, no—

Howard: What made you get that? Just out of curi-
         osity? Marketing or . . . ?

Hilton: Well, no. I started fraudulent telephone
         solicitation after I got up here. Within
         about a—

Howard: On your own?

Hilton: No, just printing invoices and selling them.

Howard: Oh, okay.

Hilton: Making up Southeast Regional Council of
         Georgia.

Bridges: During that time, did you make good money
         doing that?

Hilton: Well, yeah, but I was so drunk . . . sick
         drunk. I stayed sick drunk until September
         of '77.

Howard: September?

Hilton: And then I quit.

Howard: Cold turkey, or did you go to rehab or anything?

Hilton: No, I did. I got medical help on that.

Bridges: Where did you get that at?

Hilton: A private doctor in downtown Decatur, and what I had been doing was going to Grady because my blood pressure had gotten so sky-high, just tremendously high. Like 145/115. Just tremendously high. They were giving me experimental drugs, so I had a couple of convulsions and the handwriting was on the wall. I got married to a prostitute, and on the day I married her—you know, I had courted her and married her drunk—and . . . and the day we got married, I quit. Bad mistake, really.

Howard: Do you remember her name?

Hilton: Yeah. Yvonne. Yvonne Ball was her name. Her real name was Dina Yvonne Call, but she went by—

Bridges: Diana?

Hilton: Dina.

Bridges: Okay. Is she still around or is she—

Hilton: I haven't seen her for decades. Over twenty years. I run into her on Highland, twenty years ago. I was running, you know, down the street and I ran into her, and we . . . I just said a few words. "Hi, how are you doing?" I said. "Are you working?" and what I meant is, did she have a job? In retrospect . . . in retrospect I realized what she took that—that question to mean. She said yes.

Bridges: She was still a prostitute?

Hilton: Yeah, and then, "See you." I didn't know what else to say to her. The poor thing. I just felt sorry. She didn't have a chance in the world. That poor girl. She was dumb, man. She tried to enlist in the marines and she was too dumb to get in. Literally.

Bridges: How old was she when you guys got married?

Hilton: She was about my age, and we got married in '77. So that would have put her at around thirty-one. But I quit drinking. The problem is, I stayed sober. . . . I fell off the wagon for six months in '82, quit again, and stayed sober until 1985. Then I stayed drunk for four years, until '89, and I haven't had a single drink since '89. But the first time I quit, yes, I went to a private doctor. He put me on Mellaril. It's called an antidepressant. *(Editor's note: Mellaril is a powerful medication in the thioridazine class.)*

Bridges asked Hilton if he remembered the doctor's name who had prescribed the medication. Hilton could not recall.

Bridges: You married again in '79, didn't you?

Hilton: Yeah, and in '79, again, I was married for six months.

Howard: I'm sorry, you were only married to Dina for how long?

Hilton: Six months. We were divorced in about March, April of '78. And then I married the police officer. That's Stone Mountain Police Department. And by the way, she was grandfathered in so she was a police officer before POST (Peace Officer Strategy and Training). Okay, so she was not a POST-certified officer, although the department . . . Well, then the law had been passed. You know, everyone had to be POST, to be a Blue Light Police Officer, but she had started before them, so she was grandfathered in. And at the time I was going with her, married to her, she was not POST certified. However, she was a Blue Light Police Officer.

Bridges: You had met her there in the park?

Hilton: Yeah. Yeah. You know, I was running with her every day, and I was really good-looking, good, and everything, in great condition. After we were divorced in late '79, I started taking pills again, and the rationale was "Hey, I'm not drinking." But I was just taking every pill I could get, and that was in the waning days of the quaaludes craze.

Bridges: Right.

Hilton: As a matter of fact, you could even still get real methaqualone quaaludes. One guy with the DEA persuaded the four or five people in the world that made methaqualone hydrochloride should just discontinue production. Okay. And there was no more quaaludes. Real quaaludes. And then they were all counterfeit and made typically of diazepam, which is Valium.

Howard: Right.

Hilton: And they were great. They were great. I estimate some of those counterfeit quaaludes made of the diazepam probably had up to five hundred milligrams of diazepam in it. And, as you know, it comes in five-, ten-, fifteen-, twenty-milligram tabs, you know. I'd take some of those tabs . . . they were instant white lightning. I mean, you'd take one, and if you were an experienced down freak, you'd stay on your feet and do all kinds of things. But you wouldn't remember a damn thing of it later. I mean, these were wild. I've woken up after a night of doing those things, walked out to my Camaro that I had my spare on, looked into the trunk, and seen my original tire was totally shredded to pieces, and then a couple of hours have a guy from the Noon . . . You know, I live in Stone Mountain, have a guy from the Noonday Baptist Church at Highway 5 and 92 in Woodstock call me and tell me he found my wallet in the church parking lot, number one. I had a shredded tire and no—no memories at all of changing it out and putting the spare on. And a guy has found my wallet in a Noonday Baptist Church in Woodstock. You know, fifty miles away. You didn't really think of God-only-knows what happened that night and how many people I ran over or what. That tire was shredded so much it was like a guy had hit a curb at a hundred miles an hour. That tire was so shredded. It was wild. Yeah, those are wicked. Totally wicked.

Howard: You started doing this while you were married to Sue?

Hilton: No. No, no, no, no. I wouldn't take a pill
— or nothing while I was married. I was in my—my rebirth. When you start running . . . You see, I had a lot of experience or foreknowledge, as far as being able to run long distances, because I had learned in the army in a class of six hundred guys—okay now. And your average guy—if he's young, in good health, and not obese—your average guy can go out and run for an astonishingly long time if he doesn't sprint. I learned that in the army, so I was able to start running in 1978. I met my wife through the running at Stone Mountain. She would drive by and I never would wear a shirt, even in wintertime. Had the hairy chest and, you know, cut, and I was lifting weights, every other day, and running ten miles or more, every other day. She would drive by in her police car. She'd put the loudspeaker on where they say, "All right, everybody, disperse. This show's over." She'd put that loudspeaker on and she'd go "uh-huh," like that as she'd drive by. She just scarfed me right up because she found out I had VA benefits, and she wanted a home more than anything. What do a lot of women want? They want their home and things, and they want their kids. That's what they want, and so she was just dying for a house.

Howard: She had kids?

Hilton: Two, six, and eight. She found out that I had
          a hundred-and-fifteen-thousand-dollar VA
          loan, which was the equivalent of three hun-
          dred thousand now. That was in '78. Two or
          three times the money, and so that was
          enough. She got me married and went out
          and found a house. Got a good deal on it, too.
          Bought a house across from the school in
          Decatur. Hollywood Drive. Bought that
          house. It had been sitting empty and she
          bought that house for thirty-five thousand,
          man, and this was in '79, and that's when the
          big real estate inflations hit, man. Those real
          estate . . . that inflation of the late '70s, finally
          President Carter had to put a cap on . . .

Hilton veered off course and lectured at length about
interest rates under Carter and Ford, how the underlying
value of real estate trumped other investments, the strong
rise of the middle class in the 1970s and other social,
political and philosophical issues before Howard could
guide him back to topics more useful to the GBI.

"So she bought that thing," Hilton continued. "She
stole it from the guy. He had gotten a divorce and been setting there. She saw it just setting there, setting there, and
setting there. She got that house for thirty-five thousand.
When we got divorced six months later, she wanted to get
another five for it. I got a flying hair up my ass. I said,
"Let's advertise it at forty-five," and bigger than shit, we
advertised it at forty-five and the first person that in-
quired on it bought it. We made ten grand off that house
in six months.

Bridges: A friendly breakthrough?

Hilton: Yeah, it was. I've always been fair to my ex-wives. When I bought that house, I bought it in my name—the VA, you know—but she was my wife, and she came to the closing. I said, "Sue, do you want half that house?" and she said yeah. So I asked the attorney, "Can I give her half that house?" He said, "Yeah, I'll make you a quit claim deed right now." I gave her half the house, and I thought it was fair because she's the one that went out and got it. I mean, I wouldn't have had it. I wouldn't have made the ten thousand, you know. When we sold the house, I willingly gave her half of the proceeds.

Howard: But you were in an apartment before that? Kind of on your own? You went from an apartment to a house with kids?

Hilton: With two kids, man.

Howard: What was that like, just making that transition? It'll drive you nuts.

Hilton: Well, you see, back then I was really a pathetic guy in that the saddest thing in the world is a loner, which I was. A loner trying not to be one. What happens to sociopathic characters is all their lives, all the way up to the present day, are programmed. They're bombarded by hundreds of messages every day telling them that any activity is only valid if they do it with someone else. Every bit of advertising—every cultural message that you receive—everything is programmed to the fact that any activity you do is only validated if you do it with someone else. A good example. I had a season pass to Six Flags in the summer of '78 and I told someone I was going and they said, "Oh, who are you going with?" I wasn't going with anyone. I just had a season pass.

I'd go out there and it's a summer evening, long evenings, and I'd just go and people watch, ride rides, do what I wanted to. It was always awkward watching a single person getting on a ride. You know, it had two seats, but, hey, there'd be some other idiot there. They'd put me with them and I had a great time. I saw all these people and the colors, and sights, and sounds, of Six Flags. It was great. I'm going alone. They go, "Oh, darn." You know, but that's the attitude of society. I mean, when is the last time you went to a movie alone? Never. You'd be afraid to.

People would think you were odd. People are acculturated and programmed to believe that life is valid only if they're doing it with others. So the problem with these poor loners—these sociopaths—is they're so programmed like that, that in spite of themselves, they don't know themselves. They don't understand that they're a round peg in a square hole, and that they're never going to fit in. They don't understand that there's no way in the world that they are going to get real satisfaction out of a human relationship. They don't understand that any human relationship they have will always be less than fulfilling. They don't understand that, and they're trying to be like everyone else, but they're not. They're not going to fit in, and they're not going to be accepted. That's terrible. That's terrible.

Howard: That kind of experience.

Hilton: I didn't understand myself until '91. Actually, when I got the dog (Ranger), and all of a sudden I was no longer alone, and I didn't have that wrenching sense of loneliness and being alone. But there would be no salvation in the company of others. You're alone. Your life is empty and alone, lonely. There's no salvation or satisfaction in the company of others. It's terrible. Those are the worst kind of people. They're tragically unhappy.

Howard: So it was like trying to be with the kids and then. . . ?

Hilton: Okay, now, that's the answer. I was trying to be normal.

Howard: And you're going from your own thing to living with a . . . What were they? Boys, girls, what?

Hilton: Yeah, a boy and a girl.

Howard: Both.

Hilton: I was trying to be normal. I was involved in fraud. I didn't even have a job. I was presenting it to her that I was a self-publisher and so forth, and these deals were sponsored, and it was for real. They were real. I even had her picking up money for me at the beginning of our relationship.

Howard: Did she catch on to that or—

Hilton: When she did, she said, "Man, it's not a job. It's a con game."

Howard: Did you kind of try to keep that from her or kind of try to hold it . . . ?

Hilton: Oh, she caught on, and in the end, I think, she's probably the one that turned me in.

Howard: Turned you in for?

Hilton: Fraudulent telephone soliciting.

Howard: Oh.

Hilton: As soon as we were divorced, I got busted out. I had an office in Decatur. Got busted by DeKalb County and had a phone room. Busted me out on that. Took everything. Phones, everything.

Howard: When was this?

Hilton: That was in '79.

Howard: You got busted in '79.

Hilton: Yeah. At the end of '79, right after our divorce was final.

Howard: Did you get any time for it?

Hilton: Oh no. It was a misdemeanor. Fraudulent telephone solicitation.

Howard: They didn't give you any of your phones back or your office. . . .

Hilton: Man, they did all this work on it, including running an undercover officer through the operation. They ran a black female juvenile police officer through the operation. I had her come get a job, work a day there, and then when they came for the arrest, they showed up with crime scene vans with their own boxes.

Howard: Were you married at the time?

Hilton: No. We had been divorced a week or two or a month or whatever. I think our divorce was final in about October the twentieth.

Howard: How did the divorce go? Was it an amicable thing you both decided, or was it—

Hilton: Yeah, it was.

Howard: Did you call it quits with her, or did—

Hilton: Well, I had, and then she had. She'd had enough, too. She had been shopping around by then and she already had the next guy lined up.

Howard: How did you react to that?

Hilton: I had to laugh. You know, these girls say they're looking for a husband, and I call it "sleeping around."

Howard: It's all in your perspective.

Hilton: Yeah. She'd fucked half the police department out there already before she met me. Oh, she fucked a captain.

Howard: Did she tell you this, or is this stuff you just kind of learned over time?

Hilton: She told me. She was crazy. Good Lord . . .

Howard: Like how?

Hilton: One of her boyfriends, not a police officer, was making . . . They didn't have a video, and they were making eight-millimeter films of her dancing nude.

Howard: How did that come up in conversation with a new husband?

Hilton: Oh, that's the way it always is. Don't you

know that? You're going with someone. She's the one that's got the pussy and can fuck anytime she wants. Sooner or later she comes around to all the people she's fucked. It always ends up that way. Don't you know that? Anytime you have a relationship, you go with someone, sooner or later, they're [going to ask], "Who else have you fucked?" And almost invariably, at least with the chicks I go with, they want to tell you.

Bridges: Obviously, I missed out on an important part of the conversation.

Hilton: There's a fine distinction, for women to threaten to give it away, the pussy, I mean, and for them to let you know that they could give it away, and they have given it away, increases the value of it. It's marketing. A sophisticated woman understands that to threaten to give it away increases the value. And actually giving it away decreases the value. Some women aren't smart enough to know the difference and they fuck up that way. They all do that. Okay, the nice girls, you know how they do it? They say, "Either you marry me or forget about it. I'm going to find someone else." That's threatening to give it away, and that's how they get men to do what they want them to do.

Howard: Oh yeah?

Hilton: Always. "Either you do what I want, or, in the end, I'm going to give it to someone else." That's part of my dislike—or I wouldn't call it "hatred," but almost—for women is that they have all the advantages.

Howard: The deck is stacked against us.

Hilton: I'm telling you, man. I finally came to the conclusion . . . I mean, the last piece of ass I had, except for rape, was in '89. Was in January of '89, and I never—

Howard: You kind of dropped out of the game there.

Hilton: I was never so happy after I did that. Once you stop getting led around by the dick, and we all are—all of us are. That's why we become less than men. That's why we start doing our woman's agenda. How many little nine-year-old boys have said to their little girl, "Oh, you know, I would like to get your toy tea set out, and let's have tea, and let's get our dollies here, and have tea with our dolly." You've never seen a boy do that. But what a woman wants you to do as an adult is to play house. And to have children. I understand that for men having children is the greatest thing in their lives. Nevertheless, how many nine-year-old boys have you known that have said, "I don't want to be a soldier or a pilot or an astronaut. I want to grow up and have a family." Bullshit. That's not what men are about. But, in the end, puberty happens. The hormones rise. We start getting led around by our dick.

And in the end we become women. You look at any married couple, and when I say "any," that's a big word, *any married couple,* especially the older ones, and what you have is not a man and a woman. You have two women, and one of them has a penis, and he's the designated dick. It's like, "Honey, you know. Can you give me back my dick tonight?" And you have two women doing the things that a woman wants to do, and having the values that a woman has, and leading a woman's agenda with the so-called man giving permission to do symbolic, almost ritual, things that make him the man. It may be whatever. It may be having his collection of snap-on tools in the garage. It could be his fishing or his hunting. These are symbolic, ritualistic things that they're allowed to do to say they're men, and even the toughest generally go home to a soft house to a soft woman's environment, to a *nicey*-nice . . . Look at these damn Muslims we're fighting, man. They're tough as fucking nails. They're thin. They're wiry. They eat a handful of mud every day, and they shit once a week. They sit on the fucking floor.

Oh, man. And here our so-called men, they go home to cushy-cushy and everything's all *nicey*-nice, and it's all got the woman's touch and everything. It's two women there.

Howard: Did you realize this—

Hilton: You look at any man's home—I'll answer your question in a minute—you look at any man's home. It's a woman's home. And what is his man thing? Having a nice lawn. Oh, Jesus Christ, give me a fucking break. Out there cutting grass and digging in the dirt like a fucking animal.

Bridges: All your travels and camping and stuff, by yourself, you get a lot of time to think. . . .

Hilton: That's lawyers and everyone else constantly asking, "How come you're so intelligent? Are you well-read? Are you well-educated?" You're right. You hit it right on the head. That's very perceptive of you. The reason I'm so seemingly intelligent is that I alone, amongst almost anyone else, including you dudes, have time to actually stop and think about things. You are so busy distracting yourself because you're running from the reality of the situation, which is frantically, desperately distracting yourself with every kind of thing in the world, including your work. . . . Now again, I'm not judging you. You're just human beings. That's all you are. You're just human beings, and God bless you. I'm not judging you, but I'm just saying, you're so embedded in the matrix that you live in that you can't even see it. I'll refer you back to what they advertise. . . .

And Hilton was off on another rant on academic thought suffusing the atmosphere and advertising saturating society's thoughts to the point where there is no room for any kind of thought except what "they" provide. He, among all men, knew this; and he realized and grasped the existential terror of being and that everything, in the end, was meaningless.

"You don't even know. You can't see the forest because of the trees," Hilton continued. "That's the thing. You hit right on it. The reason I seem to be intelligent is I, alone, amongst very few people, have the time to think, and when you're into hiking, when you're into running, and you're hiking and hiking . . . or you're walking your dog every day. Two or three hours, you know, and you're walking and you're walking and you're walking, you got to stay heads up and watch the dog and make sure he don't get run over, and it's all about the combat patrol, and that you're going to have to react at any time. You may hear the clickety-clack of dog nails behind you, and spin around, and there's a shepherd in your face ready to rumble. Okay, so it is that kind of combat-patrol kind of thing, but otherwise, you got time to think.

"That's one of my first memories. I'm a philosopher. I'm a soldier. I'm a psychic, and I'm an artist. Those are all distinct personality types that represent different, distinctively different, things, and I'm all of them, and what it really means is—is—is—is two opposing pairs. You have the rational, intellectual soldier and the scientist. The coldly rational soldier."

Howard: Coldly?

Hilton: Yeah, and the coldly rational scientist. The scientist—if it can't be demonstrated, it doesn't exist. It's only a theory, you know. You got to show me the facts in science, okay? So those two are the coldly rational ones. The artist and the philosopher are interested more in the textures, and the why and wherefores behind it, you see.

Howard: So you're having to balance the two?

Hilton: I have all those there, and it's not as complex as it sounds. If you're aware that I'm a soldier, a scientist, an artist, and a philosopher—if you're aware of that—then I'm a very simple person.

Bridges: What's your artistic side? What do you mean by "artist"?

Hilton: By "artist," I mean truly in the sense of being an artist in that you see everything in terms of not the linear, but the impression of it, and so forth. People ask me, "What's your medium? Are you a sculptor or . . . ?" No, my artist . . . my art is my life, and my art is weird. My art is my life. My art is weird. (Hilton exploded in laughter.) My art is my life, and my art is weird.

Bridges: I'm actually buying into this.

Hilton: Of course. It's true. It's all true. This is true. It's real. Everything I've told you is true. Everything I'm telling you is real. It exists. It's true.

Bridges: What I'm saying is that you say your life is your medium.

Hilton: Just for an audience of one. The rest of the world, they can't really understand. I delight in representing a fantastic spectacle to people in terms of my technicality. You know, I'm all tech'ed out. I'm strapped with every kind of layer of equipment and I present this fantastical spectacle to people, but I understand. They can't understand it because it's so fantastical. It's kind of like the Lone Ranger. The Lone Ranger will come galloping into town. There will be all the same townspeople, right? And here the Lone Ranger will be wearing this mask, a skintight outfit, a really elaborate two-gun rig with chrome pistols, and it's just a theatrical outfit. He'd be mounted on this beautiful palomino. He'd have this trippy Indian named Tonto with him, and if the Lone

Ranger would ride out again, what would they always say about the Lone Ranger? You don't remember this. They would always say—

Bridges: "Who was that masked man?"

Hilton: "Who was that masked man?" Okay, that's what I do to society. They can't get their minds around it even. That's why they remember me. That's why I can't go anywhere without a hundred people calling in. I'll bet there are people who have called in that met me one time over ten years ago for five minutes.

Bridges: You're absolutely right. Which brings up something interesting that you're talking about and why. One thing I'm curious about.

Hilton: What?

Bridges: You bumped into a Cherokee County deputy up on some private hunting property back in October. It was highly publicized after we caught up with another one, and you threw it out there to him that you were a paratrooper on perpetual maneuvers.

Hilton: I thought he realized what I was doing. You know, I'm doing this day after day, and I finally realized—

Howard: Combat patrols, where you got to stay alert all the time?

Hilton: Yeah, the combat patrols and land navigation. That's exactly it. Every time I go out to walk my dog, I'm like a police officer. I understand that there's a significant chance that before I come home, I'll be fighting for my life. Every time I walk my dog anywhere. You know why? All it takes is one gate left open, one door left open. I got a Rottweiler this big. One time I had run a route for over ten years, and I never knew the dog was there, and I passed by a house and I hear a guy yelling, "Bad dog, bad dog, bad dog!" And I look, and that was this dog's name. It was a big-ass Rottweiler coming for me. He had gotten loose out of the house, and that was the dog's name, Bad Dog.

That's the way it is, man. You know, it's like police work. I mean, ninety minutes of boredom and ten minutes of utter pucker-up shit. It's happened so much that I fought, and again I say fighting, I shape the situation rather than kick ass. 'Cause when you kick ass, it's going to ruin your day, regardless. Even if you're right, it may not go your way. You don't have a badge. About 1995 or so, I realized that that's what I'm doing.

Hilton talked for some time on tactical battlefield maneuvers that he related to police work, as well as riffing on rocket-propelled grenades (RPGs) as opposed to rockets, and the tracks on various mechanized vehicles. The soldier aspect of his personality stepped out like General George Patton.

Hilton: You know, I'd get in the truck with the dog, move, get out, get my shit together, run a patrol, come back, eat. You know, sleep, move, get out, get the shit together, run a patrol. And [I] finally realized that I was just on perpetual field maneuvers, and I said, "Well, it ain't much of a life, but, hell, it's a life."

Bridges: When you throw stuff out like that, I'm just trying to figure out. You know, you call it "artistry" or whatever.

Hilton: You might call it "insanity"?

Bridges: No, I'm not saying that.

Hilton: No, you're not.

Bridges: I don't think you're insane, by no stretch of the imagination. What I'm getting at is it is almost like a little acting on your behalf to— I don't know—kind of steer this law enforcement officer away from you?

Hilton: Oh, with him? No, I was being perfectly candid with him. I steered him away from me.

Bridges: Yeah, I mean, I'm just trying to figure out what—

Hilton: Here's the thing. Police officers are individuals, so, of course, they're going to run across a whole spectrum of human behavior, but there's—there's a large number of police officers that are highly experienced. And that they are pros, and they recognize a pro when they see a pro. And I'm a pro. So I'm not some bum out there sleeping in my van. I'm a pro.

Bridges: Right.

Hilton: He saw my map collection because I was showing him maps, man. These are just maps I carry. I've got a Rubbermaid— twenty-six-gallon Rubbermaid container full of maps. Area maps, topo (topographical) maps, every kind of map.

Howard: You're not just playing around. You're training.

Hilton: I got a map collection that is so exotic. I
mean, it's wild. It's got every kind of area
map. Everywhere from Shining Rock Wil-
derness to all the way down to Ocala
National Forest in Florida. I can pull out
any map, and I got topo . . . maps of much of
the North Georgia area. Every kind of map.
I got Cherokee National Forest, Nantahala
National, every national forest.

Bridges: In the interest of time, let's—if you don't
care—let's go back to . . . where did we get
up to? The early '80s? Right after the divorce. You were still in Atlanta at that time
and you were. . . ?

Hilton: Yeah, and when I got busted I had to go
straight for six months. I got a job.

Bridges: What did you get arrested for?

Hilton: Fraudulent phone solicitation. It was a misdemeanor thing, though. Now it's a felony.

Bridges: What type of telephone fraud were you
doing at that point?

Hilton: The usual. *Georgia Veteran's Journal, Georgia
Inspector's Journal,* Southeast Regional
Council, Georgia Youth Sports Project. You
had a list of about a hundred charities.

Bridges: What year did you get arrested for that?

Hilton: Seventy-nine. Yeah, probably about November.

Bridges: November?

Hilton: So I played that out, and I went and got a
job. They took everything, and they did a
search warrant on the house, too. So I got
a job for about six months. Got a job, Fourth
of July, and by then I was long divorced.

Bridges: What kind of job?

Hilton: Industrial chemicals, long distance, on a watch line. Got that job, kept that.

Bridges: Name for that place?

Hilton: It's no longer in existence. KEM Manufacturing.

Howard: That was like what? Right after you got out, so '81-ish? Beginning of '81 or . . . ?

Hilton: I kept that until July 1980.

Howard: Okay.

Bridges: Then what did you do?

Hilton: Oh, went back to my old habits. Yeah, I actually got time in DeKalb County Jail. It was in '79. I was in there on that bust. Guy was telling me his life story, and it was just, you know, a tragedy. So I asked him, "Why do you keep doing this? Why?" You know, why? He said, "Because I can't get up and go to work," and you know, that describes most criminals.

You could say a criminal is someone that breaks the law and gets away with it, and keeps doing it until he gets caught. That's a good definition, but another good definition is one that can't get up and go to work in the morning. That's the artist. Don't you understand? That's the artist in me. Artists don't get up and go to work in the morning. So okay, once I started doing that, and I kept doing it through the '80s. I took a bust in '87. My computer printout has "theft by taking," but the actual charge was "theft by deception." Misdemeanor again. The woman lured

me over there, right in the heart of Dunwoody. A fucking yuppie woman lured me
over there to pick up a twenty-five-dollar
check and then kept me waiting for the
check. She was really good. She was pre-
tending she was on the phone, and she would
come and let me see her on the phone. Kept
me waiting there for thirty minutes. When
I told my criminal friends about it, they said
I should have never sat there waiting for
thirty minutes. Taught me a lesson. DeKalb
County North again. They showed up, arrested me. They got the check and they got
the woman complaining. They found my car.
Okay? The car I was driving was a stolen car.

Bridges: Really?

Hilton: It had been stolen from a rental company
that I had been renting from, and—

Bridges: What kind of car was it?

Hilton: It was a Chevy something—Eurosport—
and I had been renting cars from them. Fourteen [dollars] a day. Unlimited mileage.
Killer, man. I could just rent the thing once
a week and go put two hundred miles on it
for seven cents a mile. The receipt was not
only proof of ownership, but it was also
proof of insurance. They'd check if you had
purchased insurance. So I just wrote on that
slip. Had dealer drive-out tags on it, and at
that time, the drive-out tags were not the
issued. One time a cop in High Falls State
Park in Tennessee . . . I was up there with a
stolen car in the park. The police officer followed me and followed me and followed me.

I was going to the office to pick up a map there, so I pulled in and parked, and I got out. He pulled in and got out and was walking in. He asked to see the slip and says, "Is that what y'all have in Georgia there?" I said, "Yeah, that's what they use." He said, "Well, it's no good for police work." I'm thinking, "Little does he know."

Bridges: When was that?

Hilton: Eighty-seven or '88. I drove it for years.

Howard: Wait a minute. When did you rent it?

Hilton: You mean stole it?

Howard: Yeah.

Hilton: Eighty-six.

Howard: Oh, okay.

Hilton: Drove it until '89. I just took it, and would keep it washed. You're not going to charge me with this, are you?

Bridges: No, no, no, no, no.

Hilton: I shouldn't have told that story. Anyway, I kept it stashed. And, anyway, I broke my arm running. I was running along a block wall, about nine feet over a parking lot, and one of the rocks was loose, and I fell off it and fell all the way down to the pavement and broke my arm really bad right here. Then, the next year I broke it by falling off a mountain bike, same place. A displaced fracture. I had this old '77 Ford. Power steering was broken, so I couldn't drive it with one hand, and that's the reason I had been renting them, anyway, because my car was so decrepit, you know. Anyway, so I'm—

Howard: What kind of car was it?

Hilton: Seventy-seven Ford LTD. Big ol' monster.

Howard: Like a cop car?

Hilton: Yeah.

Howard: Wasn't blue, was it?

Hilton: No. The paint was all scaled. It was horrible-looking. But, anyway, the very first day I drive it to work in, you know, I was out picking up my fraudulent money, and I'm on McGinnis Ferry Road. State patrol, highway patrol, had a road check there. Came along, and right where you cross the Chattahoochee River, on the east side of the river, they had a road check set up, and you really couldn't see it because they were kind of in dead space or something. You know, that's where they have it, of course, where you can't see it two miles away. I drove into it before I knew it.

This was before computerized insurance, so you had to have proof of insurance. He said, "Proof of insurance, driver's license." So I was flipping my orange contract, which you couldn't read, anyway. It was called a copy. The date was illegible, but the legible part was that I had insurance and my name and address on it. I reckon I half-ass erased the date. It was horrible, anyway, but looked real. It's just like a third carbon or something. But you could see it was my name and address and that I purchased insurance because that box was checked, proof of insurance, and so I handed that with my driver's license. He didn't even look at it. He just sent it back to me return mail, and I drove that car three more years until I bought the truck. I bought a Mazda.

Howard: When did you get the Mazda?

Hilton: Eighty-nine.

Howard: So you got it in '86 and drive that one . . .

Hilton: I started driving it. I had it stored for several months until I broke my arm and then I just started driving it, and once I went through that road check it was okay, and it did have the drive-out tag on it. Celebrity Eurosport. The trunk was just a box. You could take a bike and take the front wheel off and put a bicycle right in the trunk. I mean, it was just a box with four doors. Just beautiful, useable space.

Bridges: Did you have any roommates back around that time, or anything?

Hilton: Twice. A guy named John Moss, back in '82. I lived with him for about six months, and Chris Johnson, who called in twelve years later to lash me. Called me a misfit with a mean streak.

Bridges: Since '97?

Hilton: Yeah. Ninety-seven, I started there, and in '98, I lived there—started living there. And in 2001 I had a six-month break I was away from it.

Howard: What did you do for that?

Hilton: Worked for another company. The guy was stealing from me the whole time, and it was a real shame. Even guys like myself who are just totally sociopathic, we still need some human to trust. Even if we're not close to them, to trust them, even if it's a business associate, and I chose to trust him. . . .

Howard: John Tabor?

Hilton: Yeah, and that's why he got away with it, you see, because when you choose to trust someone, it's kind of a dimming of awareness. It's like with your spouse. You're in love with your spouse, so you dress them up in your love, and you make them, quite often, into something that they really weren't.

Howard: Put them on a pedestal almost.

Hilton: That's what I mean. Dress up . . . Cyndi Lauper put out a song, "Gonna Dress Him Up in My Love," and I thought that's a good line. Quite often people find that their spouses really weren't who they made them out to be. *(Editor's note: The artist was actually Madonna, and the song was "Dress You Up (in My Love)" from her* Like a Virgin *album.)*

Bridges: Right.

Hilton: They find that their spouses were looking them in the eye for the whole ten years and saying, "Honey, I love you. There will never be another one." And sleeping with them, and being intimate with them, and the whole time sharing their body and their lives and their emotions with some other woman or some other man. It's an all-too-common story. It's psychopathic behavior, but everyone does it, so it's one of my favorite observations that I come to learn through my philosophical insight. Personal integrity is so hard to judge because everyone—

Bridges: So the '90s was pretty much the same deal? You were staying in an apartment up until . . .

Hilton: No, no, no. I went homeless in early '90s. The reason I went homeless is I was being investigated, again, by the police.

Bridges: For the same thing, telephone fraud?

Hilton: Yeah, and I knew what went down. I was hiring people to go out and collect. But I had the mind-set that this was a warrant or a subpoena, and I was a cop, and you know, and I looked like a cop, you know, because I was well-built and I carried myself like a cop. I'd drive up in this plainclothes police car, get out like I owned the damn place. I got my court order in my hand, and I go in there, and I pick up my five dollars. I'd risk my life. I got a gauntlet of guys hanging around in front of the liquor store. Had to walk right through them, okay. That's what you call occupying your space. That's what you call officer presence. Okay? I had it. I had a guy one time I got out of that car, and he was in the front of the liquor store, he put his hands up. He said, "Okay, you got me." I said, "I don't want you." He thought I was there for him.

Bridges: Did you carry any weapons with you? I'd have had a gun if that was me. So you went homeless?

Hilton: In 1990. I started living in storage buildings. And I would stay about seventy-five days a year in a Motel 6, free local phone, seventy-five, [or a] hundred days a year. Free local phone, and Motel 6 has been for seventeen, eighteen, nineteen, twenty dollars a day.

Bridges: Do you remember what storage facility you stayed in? Eight and a half years, I'm sure you remember it.

Hilton: It went through several incarnations. It was Pack and Stack. Now it's a Sure Guard Storage in Gwinnett.

Bridges: And that was probably all the way up through '98?

Hilton: Yeah.

Bridges: Is that when you got on with John (Tabor)?

Hilton: I moved in at John's house.

Bridges: Moved in?

Hilton: I'd been working with John since '97. John lived there before he got married in late '97. He wouldn't let me go in for a while, but he needed me too bad. I left him in early '97 and stayed away several months, and he needed me real bad—so he let me move in. By the way, you can tell John Tabor that I'm the one that killed the girl. Okay? I'm the one who killed her, but the reason she is dead . . . I want you to tell Tabor this . . . the reason she's dead. Now, I killed her. Okay? But the reason she is dead is that when I called him on Thursday or whenever—

Bridges: Thursday.

Hilton: When I called him, that girl was alive. She was in my van. She was in the parking lot at the Huddle House, and it's just like . . . I gave the girl's body up when I realized that I had been caught, fair and square.

Bridges: Right.

Hilton: That's what I told you because they had me under kidnapping, and it was going to stick. The evidence was good right out of the Dumpster. It was just a smoking gun. They had me, and on the kidnapping charge it's the same as a life sentence for me. It's either forty years first-degree or life with bodily harm, so I was getting a life sentence, and they had that, and so there was no real use in keeping the girl's body—except not to be charged with murder and everything—and I did it under those things because they had me, and I did it for the girl's family.

Bridges: Right.

Hilton: The point I'm trying to make is I gave the girl's body up because you had me. You had me, fair and square, and I was getting life.

Bridges: But you were talking about . . .

Hilton: Tabor. At that time, the girl was alive, and if Tabor hadn't have been such a little smart-ass . . . He's such a girl . . . tattle-tale's here. . . . These guys are such . . . I called Tabor and I told him I needed money, and I wanted to start working for him again, and I was really sincere in trying to start work again for him, because I saw that this robbery shit wasn't getting it, because I hadn't—hadn't gotten any money off her. You know, I hadn't got a dime. I had spent money on her. I had forty-five dollars to my name, and I had done spent thirty dollars of it driving all over Georgia trying to work her ATM card on the bogus numbers she gave me. I lost money on that deal, you know, and so Tabor had to be coy, and, you know, carry it all the way.

I asked for eight hundred. "Well, I don't know if I can give you that." I said, "Well, you know . . ." "Okay, I'll leave you a check."

Yeah, he's such a damn girl. Just a smart-ass yuppie. If Tabor—trust me, tell Tabor this—if he hadn't been trying to entrap me . . . He wanted me, you know, to come and get it at the office. He was just setting a trap for me. He's the one that called to begin with, you know. He was the first one that turned me in. If Tabor had said, "Hey, Gary, they know it's you. They're looking for you now." I wasn't in the paper that day. I had joked about it with the girl. This is the second or third day I had her. She still wasn't in the paper. I said, "You know something, no one's even missed you," and she said, "Well, I'd be mad if once you let me go, and I came back, and my boyfriend said, 'Have you been gone?' We were laughing about it because nothing appeared in the paper. I said, "They hadn't even reported you missing yet." It was like the second or third day, or third day after she went missing, something like that. The day before she was killed, okay? Tabor had already turned me in, but it hadn't hit the papers yet. It hit the papers on Friday. I got that, and it was on the front page. Well, I saw that article like two hours after I killed her. If

I had bought a paper that morning on Friday, instead of that afternoon, she would have been alive because my picture's on the front page. A color picture on the front page of the *AJC,* looking for me and everything. I wouldn't have killed her. For Pete's sake, no. And the same holds true with Tabor.

Instead of trying to be a smart-ass and lay a trap for me, if Tabor had just said, "Hey, Gary, that hiker," but she wasn't in the paper. I bought a paper the day . . . I had just bought the paper in the gas station before I went there and looked at the paper. They didn't have a pay phone at the gas station I bought the paper at, so I went across to the Huddle House to use the phone. I had already looked in the paper. I showed her the paper. I said, "They haven't even reported you missing yet. You've not even been in the paper." But if Tabor had just said, "Gary, they know it's you. . . . They're looking for you," the girl would be alive. Listen, the reason for killing the girl—it was either once you've taken someone, you're either going to kill them, or you're going to get caught. It's as simple as that. In my situation, look at me. I got the dog. I got the van. I'm me. I'm famous, anyway. Regardless, and I know it, and once you've taken someone, you either kill them, or you get caught. If you release them, you're going to get caught.

Well, she seen the van. She seen the tag. She seen the dog. All she has to do is put that out, and ten thousand people will be calling, including Tabor. He was just the first one, you know. Of course I knew it. You either kill them, or you get caught. Okay? But if you're already caught, there's no use in killing them. I didn't kill them because . . . for any satisfaction. It was distasteful. It was dreadful. Trust me, it was. Of course, I was able to do it because of my general rage against society, of course. It's because I'd become . . . Well, you get that way in Atlanta.

Howard: Smog and traffic.

Hilton: And the people think they're just fucking royalty, even though they're idiots.

Howard: I guess Tabor's kind of part of that somewhere.

Hilton: Tabor's a kind of part of that. But Tabor is a little more. When it comes to individual human beings, the answer is rarely simple. I simplify groups of human beings. You really have to, actually, to preserve your scalp, for that matter. You have to make broad judgments about groups of human beings, but always understanding that [with] individual human beings the answer is rarely simple.

Bridges: You and Tabor were pretty tight, right?

Hilton: No, I was tight with Tabor. Tabor was not tight with me, nor is he tight with anyone. I talked to him a lot, and if Tabor was screwing me, he'd screw his mother. He'd screw his wife. He'd screw anybody. He's a psychopath. I'm sure Tabor's laughing now because I called Tabor a psychopathic criminal with no heart, no conscience, and no moral compass, and I'm sure he's saying, "Yeah, look who's talking." Tabor is worse than me. He's just not dangerous like me. He's—he's just your . . . a girl. Yeah, he's a girl. I'm a

stud. Okay? So I did a crime that studs would
do. Yeah. He does a crime that girls would
do, which is lying and stealing.

Howard: Did he confess this—this bisexuality to
you, or—

Hilton: Oh, I've been around enough, man. That
older woman I told you back when I left my
wife. In 1971, she was what they call a "fag
hag." A fag hag is a woman who runs with
homosexuals, you know. And it worked out
good for them, because they . . . Everywhere
they go, there's her running buddies. Gorgeous, good-looking guys who don't look
like queers, and you know . . . at the same
time, she relates to them as a woman, not as
a man, so they can be girls with her.

Their girl side—you know what I mean?
Fags have the heart and the soul of a woman,
with the sex drive of a man, basically—
which is why they are so inordinately, fla-
grantly promiscuous. . . .

Although Gary Hilton continued to talk for another
hour, getting on the podium to give evaluations of police
procedures, the sociology of homosexuality and bisexuality, and mind over matter, he said nothing that was
relevant to the investigation.

The two GBI special agents were exhausted from listening to his disheveled thoughts and guiding him toward
more useful things rather than wade through his personal
gibberish. They had learned about Hilton's travels, where
he was during various time periods, the cars that he drove,
and his philosophy about killing kidnapped people.

He had inadvertently strengthened suspicions that
slaughtering people was not new to him: *"You either kill
them, or you get caught."*

Chapter 14

There was a feeling of angst in the Dawson County Superior Court at 1:30 P.M. on Thursday, January 31, 2008, that seemed to deplete the oxygen for those who had gathered for the sentencing phase of Hilton's murder trial. The grief had clearly wounded Meredith Emerson's parents and friends to a degree that was impossible to describe. They were suffering as they realized that no punishment would ever bring their daughter back.

Susan and David Emerson already knew what the sentence would be and had accepted it so they could give their daughter's remains a proper memorial and resting place and get on with life as best they could. Both knew there would always be an empty place in their heart, which would never be filled.

Lee Darragh, Dawson County district attorney, represented the state. Darragh, a middle-aged man, with silver hair and an elegance of movement, looked as if he had been assigned his role by central casting for a movie production company. H. Bradford Morris Jr. and Robert R. McNeill, who were seasoned trial lawyers from the public defender's office, represented Gary Hilton.

The gallery was packed with people—most attendees

were there to offer support to Meredith Emerson's family and friends. Newspaper and television news reporting on the race to find Emerson alive had captured the hearts of residents in the area and they had come to love the young woman. She was one of their own: she had lived and worked in Georgia and had graduated from the University of Florida.

Georgia trials are divided into two parts: a penalty phase, where the jury hears evidence, deliberates, and renders a verdict; it is then followed by a sentencing phase, where interested parties can address the court to offer mitigating or aggravating circumstances. Mitigating circumstances are meant to show the defendant in a favorable light and sway the sentence recommended by a jury or imposed by a judge. Aggravating circumstances are those that show the crime in its raw, unadulterated cruelty, in the hope of winning a harsher sentence.

There was no one present to offer mitigating circumstances for Gary Hilton.

Superior court judge Bonnie C. Oliver called the court to order and told Darragh to proceed.

DA Lee Darragh told the judge that the grand jury of Dawson County had returned a true bill of indictment earlier that morning against Hilton for murder. He said that the people of Georgia, Dawson County, embodied by the grand jury, "charge and accuse Gary Michael Hilton with the offense of murder" and that "on the fourth day of January 2008, did unlawfully and with malice afore-thought cause the death of Meredith Hope Emerson . . . through the commission of a forcible felony . . . aggra-vated battery, by causing blunt-force trauma to her head."

The district attorney told the judge that Hilton had entered a plea of guilty earlier in the day and that it was witnessed by McNeill, one of Hilton's public defenders. Darragh had also signed the indictment, as did Hilton and Morris, Hilton's other attorney. After going through the legal formalities, Darragh said he would present the indictment to the court.

"Your Honor, the defendant has agreed to enter a plea of guilty in return for a recommendation from the state that he be sentenced to life imprisonment, and has completed a plea petition stating so," Darragh continued. He asked the judge to allow him to present facts that supported the plea of guilty.

Judge Oliver consented.

The district attorney told the judge that Hilton regularly visited national and state parks and that he was seen the day "before the kidnapping and eventual murder" of Emerson. Hilton was seen on the Appalachian Trail, Darragh said, where Emerson had eventually been kidnapped. Hilton had intended to kidnap a woman he followed and had actually talked with, but the plan didn't materialize because she was with several other people.

"And on the next day, Tuesday, January 1, 2008, at about one P.M., Ms. Emerson arrived at the Byron Herbert Reece Memorial Trailhead parking area in Union County," he said. "There were witnesses who saw him at that location. There were also witnesses who observed Mr. Hilton following Ms. Emerson on the Appalachian Trail at different intervals. One gentleman was a former law enforcement officer and noted that the defendant was carrying a large knife and a police-style baton on his belt.

"Later that afternoon that witness found two water bottles, a dog leash, and some dog treats, along with a police-style baton, lying on the edge of the Reece Trail," Darragh continued. "He believed that the baton was dropped by this defendant and became concerned for Ms.

Emerson's well-being, and suspected a struggle at that location."

Darragh said that later investigation showed there was a struggle between Hilton and Emerson. "The defendant . . . was able to place her under his control eventually and took her down the trail back to where her car was and where his van was," Darragh said. He added that Hilton took some ATM cards, identification cards, and other items that were in Emerson's car and placed them in his vehicle.

"Throughout the next couple of days, Mr. Hilton basically rode Ms. Emerson around to various locations throughout North Georgia, seeking to get money from her ATMs," the district attorney continued. "During this time Ms. Emerson often gave him incorrect PIN numbers and he was unsuccessful. Although it is unclear, I would like to think it is because she was doing everything she could to insure that perhaps he would get caught during his efforts to use the ATMs."

Darragh talked about how witnesses saw Hilton on January 4 along the Dawson Forest Wildlife Management Area. Eventually, he said, Hilton was caught in DeKalb County, where he was trying to dispose of evidence, but he wasn't successful at that attempt.

"Evidence from his van included items containing blood and other items that were connected with Ms. Emerson," Darragh said. "Those items, through examination, DNA comparison, proved to contain some blood of Ms. Emerson. That was on Friday, January the fourth, when he was finally arrested that evening."

At the time, Darragh said, Hilton was arrested on an outstanding warrant for failure to appear that had been issued by the U.S. Northern District of Georgia, and was taken into custody by U.S. Marshals. The next day Hilton was charged with kidnapping with bodily injury, and on

Monday, January 7, 2008, Hilton was denied bond in Union County. Plea bargains were started almost immediately by the Union County district attorney and the public defender who represented Hilton at the time. Under the plea bargain Gary Hilton agreed to show the police where Emerson's remains were located—if the state would not ask for the death penalty. He told the court about Emerson's decapitation after death "for forensic purposes" and the defendant's attempt to destroy evidence, all to make it harder to identify the body. Darragh explained all of this to show that the state had followed all required procedures in striking the plea bargain and that Hilton understood the consequences. Hilton and his public defenders acknowledged that the defendant was fully cognizant of the ramifications of his plea bargain.

Following DA Darragh's remarks, Judge Oliver had a few questions for the defense.

"Were all the facts and possible defenses discussed with Mr. Hilton?" she asked.

"At great length, Your Honor," Robert McNeill answered.

"Is there any meritorious defense for Mr. Hilton?"

Both McNeill and Morris said they weren't aware of any. The public defenders also answered in the affirmative when the judge asked whether or not Hilton was competent. Having been satisfied that no stone had been left unturned that could result in a mistrial or an appeal, Judge Oliver told Hilton she had a series of questions for him.

Hilton asked, "Should I stand?"

The judge told him she had already informed the defense that he could remain seated. She asked for Hilton's full name, age, if he could read and write, and whether he was under the influence of any kind of drug, alcohol, or intoxicant. His answers consisted largely of three-word sentences: "No, Your Honor" or "Yes, Your Honor."

"Do you now suffer from any mental or emotional disability?"

"No, Your Honor."

Hilton answered in the affirmative when he was asked if he fully understood the plea bargain, confession, the nature of the charges against him, and his right to plead not guilty. He acknowledged that he had a right to a trial and that no threats, force, pressure, or any other type of intimidation had been made to persuade him to enter a guilty plea. Hilton answered yes, when he was asked if he understood he would receive a sentence of life in prison; and he said he was satisfied with his lawyers and how his case was presented.

"Did you, in fact, commit the unlawful acts set forth in the indictment against you to which you are proposing to enter a plea?"

"Yes, Your Honor."

"Do you now want to enter a plea of guilty?"

Hilton said he did.

"And how do you plead to the charge of the murder in Dawson County, Georgia, on the fourth day of January 2008 with malice aforethought causing the death of Meredith Hope Emerson?"

"Guilty, Your Honor."

Finished with her questions to Hilton, Judge Oliver directed her attention to Darragh and asked him if he knew the average length of time that it takes in Georgia to get a death penalty case to trial. Darragh said that it usually takes two to three years after an arrest to bring a case to trial, and the average amount of time spent on death row until execution is about twelve years.

The judge asked if Emerson's family was opposed to

the plea bargain. They supported the arrangement, Lee Darragh told Judge Oliver.

"Their beloved daughter went first missing only thirty days ago," he said, "and here we are before the court closing this matter.

"This is a situation that will not be over for them by any stretch of the imagination," he continued, "but through the acceptance of this plea, they can get this legal aspect of what has occurred behind them. . . . Before I made the actual offer . . . I discussed it with the Emersons very thoroughly."

Darragh said a life sentence without parole meant that Hilton would spend the rest of his life in prison.

Judge Oliver removed her glasses for a moment and looked at Hilton through narrowed eyes and then she spoke.

"Because we are a civilized society and our system of laws has many protections and safeguards built in to prevent injustice in even the most heinous of crimes, I will consider this plea." She told Hilton that the community and most of the state would consider his immediate execution as the only satisfactory penalty.

"Even the most tenderhearted among us would consider your actions deserving of the severest punishment," she said. Because it was so important for the victim's family and friends to recover her remains, Judge Oliver said she would accept the plea bargain.

Because he was sixty-one years old, with a life expectancy of seventeen more years, the judge told Hilton, it would be unlikely that he would live long enough to be executed if the death penalty was ordered.

Hilton told her there was nothing he wanted to say before the judge passed sentence. Hilton's sentence was to spend the rest of his life in a Georgia prison without the possibility of parole.

* * *

Following the sentence, Meredith's parents were allowed to address the court. They said in part:

"We stand before you as brokenhearted parents, having lost our beloved daughter to the vicious murder committed by Mr. Hilton," David Emerson said. "Our days are filled with tears, blank stares, and we constantly struggle through each day. Meredith was our shining light in our lives and now we are left with a hole in our hearts that will not heal."

Their daughter had been an inspiration for good and had treated everyone with respect and dignity. "The outpouring of love and support from friends and loved ones and countless numbers of strangers is a testimony to how Meredith touched so many people in a positive way, both in life and death," David Emerson said.

As a father who had lost his daughter so early in her life, Emerson said he would feel the grief and pain forever. Gone was his joyful anticipation of walking his daughter down the aisle at her wedding or holding one of the children whom she now would never have.

"I feel that no punishment for Mr. Hilton is too great," he said. David noted that we provide food and shelter and protection for criminals such as Hilton instead of allowing the family to administer what it considered justice.

"I only pray that he suffers immensely for his heinous acts and that even his fellow inmates recognize his evil and malevolence . . . and treat him with appropriate measures."

Barely able to hold back tears, David listened to his wife, Susan, speak to Hilton. Before addressing him, she told the judge that Meredith's brother, Mark, had found it too difficult to pen his own statement. She was also speaking for him, she said.

Susan Emerson told the judge that there was "no such thing as justice" in this case. Nothing would bring their daughter back. She did not regret that the death penalty had been taken out of consideration, Susan said. That would have been an easy way out for him; instead, she hoped that "he should stay alive and slowly rot."

She mocked Hilton's pretense of being a soldier on perpetual maneuvers:

"He is nothing more than a bully and a weak-minded man on the run," she observed. "He fancies himself a survivalist, while anyone can see he is a scared little man on the run. He is the fool who goes through life too ignorant to realize he is a fool, and Meredith has exposed him."

The grieving and angry mother said that her daughter was one of the few people who would forgive him, if given the chance.

"I have no doubt that her goodness and light intimidated the hell out of him, so he struck out in fear," Emerson said. "I'm sure he thinks he snuffed out her light, but the truth is, she is stronger and brighter than ever, while he has been diminished."

Susan Emerson posed the possibility that her daughter may have seen the capacity for evil in Hilton and "at a soul level" decided "to take him out so he could never harm another innocent person. It's the strength and the type of person that she was at the core."

Emerson said that she had been "shown a vision" of Hilton as a mass of darkness with a tiny pinpoint of light. She said he didn't have the courage to nourish the light and become someone worthwhile. "Instead, he made one conscious choice after another to become the pathetic shell of a man that he is," she said. Hilton knew this in the deepest part of his soul, Emerson said.

"God may choose to forgive him," she said. "However, he is not worth the time and energy it would take me to do so. My focus will remain on all the good Meredith stood for and still does. She lives on, and I know her energy is strong and expansive. I have seen it and have experienced it in the past weeks."

She thanked the court, and Judge Oliver offered the family her deepest sympathy.

Court was recessed and Gary Michael Hilton's trial was over in Georgia. He would spend the rest of his life in prison, but the death penalty still stared him in the face. A trial date for the murder of Cheryl Dunlap in Florida had not yet been set.

Hilton, who had spent his life on a "Deadly Run" of his own, had not won the race. He had merely dodged it.

Death still looked him squarely in the eye.

Chapter 15

Almost as soon as he left the courtroom, Hilton began plotting to attempt blocking his extradition to Florida. On February 28, less than thirty days following his guilty plea to Meredith Emerson's murder, Hilton had been indicted on charges of murder, kidnapping, and two counts of grand theft in the murder of Cheryl Hodges Dunlap. Leon County, Florida, SA William Meggs announced at that time that he would seek the death penalty in the Dunlap case.

Prior to Gary Michael Hilton's indictment, investigators had stated they knew that Hilton was in Florida when Cheryl Dunlap disappeared on December 1. They knew this because of a run-in he'd had with a forestry agent in the area of the Apalachicola National Forest. Major Mike Wood, of the Leon County Sheriff's Office, told the media that the agent ran Hilton's license plate as a "routine check" at that time and had a conversation with him, but the tag number checked out to have no reported warrants on file for its driver. Investigators later learned that Hilton had been stopped by a U.S. Forestry officer in November, approximately two weeks before Cheryl

Dunlap's disappearance, and the tag on his white van was checked, also without results at that time.

A hunter in the area also reported he had seen a man fitting Hilton's description in the national forest on December 7. He described him as "homeless-looking and disheveled." The hunter said the man had a knife. He warned the man, he said, that it wasn't very safe for him to be in the forest during hunting season. As soon as the hunter realized that he might have encountered Dunlap's killer, he quickly came forward and told the authorities about his meeting with the man who fit the description of the suspect he had seen on the news.

Because of the national coverage of the Meredith Emerson case, Gary Hilton had already achieved a great deal of notoriety. When he was officially identified as the prime suspect in the murder of Cheryl Dunlap, hundreds of other tips came in concerning the case, and over twenty people reported seeing Hilton in the Tallahassee area. Some of the sightings dated back almost ten years and were obviously a case of mistaken identity, but Leon County sheriff Larry Campbell told the *Tallahassee Democrat* that sixteen of the reported sightings had taken place within the previous three months.

"The accuracy of those sightings is absolute," he said. "No question about it."

Major Mike Wood said his department's investigation was "focused utterly and completely on Mr. Hilton."

Hilton, who was being held at the Georgia Diagnostic and Classification Prison in Jackson, was well aware of his risky position. He had nothing to bargain with in the Dunlap case. He knew that he would not be able to wrangle another deal with prosecutors in Florida, as he had done in Georgia, where he had led investigators to the location of Meredith Emerson's body in return for having the death penalty taken off the table. He began working on his plan to fight extradition to Florida.

On April 3, Gary Hilton notified the court of his intention and was given twenty days to either file a petition or retain an attorney to do it for him. On April 22, he submitted his paperwork, an Extradition Habeas Petition, to the Superior Court of Butts County, Georgia, acting as his own attorney. The petition contained a considerable amount of whining and complaining about his circumstances at the prison:

I have no access to the telephone, the Internet, and very little U.S. Mail; the stamp and envelope that I am using to mail this was given to me by another inmate, he claimed.

Hilton said he was being held in such tight security that he was unable to get an address for the court, and was not sure it was the correct address.

That means that it took me 13 days just to get this court's possible address, he complained.

Hilton also said his rights were being denied because he hadn't received a copy of the arrest warrant from Florida.

Butts County district attorney Richard Milam, handling the extradition for Georgia, said Hilton's filing was insufficient to stall the process and called it "just a delaying tactic."

On May 2, Hilton was given an eleven-minute hearing in front of Judge Thomas Wilson in the second-floor courtroom of the Butts County Courthouse. Security was unusually tight for the hearing; SWAT team members and other officers with semiautomatic rifles guarded the courtroom and were stationed outside the building.

Hilton's handcuffs were tethered to waist chains; and when he was brought into the courtroom, corrections officers sat on either side of him. These security measures served as a dramatic background for Hilton's histrionics. Still acting as his own attorney, he intended to have his say concerning the unfair treatment he believed he was receiving.

His main concern, however, seemed to be his insistence that the court should have appointed him an attorney to aid in his fight against extradition. Hilton told the judge that he thought it was clearly the law that he should have the right to a court-appointed lawyer.

"Georgia is under no obligation to provide you an attorney," replied Judge Wilson, but Hilton continued talking, saying he denied the Florida charges and challenged the legality of his arrest.

"Do not interrupt me, Mr. Hilton," the judge warned him, telling him that retaining an attorney was Hilton's own responsibility, not the court's, because extradition was a civil, not a criminal, matter.

Hilton went on to complain that he'd had no access to a telephone to find a lawyer and was locked up the majority of the time, unable to leave his cell long enough to retain an attorney.

"I haven't been able to make a phone call. How can I procure counsel?" he asked the judge.

Wilson replied that he could have written letters, since that was how he got the hearing.

In answer to Hilton's complaint that his right to have a court-appointed lawyer had been violated, Wilson told him that the only matters in question concerning his extradition were that there was a valid indictment against him in the state of Florida, and that orders for his extradition had been signed by both Georgia's and Florida's governors.

Then Wilson issued his decision: Hilton was ordered to be extradited to Florida, but would have thirty days in which to file an appeal.

There was disappointment after the hearing among the authorities who had come prepared to transport Hilton back to Florida. Both William Meggs and Richard Milam felt that Hilton had stalled long enough, but they knew that there was only another thirty days left for them to wait if Hilton failed to file his appeal on time.

When the filing deadline approached and nothing had been received by the Butts County Superior Court, officials grew hopeful that time would expire and Hilton could finally be transported to Florida to face the charges there.

Two days prior to the deadline, no notice of an appeal had arrived and court officers had not notified either Milam or Meggs of any developments. The Georgia State Attorney's Office had not notified the Leon County, Florida, Sheriff's Office about any pending plans to transport Hilton, and a spokesman for the sheriff's office said that they planned to make arrangements for transport as soon as they got the go-ahead. Just to be on the safe side, the Georgia attorney general decided to wait a few days past the deadline before releasing Hilton to Florida in case his appeal had been mailed prior to the deadline but had not yet arrived at the court.

"As long as the document is received by the prison on the thirtieth day," said Georgia Attorney General's Office communication director Russ Willard, "then it will have satisfied the requirement."

Willard said his office was not sure if anything had been submitted to be mailed by Hilton at the prison, and Hilton would be sure to press charges against the Georgia

Department of Corrections (DOC) if his paperwork was delayed at the prison and he did not get to exhaust his right to appeal.

Finally, since no appeal was received within several days past the deadline, and there was no indication that Hilton had made any attempt to file one, a group of six Leon County SWAT team officers took custody of Hilton and left the prison in Georgia in three unmarked cars en route to Tallahassee, taking their prisoner to face trial for the murder of Cheryl Dunlap.

Leon County sheriff Larry Campbell told the press that Hilton had fought extradition to Florida for quite some time, but his efforts had been in vain.

"We've sat patiently waiting for him to go through the legal process in North Carolina and Georgia, and now it's our turn," he said.

Campbell also said that Willie Meggs planned to prosecute the case personally and would seek the death penalty. Hilton was calculating, ruthless, and dangerous, Campbell said, and had roamed through society preying on unsuspecting people.

Hilton had done everything he could to keep himself from being apprehended and prosecuted for his crimes, Campbell said, including destroying evidence and dismembering his victims. His efforts had proved useless, however, in keeping him from arrest and extradition.

"He should have stayed out of Florida," said Campbell.

Around five hours after leaving the prison in Georgia, Hilton's motorcade arrived at the Leon County Jail. Cuffed to a waist chain and wearing leg irons, Hilton walked into the jail without commenting to the reporters who waited, hoping for a word from him. He was due for his first appearance in court the following morning, to have the charges against him read. The two assistant public defenders who had been appointed for him, Ines Suber and Steven Been, were both specialists in cases of capital murder.

After Hilton had been booked into the jail, Sheriff Campbell held a press conference to answer questions from the large number of reporters who were waiting for information. Campbell told them he didn't plan to put Hilton in solitary confinement, but would probably place him in a pod for inmates charged with the most serious crimes.

"I don't want him to have a private room," Campbell said. "He'll be right out there with the rest of them. We don't want him to have cruel and unusual punishment. We want him to be with his peers."

Campbell acknowledged that it was possible that Hilton would be connected with yet more crimes, possibly crimes that were thus far undiscovered. And in answer to questions about the expense incurred by the state of Florida in trying Hilton for the murder of Cheryl Dunlap, when he was already serving life in prison in Georgia for Meredith Emerson's death, Campbell said that money was not the point.

"This isn't about money. This is about justice," Campbell said. "This is about the lady that he murdered very viciously, in cold blood, in our state."

Chapter 16

While Hilton waited in jail for the wheels of justice to grind their way slowly to his trial and punishment date, he was interviewed by Captain Dewey Smith, of the Pickens County Sheriff's Office, South Carolina. Smith hoped to get any scrap of information to help solve the disappearance, ten years earlier, of Jason Knapp, a young man who had gone missing at South Carolina's Table Rock State Park. During the interview Hilton made some chilling comments that revealed details about Cheryl Dunlap's murder that had not, at that time, been released to the press. He showed his intent to try bargaining his way out of the death penalty, if at all possible.

Hilton had denied any knowledge of Jason Knapp's disappearance, and in regard to his other alleged victims, Smith told him that he hoped Hilton would someday "come to peace with all the officers and courts" so he didn't leave other grieving families with no closure.

"Yeah, yeah," Hilton said, "that's up to them, though. That's up to them. Because if they're gonna try to kill me, of course I'm not gonna give them nothing. What would you do? You'd be pissed off. You'd fight everything. Everything is gonna be a big deal, starting with from extradition to whether I got enough blankets in jail. I am gonna fucking raise hell. Total hell. I told my Florida lawyers, I won't be happy unless it takes three to four years to go to trial, and unless we have a one-thousand-person jury pool, and unless we have at least two changes of venue. And that's just to begin with."

Hilton went on to tell Smith what a long, drawn-out, expensive trial he planned to have, how he might not be able to get out of bed to go to trial because "I got MS, and if I say I can't get out of bed, I can't get out of bed, man."

Hilton said that since he already had life in prison, he'd offered the state a deal to give the family closure; but if they wanted to do it the hard way, then that was how he would do it.

"And if that's so, if the way we're gonna do it is the hard way, we're gonna spend four million dollars and fifteen years" to try, convict, and execute him and never know the truth about what happened to Cheryl Dunlap.

"They may in Florida . . . there may be missing body parts. They may have recovered body parts. They could be missing [some]."

Hilton then told Smith that Cheryl Dunlap was decapitated, claiming that was a well-known fact about the case.

"Well, they may be missing her head," he said. "And if they were missing her head, and if I did it, I could give them that head and I'd be happy to do it. But if they don't want to get her head, et cetera, and they want to kill me, instead, and spend four mil, et cetera, et cetera? Bring it on!"

He was sixty-one years old, Hilton told Smith, and had seventeen years' life expectancy.

"Bring it the fuck on! If you want to get me into the execution chamber when I'm almost eighty years old, hey, knock your fucking self out! You got a fight on your hands."

Smith asked Hilton how he knew that Florida planned to seek the death penalty.

"I actually don't know that," he said, but he indicated that he had a fairly good idea that was what would be in store for him in Florida.

"I've offered Leon County detectives the deal," he said. "I know they're not the state attorney, but I told them to take it back to him."

Hilton said that since he already had a life sentence, they couldn't give him another day.

"So what does that leave?" he asked. "Why are they extraditing me when I said, 'You don't have to bother with that.'"

He liked Georgia prisons, he said, and wanted to stay in Georgia because "they understand that a prisoner who is reasonably happy is not likely to assault guards."

During the course of his interview seeking information about Jason Knapp, Captain Smith had also gleaned some very telling details from Hilton from the implications he had made about the Cheryl Dunlap case—details that Hilton would have been hard-pressed to know if he had not had firsthand knowledge of the crime.

In late September 2009, Hilton's trial date still had not been set. Leon County Circuit Court judge Terry Lewis had attempted to move the proceedings along earlier in the year by giving his approval for discovery materials—except for those things that either the prosecution or the defense felt might prejudice potential jurors when the case came to trial.

This situation did not sit well with the *Tallahassee Democrat,* and a motion was filed by the newspaper's attorney, Michael Glaser, for access to the pretrial evidence and to those items that were normally released.

Glaser said the public was entitled to have access to the withheld items prior to the trial, as was customary in such criminal cases.

"What's important about this is that it deals with the public's right of access," he said, adding that his motion was not about the newspaper, but about the public's rights.

Hilton's attorney, assistant public defender Ines Suber, was opposed to the release of those items of evidence she had asked to be withheld from the public, and blamed Hilton's many mentions in the news for the need to withhold them. She said that reporters "had the nerve to do their own investigation," and had been harassing witnesses when attorneys were not present to inform them of their right not to talk.

Judge Lewis told both sides of the case to advise him as to which items of information they believed should be closed, and to meet with him again the following month, on October 23, after which he would decide what would be released. He also hoped to set a trial date during the hearing, but Suber claimed she couldn't get ready to go to trial until 2011 because of what she claimed was a huge amount of evidence and unusually large number of witnesses involved in the defense. However, Assistant State Attorney (ASA) Georgia Cappleman told the judge she saw no reason why the trial couldn't begin the following spring.

"Two thousand eleven seems like an awful long time to get ready," the judge told Suber. "If you have a lot of witnesses, you want to lock them in on a trial date."

Chapter 17

After much legal wrangling and arguments back and forth between the defense and the prosecution, with the trial delayed while the defense's claims of not having enough time to prepare were heard, Hilton's trial date was finally set for July 12, 2010. A continuance was granted, however, and the date was set once again, this time for January 31, 2011.

As that time drew nearer, Suber still contended that she hadn't had time to deal with all the witnesses. She told the press she had interviewed around 150 people, but had "hundreds more" to talk to before the trial. She argued that in a death penalty case, it was her job to find out what each of those witnesses would be testifying to.

"Back in June, I told the court there was absolutely no way" to be ready for trial by January, she told the media. Suber filed a motion asking circuit court judge James Hankinson for a continuance until April 2011. The judge responded that he would hear arguments on her motion on October 22, three months prior to the time set for the trial to begin.

"This isn't rocket science. They should be ready," said Georgia Cappleman, the prosecutor. "They may be trying to wear us down so we'll offer a life sentence, but that's not going to happen."

When time came for the arguments to be heard, Judge Hankinson denied the motion for a continuance, despite Suber's claims that she needed more time to prepare. Hankinson said that he felt three years was plenty of time to prepare for a murder case, and his decision on the January 31, 2011, trial date would stand.

Suber was disappointed, but not surprised, according to her statement to the press following the hearing.

"[Judge Hankinson] knows the importance of allowing enough time for the lawyers to prepare," she said. "His decision is that I have had enough time. I disagree respectfully with him." She went on to say her reason for needing more time was because she had not been able to get to the 632 witnesses expected for the trial. She also claimed that the prosecution had not given her all the documents required to be turned over to her; therefore she would be neither ready nor "efficient" to go to trial in January.

Cappleman, however, said the prosecution had fulfilled all their obligations to turn over all the required documents to Hilton's attorneys.

After only a couple of weeks passed, in mid-November, another session of court appearances began. This time these were not attempts to postpone the trial, but rather an extension of arguments that were initially held behind closed doors over where Hilton should be taken for a battery of pretrial mental-health tests. Suber told the court that she had contacted scores of medical facilities all over Florida, and there was no closer, qualified place to send Hilton for the testing than Gainesville. The prosecution objected, on the grounds that the tests could be done in

Tallahassee without posing the security risk that a trip all the way to Gainesville would produce.

Judge Hankinson issued a ruling that the location of Hilton's testing should be made public, but the time and date would not be. This came in response to an argument by attorneys for WCTV, a CBS affiliate, and the *Tallahassee Democrat* who contended that the hearing should not be held behind closed doors.

At the hearing, officers who had been in recent contact with Hilton testified, as well as Leon County Sheriff's Office lieutenant Tim Baxter, one of the deputies who brought Hilton back to Florida after his extradition was approved in 2008. He described the trip's security measures, saying that three deputies rode in Hilton's car that day, with another car in front and two additional cars behind them. Their route was planned in advance, he said, along with one rest break, and Hilton was put in handcuffs, a waist chain, and leg irons. The prisoner remained relatively quiet during the trip, he said, with no threats or other problems.

The court then heard from an officer supervising Hilton at the Leon County Jail, who said he was posing no problems there, but said he was on what he called confinement status, used for high-risk inmates. Hilton was in a cell by himself, checked every thirty minutes, and only allowed out of his cell for an hour each day. Most of the prisoner's time, said the officer, was spent sleeping and reading.

When Prosecutor Cappleman addressed the court, she argued that taking Hilton to Gainesville would not only be a risk to public safety, but a "great expense and a great burden" to law enforcement.

The judge settled the matter by ordering the defense, the prosecution, and a representative from the sheriff's office to meet, go over all their available options, and come up with a plan to transport Hilton for his testing, and to have their plan ready by the week after Thanksgiving.

The hearing to present their plan to the judge was canceled, however, when the group successfully came up with a suitable plan. The details of the arrangements were not announced, and that began a great deal of speculation on the scores of Internet crime blogs. Hilton might not be held in the Leon County Jail at all, one entry said, and might not even be in Florida. Another claimed to have "inside information" that Hilton had been taken in secrecy to Shands Medical Center in Gainesville. Other bloggers complained about the defense's continual delaying tactics, motions, and requests.

But right after it was disclosed that there had been an agreement in the transport plan, Hilton's attorneys were back with yet another motion aimed at the news media and their right to inform the public.

Ines Suber had already made it clear that she felt all proceedings prior to the actual trial should be closed to the public. She claimed Gary Hilton had gotten far too much publicity already. If the pretrial hearings were to be made public, she was expected to request a change of venue for the trial. Attorneys for the *Tallahassee Democrat* and WCTV felt this was an overreaction on Suber's part. They said that publicity for the case had cooled down after three years, so their contention was that the request for a closed courtroom was unreasonable.

During the hearing Suber called an investigator for the public defender's office to the witness stand and spent over an hour relating the thousands of items posted about Hilton on the Internet and other sources. There were 150,573 online name views about Hilton evidence, she said, and only 141,526 available jurors in the county.

Almost everyone, she said, knew about Hilton, the murder of Cheryl Dunlap, and Hilton's earlier conviction and the suspicion that he was responsible for several other deaths or disappearances.

Suber told the judge that the thirteen motions he had earlier sealed at the defense's request should remain sealed, despite requests by the media attorneys that they be made public.

When this hearing continued on December 12, Suber changed her tactics slightly, saying that she only meant that the media, and therefore the public, be excluded from any hearings dealing with evidence, not all of the hearings involving Hilton. Her arguments would end up concerning the thirteen sealed motions, and her claims that comments by the public that had been printed or broadcast would make it impossible for Hilton to have a fair trial.

"The comments call him evil, serial killer, a dirty old man that deserves to be sent to Apalachicola and be beheaded," she said.

Chapter 18

When Judge Hankinson announced his decision, the arguments of the defense had failed to have its desired results. Ten of the thirteen motions that Suber had hoped would remain sealed were made public.

The unsealed motions had requested the court to disallow any mention during the trial of the following:

Motion1: Evidence from the North Carolina case of the murder of Irene and John Bryant,

Motion 2: Details of the movie *Deadly Run,* for which Hilton had allegedly suggested the plot and furnished much of the background story,

Motion 3: Evidence from the case of Patrice Endres, a Georgia hairdresser kidnapped from her shop and murdered,

Motion 4: Evidence involving the disappearance and likely murder of Rossana Miliani in North Carolina,

Motion 5: Evidence from the Michael Scot Louis beheading murder in Florida,

Motion 6: Evidence from the Levi Frady, disappearance and murder case in Georgia, where young Levi was taken while on his way home,

Motion 7: Evidence from the investigation of the disappearance of Jason Knapp in South Carolina,

Motion 8: Use of the derogatory term "serial killer" by prosecutors or witnesses during court proceedings and testimony during the trial,

Motion 11: A book found in Hilton's belongings called *Cannibals and Kings,*

Motion 13: Tool mark evidence from a U.S. M7 bayonet, allegedly belonging to Hilton.

The majority of the motions had originally been made in an effort by the defense to bar the introduction of any evidence in seven killings that took place in four states over a period of eleven years. Clearly, Hilton's defense team was aware of the striking similarities to the Dunlap case in some of those murders and disappearances. Most of them involved incidents that took place in state or national parks, including the use of victims' ATM cards, kidnappings, and even beheading. The crimes might very well seem to a jury to be far more than just coincidental.

On January 6, 2011, the judge ruled that the prospective jurors would be questioned individually, behind closed doors, about their knowledge of the case and any news items concerning Hilton that they might have seen. He ruled against another request from the defense, which wanted to question the jurors individually about their feelings about the death penalty and whether or not they felt they could impose it.

The following day, on January 7, the judge, who had asked to have a jury pool of 220 potential jurors summoned for jury selection starting on January 31, denied a request from the defense to have questionnaires sent out in advance to those prospective jurors in order to speed up the selection. The judge did not like that idea. It could tip off those who were summoned that they were going to hear the Hilton case, he felt, and therefore make it harder to seat a jury. People might try to come up with ways to get out of serving, he said.

"People aren't stupid. They are going to know this is something out of the ordinary," he said, adding that sending out the questionnaires "will alert the jurors they are coming to hear this case, even if it doesn't have [Hilton's] name on it."

The judge was very likely right in his assumption. A comment following an Internet story about the date set for the trial and the jury selection said: Uh, oh, I just got a summons and it's for January 31!

Court administrator Danny Davis verified that the judge requested four panels of fifty-five potential jurors. Five hundred thirty summons were mailed out in hopes of getting the total of 220 that was requested.

During that same court session Hilton's attorneys also tried to challenge some of the evidence the prosecution was planning to present. A bayonet that the state claimed Hilton had used to slash a tire on Cheryl Dunlap's car was contested. Tool mark expert Dr. Adina Schwartz stated there were no forensic means to prove that a particular instrument was used to leave a mark. An analyst was only able to verify that a particular type of tool was used, not the individual instrument.

"It's very difficult, because you get marks in tires. You don't know what tool made it," Schwartz said. "You don't know what pressure. You don't know what angle of attack."

The prosecution's expert witness, firearms analyst Jeff Foggy, testified that he had done the lab work on the bayonet that Hilton was accused of using to slash the tire. When prosecutor Georgia Cappleman asked Foggy if he had been able to make an identification based on microscopic imperfections, Foggy said that he had.

Judge Hankinson said he would wait on making a decision about whether or not to allow the bayonet to be admissible until he reviewed several rulings and studies.

On January 10, Hilton's attorneys filed a thirty-page request for a change of venue because of what they called the "intense publicity" that had been ongoing in Leon County since Cheryl Dunlap's murder.

Judge Hankinson said he would attempt to seat a jury in his court first, before considering a change of venue. "I would like to seat a jury in Leon County," he said. "I don't know if we can do it or not, but I'd like to try."

Cappleman also voiced her objections to a move. It would be cumbersome and expensive to hold the trial in another area, she said. The prosecutor also thought the case should be tried in the community where Cheryl Dunlap lived and died.

Along with the thirty-page request from the attorneys, Hilton himself also submitted a letter asking for the change of venue: *All of the publicity and comments thereof show that Tallahassee and Leon County has a bias in favor of Ms. Cheryl Dunlap and against me. I do not believe that these communities can fairly and impartially decide my guilt or whether I should die.*

Judge Hankinson remained determined to try to seat a jury before considering any request for change of venue.

On January 20, Hilton was in court once again, to answer questions from the judge. These were routine procedural questions about a deposition, but his attorneys were at the ready, with a stack of motions they wanted to submit before the January 31 trial date.

One motion objected to the prosecution's attempt to get several years' worth of Hilton's medical and mental-health records from many law enforcement agencies, dating back to 1974. The intent was to determine if Hilton had been treated for any medical or mental illnesses while in the custody of any of those agencies. The prosecution contended that if Hilton's defense attorneys planned to call his sanity into question, the state had a right to know his past mental and medical history.

"We anticipate the defense will present a mental-health expert in the penalty phase of this trial," Cappleman said, "and so it would be important to know."

Defense attorney Robert Friedman told Hankinson that prosecutors were going on "a fishing expedition" and should have to show that the records they wanted were relevant to the case at hand.

Hankinson ruled that even though the insanity plea had not been brought to the table at that point in the proceedings, the prosecution had the right to obtain the records in case the defense chose to use that tactic later in the case. He would determine during the trial, he said, if the records had any bearing on the case.

The defense then addressed the motion they had filed

asking the judge to ban cameras from the courtroom during the trial, saying cameras would disrupt the defense, impact their effectiveness, intimidate potential jurors, and hamper Hilton's ability to get a fair trial. The defense also asked the judge to ban the use of all devices such as smartphones, laptops, and iPads by jurors during jury selection, the trial, and final deliberation because they would allow the jurors easy access to media reports on the case.

The defense made another futile attempt to completely seal four defense motions, one of which dealt with keeping the condition of the bodies of Cheryl Dunlap and Meredith Emerson from being used by the state to show aggravating circumstances during the sentencing phase of the trial. Another motion would have limited the victim impact statements so that jurors wouldn't be unduly prejudiced during sentencing.

Chapter 19

Minutes after 9:00 A.M. on January 31, the first fifty prospective jurors were seated in room 3G at the Leon County Courthouse. They and the rest of the 220-member initial jury pool would be questioned that day and the following day about publicity, and those who remained in the jury pool were to be brought back on Wednesday to be questioned further.

Suber again requested a delay of the trial, which was denied by Judge Hankinson, and asked once again for a change of venue, which was also denied. Hankinson told the prospective jurors that those selected would not be sequestered during the trial, but would be during deliberations. The trial, he said, could last three weeks once a jury was struck.

Questioning of the jurors was done individually, to determine their knowledge and opinions about the case. They were called, one at a time, into an adjoining room and were seated at a table, along with the prosecution, the defense team, the judge, and Hilton—who, the jurors said, sat only three feet away, tapping his feet, staring ahead, and sometimes glancing over at them. Several said they were extremely unnerved to be so close to him as they answered questions about the case and whether they thought Hilton was guilty or innocent. Many admitted knowing quite a bit about his criminal history; others denied any knowledge of the cases he was a suspect in. Many said they had already made up their minds that he was guilty.

Out of the total of 110 jurors who were summoned on January 31, forty-seven were asked to come back on Wednesday, and thirty-six were excused because of hardship or exposure to pretrial publicity about the case.

On February 1, as the second day of jury selection continued, Judge James Hankinson stated that any prospective jurors who were aware of Hilton's conviction for Meredith Emerson's murder in Georgia would be excused. However, if they were only aware of the case but did not know Hilton had pled guilty and had been convicted, they wouldn't necessarily be excused.

As the interviews continued privately, one at a time, one potential juror was immediately excused from the jury pool when he revealed that he and his wife had spent a week hiking in Georgia, in the mountains near the area where Meredith Emerson had disappeared. That case had happened during the time they were there, the man said, and he and his wife had seen Hilton at a camp store. That surprising revelation earned the juror a quick excuse from courtroom 3G.

Defense attorney Ines Suber once again requested a change of venue, but Hankinson turned her down and repeated that he hoped to have a jury seated by the end of the following day. He remained determined to try and keep the trial where he believed it belonged, in Cheryl Dunlap's home county, where the murder had occurred.

As jurors continued to be questioned individually, another surprising revelation came from one woman who said during her interview that a friend of hers, a law enforcement officer, had talked with her about the murder. He had worked the scene where the body of Cheryl Dunlap had been found, she said, and he had told her that the body had been dismembered. Instead of dismissing her, however, Judge Hankinson asked her to return the following day for further questioning.

By the end of the day, all prospective jurors had finished their first round of questioning, and a total of eighty were instructed to return the following day for more questions, which would include their personal beliefs on capital punishment.

On the third day of jury selection, only a few of the potential jurors said they couldn't sentence someone to the death penalty. One said she wasn't sure she could live with having to make the decision whether or not someone should live or die; most of the other jurors said they could.

SA William Meggs told them they wouldn't be judging Hilton; they'd be judging the evidence and the facts. Meggs warned them the case wouldn't be concluded quickly.

"This is not *CSI*," he said. "We're not going to get this done in an hour."

When defense attorney Ines Suber spoke to the jury, she told them she had tried to speak without her heavy accent, but she found it impossible. Suber, a Colombian native, had been in the United States since 1968, and said she was a United States citizen. She asked the jurors to let her know if, at any time during the trial, they had any trouble understanding her.

Suber went on to ask if any of the potential jurors who had attended FSU, where Cheryl Dunlap had worked, would be influenced by that, or whether any of them had camped or hiked in the Apalachicola National Forest. None said the university connection would prejudice them, and several others said they had either camped or hiked in the forest. Those who said they had been to the forest were asked several times by Suber if they took rubber bands to secure their pants legs, and all said no. Suber also asked the jury not to be prejudiced against Hilton by viewing the gruesome photos from Cheryl Dunlap's autopsy and from the scene of the discovery of her body.

"So there will be a lot of pictures," she told them. "Do any of you have a problem viewing that type of photograph?"

As the questioning had progressed, the jurors began to understand why Suber had made a point of mentioning her heavy accent. Those who would be finally selected for duty would come to be very familiar with that accent before the conclusion of the trial.

Following their return from the lunch break, the prosecution gave their witness list of sixty-six potential witnesses, which consisted of law enforcement officers from Florida and Georgia, a forensic anthropologist, Cheryl Dunlap's two sons, and more.

Hilton's defense team had submitted a list of sixty-five witnesses, with their own doctors, tool mark experts, and more, coming from several states, and even one witness hailed from Argentina. It remained to be seen whether or not they would all be called.

When the day ended, a jury of six men and six women, plus two alternates, were selected to serve at the capital murder trial of Gary Michael Hilton, which would begin the following morning, Friday, February 4, 2011, at eight-thirty. WCTV, in Tallahassee, announced its live streaming video of the trial would begin—gavel-to-gavel coverage—at that time on their website. This was great news to the hundreds of true-crime fans, amateur sleuths, and others who were interested in the case, almost six hundred viewers at times. They would avidly watch and listen as the proceedings went online.

Cheryl Dunlap's family and friends were very anxious for the trial to begin and expected Hilton to be found guilty, but they dreaded having to hear what their loved one had suffered.

"It would have been better if he just—if he were going to kill her—just do it right then and not put her through anything," Cheryl's cousin Gloria Tucker told the media. "I don't want to know what she had to go through."

With the trial about to begin, the audience area was filled with spectators that included Cheryl's aunt and cousin, along with several of her closest friends. Some of them couldn't contain their emotions and began to cry when Gary Hilton was brought into the courtroom. He was seated at the defense table, but he turned around in his chair to look over the audience. His appearance had changed dramatically since his arrest for Meredith Emerson's murder. Then he looked like the fit, tanned outdoorsman that he claimed to be. Now he entered the courtroom, plodding along in an outdated suit, pale and thin, like a weak old man.

Suber tried again for a trial delay, claiming once more that she hadn't had enough time to prepare. Judge Hankinson refused the delay. Then she tried to unseat two of the jurors she claimed were aware of Hilton's connection to the murders of Meredith Emerson and the Bryants. Hankinson turned her down again, refusing to disqualify the jurors.

After the jury entered the courtroom, the prosecution outlined some of the evidence that the jurors would hear and see, and Suber went on the attack, trying to refute much of the evidence.

Prosecutor Georgia Cappleman said that Hilton had kidnapped Cheryl from Leon Sinks, kept her prisoner for possibly as long as two days, killed and beheaded her, then burned her head and hands, which he had also removed, in his campfire. There were also self-made videos, DNA and blood evidence, and much more that would prove Hilton's guilt, she told the jury.

Suber claimed it could not be determined if a number of human head and hand bones that had been found in the burn pit at Hilton's campsite were those of a man or a woman. Suber also disputed the surveillance video evidence of a disguised man in a striped dress shirt who used Dunlap's ATM card. It could not be proven that it was Hilton, she claimed. And some plastic beads found in Cheryl Dunlap's car, more of which had been found at the campsite and in Hilton's backpack, had "suddenly appeared" during a second search of the car, she claimed. She was confident that the jury, she said, would have a reasonable doubt about Hilton's guilt.

When the testimony began, the first witness called to the stand was Tonya Land, who was one of the first persons who had reported Cheryl Dunlap missing. She gave her report that day to Captain Steven Ganey, of the Wakulla County Sheriff's Office, who later went to look at an abandoned car parked on the side of the Crawfordville Highway, which turned out to be Cheryl's.

Ganey said that right from the start, he felt that the slash mark in the car's tire looked staged.

"What it appeared to us," he said, "is that someone had

punctured the tire in a place to make it look [like the car] was disabled on the side of the road."

Another of the early witnesses for the prosecution was Michael Shirley, who said that he and his wife often hiked in the Leon Sinks area of the Apalachicola National Forest, an area where there were limestone sinkholes. He said that on December 1 they had seen Cheryl Dunlap sitting, reading a book, on one of the hiking area's boardwalks. They were shocked, he said, to see her picture and an account of her disappearance a few days later: "I looked back at the photograph and immediately recognized it as the woman we had seen at Leon Sinks."

Michael said he and his wife had gone back to the Sinks to see if maybe Cheryl had fallen into one of the holes. They didn't see anything in the crystal-clear waters of the sinkholes; but as they were leaving, they saw the red book that Cheryl had been reading. It was lying on the side of the road near where she had been sitting and reading it, on December 1, when the Shirleys had seen her.

Shirley said he immediately went to a location nearby where the search for Dunlap was underway. He told the deputies on the scene that he and his wife had seen her reading her book on December 1, and told the deputies where the red book was lying.

Other early witnesses included two of Cheryl's friends. One had first reported her missing when she was unable to contact Cheryl, and the other was scheduled to go out for dinner with Cheryl on the night of December 1. Cheryl had never called or come by, she said, and she, too, had become alarmed.

Following the court resuming after the day's lunch break, Teresa Denise Johnson took the stand and testified that she was at an Express Lane convenience store on

Highway 20 in Bristol, Florida, when a man she identified as Gary Hilton had approached her. They talked briefly, and Johnson said that Hilton had said, "Isn't that bad about that girl who was murdered?" Johnson said yes, it was; then Hilton told her that she looked like Cheryl Dunlap. He then followed her to the cash register, still talking, before she left the store. If circumstances had been different, Hilton might have found another victim that day, but the lucky woman got into her vehicle and left without having any idea of the danger that she might have been in.

Others who unknowingly had dangerously close encounters with Hilton were Loretta Mayfield, who, along with her aunt, was going out to help with the search for Cheryl Dunlap. They ran into Hilton at Glenda's convenience store in the Crawfordville area. His white van was parked near where he was trying to use the pay phone—his dog, Dandy, was at his side.

"He said, 'You know, you can get out and pet him if you want to, he's not going to bite.' His dog was in the passenger seat, and I told him that was okay."

Mayfield stated that she told Hilton she and her aunt were going to help in the search for Cheryl Dunlap.

"He said, 'You never know people in this world'—is basically what he said," Mayfield testified.

While she and her aunt were searching on the dirt roads in and around the forest later that day, Mayfield stated, they had passed Hilton in his van two other times, both times inside the forest.

Another witness, George Ferguson, might also have had a close call; he testified that Hilton had flagged him down and told him his van wouldn't start. Hilton asked if he'd help him jump the van off. It was parked off L. L. Wallace Road, Ferguson said. Ferguson became suspicious that there wasn't really a problem with the van when it started immediately and gave no signs of trouble. He believed, he stated, that Hilton had faked the incident.

The testimony of Ronnie Rentz brought everyone in the courtroom to attention when he described what happened on December 15, 2007, when he stumbled upon Cheryl Dunlap's headless, handless body while on a hunting trip in the forest. When he got to the place where he customarily unloaded and released his hunting dogs, Rentz said, he noticed buzzards circling overhead. He began to investigate and quickly spotted a body in the undergrowth, partially covered with palmetto leaves and brush.

"I could see to the waist," he said, "and as I got closer, I bent over and looked, and could see the legs and feet of a body."

Rentz said it shocked him so much that he backed up for a moment, trying to think what he should do. He called the police as soon as he regained his composure, and they arrived on the scene to find that Rentz had discovered the dismembered body of a white female.

Rentz told the court he'd hunted in the Apalachicola National Forest for years but never had an experience like that. It was something he would never forget.

Chapter 20

On the second day of the trial, Prosecutor Georgia Cappleman came to court barely able to speak, having begun to lose her voice after the previous day's activity. She soldiered on, however, and was ready to call her witnesses.

Some of the first testimony concerned the ATM photos of the masked man wearing a striped dress shirt who had used Cheryl Dunlap's ATM card on three consecutive days following Cheryl's disappearance. The photos had been taken at the Hancock Bank on West Tennessee Street, and Agent Ronald Weyland, with the Orange County Sheriff's Office (OCSO), had analyzed the surveillance film. He had captured several still photos from the video, and said the man shown doing the withdrawals had worn the same shirt every day. However, on the first two times, after dark, the man had what appeared to be a homemade mask over his face. The third day, however, it was daylight and the man held a cloth over his face, instead of donning a more noticeable mask.

Weyland also told the jury that it appeared to him that

the man was carrying a holstered gun on his left hip. Weyland told the jury that he had not been able to estimate the height and weight of the man shown on the tape.

Cherokee County, Georgia, deputy William Ballard testified that he had seen Hilton in October 2007 and told him he couldn't camp in the Wildlife Management Area where Hilton had parked his van. Hilton told Ballard to "be safe."

That afternoon one of the hunters and hikers testified about seeing Hilton in the forest; when one of them took authorities to the place where he had spotted Hilton, they found a beheaded dog at the site. Speculation on the message board, running onscreen alongside the live video coverage of the trial, immediately ran wild. Consensus of opinions was that a dog had come sniffing around the area, attracted by the scents it was picking up from what had happened there, and Hilton killed it to keep it from drawing attention. He had bragged many times about killing dogs that he thought were threatening to attack him. This was strange behavior from someone who evidently loved his own dog, Dandy, to distraction.

Hilton had evidently had two different campsites, one off L. L. Wallace Road and another off Joe Thomas Road, according to testimony. Several of the hunters and hikers who were questioned had reported encounters with Hilton near both areas. One, who had stopped to ask him how far it was to another location in the forest, said Hilton had told him the distance in paces instead of miles, and also told him there was a limestone sinkhole nearby.

Another man said that when he spoke to Hilton and

told him that hunting season was about to begin, Hilton appeared to be worried about that.

Brian Bauer testified, "He asked me if there was going to be a lot of hunters in the woods that next day, and I said, 'Yes, there's going to be a lot.'"

Hilton then swore, turned away, and he and Dandy walked off.

All those who had encountered Gary Hilton in the forest had described him as being friendly and talkative, but Bauer had evidently told Hilton something that caused him concern.

When testimony began about items found at Hilton's campsite's fire pit, Leon County Sheriff's Office detective William Punasuia was one of those who recovered some of the bone fragments. When Suber cross-examined him, she asked if any of the items he recovered had been tested for fingerprints. He told her they had not by his agency, but they might have been processed by another agency or detective.

Florida Department of Law Enforcement crime analyst Amy George testified about what she found when she was brought into the case when Cheryl Dunlap's body was found.

"Her body was covered with limbs, tree limbs, and palmetto fronds," George said, "and was decapitated and her hands were missing."

When George processed the fire pit at the Joe Thomas Road campsite, she found hand and skull bones, she said, along with a bead and some pieces of metal. A photograph of the bead was shown, along with photos of similar beads found in Cheryl's car. Apparently, the beads in the car had been overlooked by investigators until the matching bead was found at the campsite; then George went back and processed the car herself and found the other beads.

After the photos of the beads were revealed, the Internet message board was again flooded—this time with opinions about their origin. Everyone's comments indicated that the beads looked to them like those that were frequently used in Sunday school and Vacation Bible Camp craft projects: **One of Cheryl's Sunday School kids probably made them, that breaks my heart.**

Other items that Amy George had processed were a beige Publix plastic bag that held feces, newspaper, and paper towels. The newspaper, George said, was the December 11, 2007, issue of the *Tallahassee Democrat*.

Good use for the Democrat, someone posted on the message board.

The following day's testimony began with the cross-examination of FDLE crime analyst Amy George. Defense attorney Ines Suber questioned George about how Cheryl Dunlap's car was examined and processed, and went into detail about how a sexual assault kit was processed. Suber's heavily accented speech made the testimony slow because of the time it took her to choose the correct wording for her questions.

The next witness called to the stand was associate medical examiner (ME) Dr. Anthony Clark, who conducted the autopsy of the unidentified torso of a woman found in the forest, which was soon officially identified as Cheryl Dunlap.

Clark had submitted X-rays that showed that the body had been decapitated at the C7 vertebra, and also photos of her body without head and hands.

Suber called for a sidebar meeting with the judge and objected to the admission of the autopsy photos; the judge denied her objections and admitted all the photos. Clark continued his testimony, but Suber made it difficult to proceed by objecting to nearly every question Georgia Cappleman asked him. Clark was able to confirm that the bones in the fire pit were all human head and hand bones, similar to those missing from Cheryl Dunlap's body. Suber objected, and was overruled. Clark said he had sent the bones to a forensic anthropologist to be tested in further detail.

On cross-examination Clark told Suber that he could not determine from the rape kit whether Cheryl had been assaulted premortem, and said there were no premortem injuries to the vaginal area. The decapitation had occurred postmortem, he said, according to his December 16 autopsy.

Clark also said that Cheryl had died from seven to ten days prior to her body being found, based on decomposition and insect activity. He had listed her cause of death as undetermined homicidal violence, saying that he felt Cheryl might have been beaten, strangled, or suffered head trauma. Again, the condition of the bones after having been burned made it difficult to precisely pinpoint the cause of death.

"Would it be safe to assume that whatever caused her death probably occurred to her head?" Cappleman asked.

"Head or neck, yes, ma'am," Clark said.

The autopsy had revealed a deep bruise on her right buttock, Clark said, and a second autopsy, on December 20, determined it was from blunt trauma, not a fall.

By that point Suber had interrupted the questioning of Dr. Clark so many times during his testimony that Judge Hankinson finally lost patience completely.

"Ms. Suber, would you quit interrupting counsel and *sit down*!" he thundered.

Suber did so, but began plotting to use the judge's orders to her client's benefit.

The next witness was a young man from Georgia named Steven Scott Shaw. He testified to what he saw on January 4, 2008, at the QuikTrip convenience store in Cumming, Georgia. He was sitting in his truck, on the cell phone with his cousin, he said, when he saw Hilton, wearing bright purple-and-green clothing, out in the parking lot beside the store. The bright clothing was what first caught his attention, he said, and he described it to his cousin.

As Shaw started to back out of the parking lot, he said, he saw Hilton going toward the Dumpster carrying something. Shaw said he couldn't see what it was that Hilton was carrying, but the whole thing struck him as very suspicious, and he called the police. Shaw identified Gary Hilton in court as the man he had seen.

Suber declined to cross-examine the witness, and there was a recess, during which the message board carried items from a couple of people who apparently had a great deal of knowledge about the Meredith Emerson case: Hilton kept his trash in black garbage bags; the stuff he wanted to keep or cared about, he kept in white bags. Meredith Emerson's head was found in a white garbage bag.

That post went on to say that had Hilton not been caught by police, he had reportedly planned to return to Blood Mountain to retrieve the head.

* * *

When the trial resumed, Suber immediately moved for a mistrial on the grounds that the judge had prejudiced the jury against Hilton when he had told her to sit down and be quiet when she had tried to voice so many objections during the questioning of Dr. Clark.

Saying that Ms. Suber's behavior had been unprofessional when she repeatedly continued to interrupt the prosecution's questions, Judge Hankinson denied her motion.

Georgia Bureau of Investigation special agent Mitchell Posey took the stand and described some of the contents of the eight trash bags that had been collected from the QuikTrip Dumpster on January 4, 2008. There was an enormous amount of items bagged and tagged for testing, and Posey said that they included a sheath of the type that would fit Hilton's bayonet, and a Forest Service citation for illegal camping.

Suber popped to her feet and objected to each of the items, hoping to have them ruled inadmissible, but to no avail. Other items from the huge mountain of plastic bags with red evidence tape that were ruled admissible—despite Suber's objections—were a black pillowcase that contained three heavy chains, a pair of "hobo" gloves with the fingers cut off, a half-dozen padlocks, a pair of black nylon pants, and a collapsible nightstick.

Following the lunch break, Ines Suber immediately challenged Posey's testimony, saying he wasn't on the state's witness list and she was not notified that he would appear; therefore she couldn't prepare. She yet again requested more time to prepare, or said the court should strike his testimony.

The prosecution admitted that Posey was not listed as a "Category A" witness and should have been. They claimed, however, that Suber was given several reports with Posey's name as the primary case agent in charge of the items from the QuikTrip Dumpster evidence, and all of the evidence was reviewed by both parties in November 2010 at the Florida Department of Law Enforcement. Not seeing Posey as a potential witness was an oversight on Suber's part, Georgia Cappleman told the judge.

Suber argued that the fact that Special Agent Posey's name was not on the witness list was not fair to Hilton, and she wanted two days to prepare. The state had 650 Category A witnesses, she said, and it was not her job to go through reports to find other potential witnesses.

Posey told the judge that he had received a document request from Suber in 2008, and the judge ruled that it was not a willful violation on the part of the prosecution; therefore his testimony would not be struck. He then dismissed court for the remainder of the afternoon so that Suber would have at least some of the time, which she had requested, to prepare.

Chapter 21

The fourth day of testimony kicked off with an argument before the jury was seated about some of the things that Gary Hilton had voluntarily said to the Leon County deputies when they went to collect DNA evidence from him during his transport to Tallahassee.

Sergeant David Graham was one of the officers who went to Georgia on both occasions, and he had stated that he and the other sergeant who accompanied him were told not to talk with Hilton or ask him any questions. Graham said, however, that Hilton kept up a running commentary throughout almost the entire time they had spent in his company.

The prosecution claimed that Hilton had told the officers: "If they want to give me immunity, I will give them a full and complete statement." The defense, in their objection to that remark, said that his reason for saying this was that he had been able to enter a guilty plea in Georgia to avoid the death penalty and hoped that Florida would do the same.

Other comments he made on that trip that drew objections from the defense included: "It'll take four years to take me to trial, fifteen years to execute me. That's nineteen years, and my life expectancy is seventeen-point-one years," and "It's gonna cost you ten million bucks, and I'll fight it."

The prosecution also said he told the deputies: "I started in September of last year (2007), nothing before that," and "I started hunting in September."

Suber immediately objected. Those statements and the others, the defense claimed, referenced other crimes and were highly prejudicial.

Judge Hankinson ruled to admit Hilton's statements to the deputies about hunting because they were highly relevant, but he agreed that Hilton's comments about pursuing appeals and what his execution would cost taxpayers were, indeed, prejudicial and would not be presented to the jury.

When the trial resumed, evidence testimony was given by several witnesses for most of the morning, with Special Agent Mitchell Posey re-called to testify about the DNA sample he had obtained from Hilton on February 12, 2008. Posey said Hilton had swabbed the inside of his cheek in the presence of two Leon County deputies, but Judge Hankinson would not admit the DNA sample until an FDLE analyst testified on DNA evidence later.

Posey told the defense, on cross-examination, that the hiking boots that were recovered from the Dumpster at the QuikTrip were lying loose in the Dumpster, not in any of the eight trash bags.

When Special Agent Clay Bridges, of the GBI, took the stand to testify about his interviews with Hilton following Gary's arrest in Georgia, he was asked about statements Hilton had made during the second interview. Hilton had initially refused to talk without an attorney present during the January 4, 2008, interview. However, when Bridges spoke to him again, on January 7, an attorney was present; and Bridges said Hilton had already made a plea deal to avoid the death penalty. Hilton told him at that time, Bridges said, that he had used a bayonet to kidnap Meredith Emerson. Hilton gave him directions to the bayonet's location on Blood Mountain and also to where Meredith's body could be found.

Hankinson ruled that the statements were not admissible at that point because there was no paperwork to indicate whether a plea bargain was made until several weeks later.

Also called to the stand was Jeff Branyon, a former GBI crime scene specialist who worked the scene at the Dumpster and Hilton's van on the night of his arrest in Georgia. Hilton had been arrested, Branyon said, on Ashford Dunwoody Road at a Chevron station, where he had parked by the vacuum cleaner unit. There were many items piled outside the van at the time, Branyon said, and even more had been left in the gas station's Dumpster. The list of items collected as evidence included a pink nylon jacket, a purple fleece jacket and pants, two yellow jackets, a black fleece jacket, three sleeping bags, a black baton case, teal pants, two duffel bags, and some lottery tickets.

All the items collected at the Chevron station and the QuikTrip Dumpsters had been tagged, bagged, and sealed, and were piled high on tables, under tables, and in boxes that literally filled the front, sides, and every other available space in the courtroom.

There were bones from at least two human hands—those of an adult man or woman with small hands—in the burn pit of Hilton's camp, according to Dr. Anthony Falsetti, an expert forensic anthropologist. He confirmed the charred bones included skull and wrist bones, in addition to the hands. They were all burned to the point that even those less damaged were too burned for DNA identification. Falsetti also received bones from a neck vertebra to look for signs of damage. He told the court that there was a sharp-force injury to one, along with six other cut marks. Four of the five wrist bones sent to him also had cut marks, he said.

When Patricia Aagard took the stand as the next witness, she confirmed that there was no DNA to be found in the fire pit bones. An FBI forensic mitochondria DNA examiner, Aagard testified as the state's expert. The bones had been subjected to such high temperatures that there were no longer any living cells to test for DNA. It would be said later that the fire pit burned so hot that the trees above it were scorched.

When Georgia investigator Mark Cecci was sworn in, he was immediately asked by Cappleman about a bayonet that he recovered from Blood Mountain. Before the recovery site was mentioned, however, Suber objected, and the attorneys went to sidebar. Judge Hankinson sent the jury out of the courtroom and the matter of the bayonet was argued, with Cecci being questioned further.

The bayonet was found on the same trail where Meredith Emerson and Hilton were both seen by witnesses, and Cecci said Hilton's statement led the investigators to the location where they also found an expandable baton. Special Agent Clay Bridges had found out about the bayonet from Hilton's statements, but neither the prosecution nor the defense knew whether those statements were protected under immunity.

Judge Hankinson said that he would have thought Suber would have found out from Hilton's Georgia attorneys whether or not there was immunity at that time, and said he would have to settle that issue before he put the bayonet information into evidence. It would be "foolhardy" for him to do otherwise, he said.

When Matthew Ruddell, an analyst for the FDLE
Crime Lab, was called to the stand, he said he had been
asked to check a Sony memory stick that had been recovered. Suber immediately objected. There was a question
about the chain of custody, and the judge said he wanted
documentation to be sure the memory stick had not been
tampered with along the way. It was not admitted into
evidence at that time.

Following Ruddell's testimony, a very tired jury was
sent home for the day and was instructed to return the
next morning at eight forty-five. The attorneys, however,
remained in the courtroom. Suber began objecting hotly
to the presentation of an audio recording made while
Hilton was being transported to Florida following his extradition. Suber claimed that the prosecution wanted to
edit the four-and-a-half-hour tape and only pick and
choose the parts of it they wanted the jury to hear. She
said the statements needed to be reviewed because Hilton
was talking out of frustration, rambling on a wide variety
of topics not related in any way to the case, and the prosecution's selections were taken out of context. As such,
Suber claimed, they would be inflammatory and were not
an admission of guilt.

The statements that she was concerned about on the
tape included:

"I'm not all bad. No, I'm not all bad. I just lost my grip
on myself."

"I just lost it."

Hilton stated that a "sense of victimization" set him
off. He also went into detail on the recording about his
bayonet training in the military:

"The drill sergeant would shout, 'What's the spirit of
the bayonet?' and we would answer, 'To kill!'"

Hilton also told the officers he wouldn't refer to himself as a "serial killer" because he had only been *accused* of being a serial killer.

Judge Hankinson ruled that the jury would not hear the complete taped conversation, but they would at some point be allowed to hear certain portions. Hankinson said that though the statements were disturbing, "he says he went off, and that's why he murdered her, and I can't imagine anything being more probative."

When testimony began on the fifth day of the trial, February 20, 2011, FDLE special agent Annie White told the jury of her trips to Georgia to collect evidence. Her first trip, to pick up a bayonet and a couple of other items, was made by car. The next time, it took a semi-truck.

Along with Hilton's white Astro van, the truckload included hiking boots, jackets, sleeping bags, backpacks, and a digital camera.

When FDLE digital evidence analyst Matthew Ruddell took the stand again, the judge was now ready to hear about the contents of the digital camera's memory stick. Ruddell had been able to retrieve the contents of the memory stick, both audio and video, even though Hilton had deleted them. There were several clips that were relevant to the investigation, Ruddell said, with one of them dated December 3, 2007, at 5:49 P.M., just two days after Cheryl Dunlap disappeared. Hankinson admitted the contents of the memory stick into evidence, despite Suber's objections, but he said he wanted to see all the clips before showing them to the jury. After he reviewed them, the jury returned to the courtroom and the videos were shown.

The videos, made prior to December 3, 2007, contained a confrontation with a Papa John's pizza employee, with Hilton complaining about a delivery driver and telling the man, "You tell these guys to quit terror driving. You tell them to keep at least a vehicle away."

Another clip shows Hilton arguing with police, saying that "[other officers] stopped me right there, on foot, jogging with my dog." In both clips Hilton is talking very fast, gesturing, and using a very confrontational tone.

In other clips Hilton posed with his dog, Dandy, hugging him and saying, "This is my baby." Then Gary showed off his physique for the camera, saying, "I've gained twenty pounds in three or four months, one hundred seventy-one pounds." He made statements along the lines of "We got to document it" and "We're having a good time."

In the video clips Hilton is seen wearing the purple-and-green clothing that was described earlier in the trial by witness Steven Scott Shaw, who saw Hilton at the QuikTrip Dumpster.

Then came two videos that contained almost no images on screen; it appeared that Hilton might not have known the camera was on at the time. Both were recorded on December 3, 2007, during the afternoon of the day it is believed that Cheryl Dunlap was murdered, and they were the ones that the prosecutors most wanted the jury to hear. Both contained a great deal of Hilton's bizarre humming and singing, talking to Dandy, driving, stopping, and driving some more. The enhanced audio revealed rustling noises like plastic sheeting or bags being moved around, grunting noises, mumbling, and lots of other sounds, as though Hilton was exerting himself in some way.

Bloggers on the live video feed, provided on the Internet by WCTV, went wild:

> Oh my God, that sounds like sawing!
> What is he doing? What are those noises?
> Did he just say something? Is he still talking to the dog?

Then Hilton was heard making several remarks which, when enhanced, were intelligible enough to cause an uproar on the message board: ". . . Killed those bitches," he said; then ". . . Killed them with this." After several more minutes of driving around on what sounded like unpaved dirt roads, he said to Dandy, "Okay, we're going to the park. We're going to the park, but first I've gotta go hide this somewhere else."

One blogger observed, This is it! This is it! He's hiding her body.

While the audio was being played, Hilton had sat in the courtroom, fidgeting, moving around in his seat, leaning back, rocking, and continuously moving his lips, clearly uneasy with what he was hearing but attempting to hide his nervousness. The rocking and lip moving had been constant throughout the trial; but at that point Hilton ratcheted it up quite a bit as he watched and listened to himself.

When the trial resumed after a lunch recess, the jury remained out of the courtroom while the state placed a phone call to Stan Gunter, a Georgia attorney who worked on the Meredith Emerson case with the GBI. Gunter brokered the deal with Hilton and Neil Smith, his Georgia attorney, that he would recommend that Hilton get a life sentence instead of the death penalty if he would tell the authorities where to find Emerson's body and give a full confession.

Hilton told investigators the location on Blood Mountain where he had hidden the body, but they could not find Emerson's head, so Hilton was taken to the site, where he led them to the correct location.

The defense then phoned Neil Smith, with the public defender's office, to testify that the statements Hilton made to the agents in the car en route to Blood Mountain were a part of his plea agreement. Suber contended that the bayonet would not have been found—except for Hilton's statement at that time—and said that it could not be connected to Hilton by blood evidence or fingerprints. It was only by those statements that were allegedly part of his plea agreement.

Hankinson ruled that Hilton's statement to GBI agent Clay Bridges leading to the finding of the bayonet could be admitted; the prosecution's contention was that it was the same bayonet used to slash the tire on Cheryl Dunlap's car.

The jury came back into the courtroom to view and hear descriptions of the mountain of evidence that was, at that time, piled in bags and boxes that filled the courtroom.

FDLE agent and crime analyst Amy George described all the items she had recovered from the van, which included paper towels, burned pieces of rolling papers, nicotine gum, a piece of palmetto leaf, and more, recovered from beneath the van's driver's seat. George also presented a seat belt, the visor from the driver's side of the van, the back of the passenger seat, and the trim from the side of the van that appeared to have bloodstains. Suber objected to each of the items George submitted, calling them "irrelevant," and Hankinson promptly overruled her objections and admitted all the items.

The jury inspected the items, passing them around so everyone could get a close look. A ceiling compartment from the van suspected of having bloodstains also had been collected, along with twenty-five swabs of blood from the inside of the van. And while the jury took an afternoon break, the prosecution and defense both spent the time looking through the piles of evidence bags and boxes, planning their next moves.

* * *

When the jury returned from their break, FDLE Crime Lab fingerprint analyst Marvin Lee Stephens was sworn in. Stephens told the court he had been with the FDLE for thirty-three years, was a senior analyst, and had been trained by the FBI as an expert in latent prints. Stephens went into detail explaining to the jury about latent finger-printing, and told them the many factors that make latent fingerprints sometimes very hard to find. Such things as dry hands, calluses, surface on which the prints may be, and the type and amount of weather they had been exposed to can keep prints from being useable. Regarding the thousands of items he had fingerprinted for the case, he was unable to locate any prints for Cheryl Dunlap because he had nothing for comparison. He tested some items from the Dunlap home, but could not find enough good prints to have a complete set. Because of exposure to the weather, none of the items from the Joe Thomas Road campsite had any prints at all. Hilton's van was tested for prints, but because of lack of fingerprint standards for Cheryl Dunlap, he was unable to identify any of the prints as hers. Her Camry didn't have any of Hilton's fingerprints, and on cross-examination by the defense, Stephens also said he could not find prints on any of the chains, dog food cans, duct tape, or paper items from the Georgia Dumpster.

Next on the stand was GBI agent Clay Bridges. Suber immediately called for a mistrial because two of the jury members knew something had happened involving Gary Hilton in Georgia, and now, Suber said, the rest would also know.

Hankinson was clearly irritated because of Suber's request, and denied a mistrial, but the judge gave Bridges and all others in the courtroom a loud warning to "Stay away from [Hilton's] rights!" and not disclose that Hilton had been involved in any other crimes.

Hilton had told him he lost the bayonet on a hiking trail in Georgia, Bridges said, without mentioning any more about why Hilton had been talking to him about the bayonet. He then said that he had asked another officer, Mark Cecci, an investigator with the Union County, Georgia, Sheriff's Office, to go and find the bayonet, which he did.

Cecci was then called to the stand and identified the bayonet in the courtroom as the one he had found. It and the photos taken of it at the site were allowed into evidence.

When FDLE Crime Lab firearm and tool mark specialist Jeff Foggy testified, he concluded that he had tested sections of Cheryl Dunlap's tire to try and determine what type of tool had slashed the tire. He had no tool to compare it to, and chose a bayonet because of how the tool had entered, and then left, the tire. He testified that his testing showed a bayonet-type tool had been used on the tire, and he told law enforcement that was what they should be looking for.

When the bayonet that was recovered from Georgia arrived at the lab, he used it to cut into a test tire, compared the results, and determined that the bayonet found by Cecci in Georgia had made the cut in the tire. Foggy also said the lab had been sent vertebrae bones to be tested, but the tool marks on the bones were insufficient to identify what type of tool had made them.

On cross-examination Suber challenged Foggy's abilities because of his inexperience. She told the court Foggy had only been *training* in the tool mark testing of non-firearms. Foggy told the court this was true. This was the first case he had testified in that involved a bayonet. However, he said, the marks were very sufficient for identification and he was sure of his conclusion.

Chapter 22

When court was called to order the following morning, Judge Hankinson told the jurors that the prosecution expected to finish calling their witnesses by the end of the day, and the defense would probably begin presenting their case on Monday, February 14. They might begin their deliberations, he said, by as early as Tuesday afternoon.

The first witness, LCSO sergeant David Graham, was one of the officers who went to Georgia to get DNA swabs from Hilton in February 2008. The jury would now get to hear the recording of a very one-sided conversation—almost a monologue—that was made during the time Graham spent with Hilton that day.

Hilton started by asking Graham about the weather in Tallahassee, saying old folks like him liked it "because it's real flat," and calling it "God's country." He then jumped to the Georgia/Florida/Alabama water controversy, accusing Georgia of taking up all of Florida's water, and said how "greedy pigs," real estate developers in the Atlanta area, were engaged in excessive building.

Hilton then moved on to talk about the charges against

him in Florida, telling Graham, "If they want to do immunity for me, I will be happy to give a full and complete statement." He also said that he had committed no other crimes prior to September 2007: "Nothing before that. I started hunting in September."

Graham said he was also one of the deputies that brought Hilton back to Florida after his extradition in June 2008. At that time the officers had been instructed not to engage Hilton in conversation or ask him any questions. Gary Hilton was only too happy to do most of the talking himself on the four-and-a-half-hour trip. He told the officers, "I'm not all bad, as I'm sure you can see. I'm a fucking genius, as I'm sure you can see. I'm not all bad."

According to Graham, Hilton said at one point that he was a "sociopath character" who "got old and sick and couldn't make a living," and went "into a rage against society."

"I just lost, flat lost my fucking mind for a while, man. I couldn't get a grip on it," he said.

When talking about his military experience, Hilton said his trainer in bayonet fighting had taught the recruits how to kill, saying that there were only two kinds of bayonet fighters, "good ones and dead ones."

Since the prosecution had played only about six minutes of the conversation, Suber asked what else Hilton had talked about during the ride. He had run the gamut from one topic to another with lightning speed, Graham said, including gas prices, the Vietnam War, the housing crisis, the atomic bomb, marriage, Hurricane Katrina, credit card debt, volcanoes, interest rates, earthquakes, the Kennedy assassination, politics, and much more.

When the defense was finished questioning Graham, and the prosecution called their next witness to the stand, it set off a heated set of objections from Ines Suber. The jury was sent from the courtroom.

Caleb Wynn, a former Leon County Jail corrections officer, was not listed as a witness, Suber said, and also claimed it was done "deliberately and calculatedly" by the prosecution. Furthermore, she said, they had done the same thing earlier, with another witness.

Prosecutor Georgia Cappleman told the judge that Wynn's testimony had been mentioned in opening statements. He had been spoken of during jury selection, and Cappleman claimed that Hilton's attorneys had scheduled Wynn for a deposition the previous week, but then had called it off.

Suber claimed Wynn's deposition was canceled because she had not had time to check to see if Wynn had a prior record. This comment brought many indignant responses on the message board, where a relative of Wynn's posted: **She has to know he doesn't have any sort of record at all, or he wouldn't be in law enforcement!**

Suber also contended that she had requested records about the jail's intercom system's maintenance, which she had not received, and needed time to depose Wynn about that, too.

Hankinson chided the prosecution, ruling that they had indeed violated discovery rules but hadn't made any effort to hide Wynn or his testimony, having given Wynn's report to the defense several months earlier. Suber would be allowed twenty minutes to question Wynn. In the meantime the judge wanted to hear for himself what Wynn had to say before the jury was brought back into the courtroom.

On August 21, 2008, Caleb Wynn had been on duty in the jail and was monitoring activity in the cells through the intercom system, which was done regularly. He heard Gary Hilton talking to another inmate, Fred Summers, saying that if the state would give him life, he'd "tell them where the head was."

"Did Mr. Hilton say anything about whether he has any regrets about killing Cheryl Dunlap?" asked Cappleman.

"Yes, ma'am," Wynn said.

"What did he say?" Cappleman asked.

"He said that the only thing he regretted is getting caught. If he had a second chance, he'd do it right. He said he kicks himself in the ass every day for it," Wynn told her.

Wynn also heard Hilton say he was "very selective" in choosing a victim. He told the other inmate that Cheryl was a Sunday school teacher and "plenty of guys would have wanted her." When the inmate asked Hilton what it was like to kill, and if it was a "rush," Hilton told him it was more like being in the military, when you went in and destroyed the whole village.

After hearing what Wynn would be testifying to, Judge Hankinson denied the exclusion of Wynn's testimony, but he ruled that he would not allow Hilton's comment about being "selective," because it could imply that there had been other victims besides Cheryl.

After the defense team interviewed Wynn, they claimed that he couldn't say if Hilton's comments about getting caught and telling law enforcement the location of the head were referring to Cheryl Dunlap or Meredith Emerson.

Wynn took the stand, however, and the jury was brought back into the courtroom to hear the same testimony that Hankinson had heard, with the exception of Hilton's comment about being selective.

When court resumed after the lunch break, Suber moved for a mistrial on the grounds that the jury was contaminated because they knew Hilton had committed a crime in Georgia and had been arrested for it.

The judge denied her motion, and the state called their final witness, who would also be the person who would provide the most damning evidence of the entire trial: proof that directly linked Gary Hilton and Cheryl Dunlap by unshakeable DNA and blood evidence from many of the over 750 items tested for the case.

Jo Ellen Brown was introduced to the jury as an FDLE Crime Lab analyst specializing in bodily fluid DNA analysis and population statistics. Brown was careful to present her findings and to answer questions in a way that was easy for the jurors to follow, despite the technical complexity of DNA analysis. Her testimony was unimpeachable, and her findings were solid and conclusive proof that Cheryl Dunlap had been in Hilton's van and at his campsites.

The witness told the jury that she had been able to make a standard set of DNA from Cheryl Dunlap by comparing findings from Cheryl's toothbrush to those from a sample of muscle tissue taken from Cheryl's thigh. In Hilton's case she developed a full DNA profile from swabs from the inside of his cheek. On the items tested, she said, she was primarily looking for blood in order to extract DNA and try to determine whose it was.

Swabs from Dunlap's car were taken on the steering wheel and driver's-side control panel. They were Dunlap's DNA, primarily, but there was a minimal amount from a man—not enough to identify, however. A cigarette filter from the L. L. Wallace Road campsite was tested, along with pieces of plastic sheeting and paper towels. All tested positive for blood, but there was no DNA to be found because the items had been out in the weather, which degraded DNA.

The Joe Thomas Road campsite included some broken

glass with unidentified female DNA, but no blood. A butt from a hand-rolled cigarette had partial DNA from Hilton, but the bayonet, too, had been left out in the weather. Although Brown had found blood, there was no useable DNA.

There were many items from the QuikTrip Dumpster that showed a mixture of DNA from two or more people, with Hilton included as one of them. The fingerless gloves and eight different areas on the hiking boots carried such DNA mixtures of Hilton and another person. After testing the blood found on the boot strings, Brown found a mixture of three people, with Cheryl Dunlap being the major contributor. A mixture of DNA from Hilton and Cheryl was on a black duffel bag.

Brown spent a great deal of the afternoon on the stand while jurors heard her testimony and passed around the items she described, looking at them while she gave her findings. They heard that several items showed indications of blood, but DNA could not be extracted. Those items included yellow overalls, a green-and-purple hat, a lime-green-and-white string from Hilton's van. Items that tested positive for both blood and DNA that matched Hilton's were a pink jacket, purple pants, a teal shirt, and three pairs of teal pants. A blue sleeping bag revealed blood, which was tested in nine different areas of the bag. At least two sets of DNA belonged to Hilton, with the other primary contributor being Cheryl Dunlap, and a purple sleeping bag contained blood and a mixture of DNA, one possibly being Cheryl's.

The analyst testified that when she was testing the black backpack, on which she found blood, she also found several items in the pack, which were plant material, a rubber band, masking tape, a stick, and a bead. The bead, which matched the others found in Cheryl Dunlap's car and at the fire pit, was entered into evidence.

Brown's final test results were on swabs from Cheryl Dunlap's thighs. She found foreign DNA, which she said was very degraded due to the length of time that had passed from the time of death to the time Cheryl's body was discovered. However, the foreign DNA, she said, was a possible match to Hilton's.

When Brown was excused from the stand, after a long and extremely well-presented testimony, Judge Hankinson turned to Georgia Cappleman and said, "You may call your next witness."

"Your Honor," Cappleman told him, "the state rests."

Chapter 23

The defense began presenting its case on Valentine's Day, February 14, 2011, as Judge Hankinson had predicted. There was business to take care of before the jury was seated. The morning began with Ines Suber's customary motions and objections, which this time included a move for a judgment of acquittal, concentrated mainly on the charge of grand theft auto.

Hankinson denied it.

Suber next moved for a mistrial, using a laundry list of grounds that included several of her previous objections to admitting bone fragments and beads as evidence and objections to the testimony of several of the state's witnesses.

Again, Hankinson denied it.

During this time there was a lot of delaying—a total of forty-five minutes—while members of the defense and the prosecution walked around, looked at evidence, and talked. When court resumed, still without the presence of the jury, the prosecution and defense argued about the qualifications of the first witness Suber planned to call, Dr. Adina Schwartz, whom she described as being an expert in tool mark identification literature.

The prosecution objected to her testimony, saying she was neither a tool mark examiner nor a tool mark expert and did not have any information that pertained to the case. Defense attorney Paula Saunders told the judge that Schwartz was qualified as an expert based on her academic research, teaching, study in the field, and more. The prosecution objected to the defense's intent to disqualify the earlier testimony of FDLE expert Jeff Foggy, saying that Schwartz could not judge his work because she didn't understand "the science of tool mark identification."

After reading about some of the previous cases Schwartz had testified in, Hankinson decided to allow her videotaped testimony and ordered the jury to be brought in.

On the video Schwartz identified herself as a City University of New York (CUNY) professor at John Jay College, with a specialty in evidence law, forensic computing, and as an expert in evidence and forensic science. John Jay College, Schwartz said, was the only liberal arts college in the United States devoted to criminal justice and offered degrees from bachelors through doctorates. Schwartz said she currently taught doctorate students on forensic identification.

On the message board, one blogger wrote: **She teaches how to discredit.**

Schwartz proceeded to give an hour-long testimony, which had been filmed in her office in New York on January 26. She claimed that Jeff Foggy's analysis of the slash mark on Cheryl Dunlap's tire having been made by Hilton's bayonet was "subjective." She said the slash mark on the tire was made by stabbing, but said there was no way of proving Foggy's findings because of differences in the composition of tires and the unknown angle of attack when the mark was made.

The testimony, which at times was so technical that it

was hard for courtroom observers and message board bloggers to follow, seemed to go on much longer than an hour. Then when time came for cross-examination, Schwartz admitted to the questioner for the prosecution that she hadn't examined either the actual bayonet or the tire in the case. She was asked if she had been paid by the defense for her testimony, and she said yes. When asked the amount of her payment, she said, "Nine thousand dollars."

The video finally came to an end, and before Hankinson could tell the defense they could call their next witness, a shocking announcement was made:

"Your Honor, the defense rests."

The people inside the courtroom were surprised into silence, but the announcement set the message board bloggers on fire:

> That's IT? They're only going to call one witness? That's incredible!
> Surely there was someone else they could have called from that long list of witnesses they presented; I can't believe they rested!

Suber gave it one more shot, asking yet again for an acquittal. Hankinson, yet again, told her, "No." Then he asked Hilton if he wanted to testify.

Hilton stood and told the judge that he did not. Hankinson asked Hilton if he had been advised of his right to testify on his own behalf, and he again said that he knew his rights but did not choose to testify.

Hankinson addressed the jury and asked them if they wanted to finish that afternoon, hearing the closing statements, or if they preferred to come back the following morning for closing. Since it was nearly time for a lunch break, he told them, "Either go home and get some clothes and come back and be sequestered overnight, or come back tomorrow morning at eight forty-five to hear closing arguments and go into deliberations."

The jury left the courtroom to decide what they wanted to do, and a discussion began of jury instructions and definitions for the jury of all possible verdicts in the case. After a very short time the jury sent the bailiff in with their decision; they would go home and return the following day, ready to begin their deliberation after closing arguments and jury charges. There was nothing left for the court to do but wait until the next morning.

The court session held on Tuesday, February 15, 2011, began with the prosecution piling up charts, screens, and evidence bags in preparation for their closing argument. Prosecutor Georgia Cappleman, wearing a bright red "power suit," looked very relaxed and confident, ready to present the state's case against Gary Michael Hilton.

"Are there any last-minute issues on jury instruction?" Judge Hankinson asked. "If there are any new objections, they'll be heard at sidebar after closing."

Hankinson addressed the audience in the courtroom.

"Once we're started on closings, I'm going to instruct the bailiff to lock the doors to the courtroom so there will be no coming and going to distract the jury."

When the judge ordered the jury to be brought into the courtroom, he asked them, as he had each day, if they were all still unexposed to anything about the case that could disqualify them from jury service. He thanked them for their attention; then he began instructing them on the coming procedures. A printed handout had been prepared for each juror, and Hankinson asked them to follow along as he read the entire handout aloud. Among the instructions were the explanations that the jury's first job was to decide if Hilton had committed the crimes he was accused of, and then to decide the degree of each crime that they found him guilty of. The judge explained what would have to be proved in order to find him guilty of murder, kidnapping, grand theft, and grand theft auto.

Then, when the instructions had been given, the doors to courtroom 3A were locked, and the prosecution's closing arguments began.

Georgia Cappleman began by telling the jury, "The man sitting here in the courtroom is not the real Gary Michael Hilton. You have had a glimpse of the other Gary Michael Hilton. He was a fit survivalist, a bayonet fighter, a hunter, hunting not deer or birds. He was hunting Cheryl Dunlap.

"She would have been easy prey for a friendly man with a beautiful dog," saying that it might never be known how Hilton had kidnapped Cheryl, maybe asking for a jump for his supposedly disabled van, or perhaps offering to let her pet Dandy.

Cappleman told the jury that Hilton had likely held Cheryl prisoner for at least thirty hours, until he made the first withdrawal on her ATM card and was sure she had given him the right PIN number. Hilton, she said, had told a fellow prisoner that he'd kept Cheryl captive for days.

"Cheryl Dunlap ended up in his clutches," she said, "wondering what her fate would be."

Cappleman described all the items of evidence that had pointed directly at Hilton as having murdered Cheryl. Maybe, she said, Cheryl was in [Hilton's] van while he was moving her car. He was seen rifling through the vehicle, getting her ATM card or whatever else. There was a trail that led from the car back into the woods. Cappleman said that the car could not have been left in the parking lot at Leon Sinks; it would have been checked very soon.

"What we're here about is first-degree murder, with Cheryl Dunlap killed in the commission of a kidnapping. Gary Michael Hilton had already formed his intention to kill before he took Cheryl Dunlap on December 1, 2007. Over thirty hours later he made the first ATM withdrawal."

Cappleman reminded the jury of Hilton's statement, on his own deleted video, made on December 3, 2007, when he said he had to "hide something," and another snippet of mumbling to himself or to his dog: "She was runnin' and prayin'." Cappleman pointed out again that from the time Cheryl was taken, until the first time the ATM card was used, forty-eight hours had passed.

"Cheryl Dunlap spent forty-eight hours with Gary Hilton," she said, "Forty-eight hours wondering what was going to happen to her next."

Hilton got seven hundred dollars from the ATM: "A fraction of what the defense paid out for his 'expert witness,'" Cappleman told the jury. She pointed out the piles of evidence that had been assembled earlier that morning, which included the hiking boots, a pair of blue pants, and a sleeping bag—all of which had Cheryl Dunlap's DNA on them.

"What are the chances the DNA [on these items] is not Cheryl's?" she asked. "One in eleven trillion. There are not a trillion people on the face of the earth.

"How else can we tie Gary Michael Hilton to the murder? He was seen by a witness on December fifth at Glenda's store, where he talked to that witness while wearing the same outfit seen on the ATM video."

Hilton offered to let the witness pet his dog; then she saw him twice more that day as she drove through the forest, searching for Cheryl Dunlap. She passed him in his van on the dirt roads in the forest, and Cappleman speculated he was lurking around the area to see if someone would find Cheryl Dunlap's body, which he was believed to have hidden two days earlier.

"How can we put Gary Hilton at the other scenes?"

Cappleman named off the items of evidence: tobacco and cigarettes at two camps, in the van, and in the Dumpster; paper towels, dog food containers, duct tape. The L. L. Wallace campsite was close to the scene where Cheryl Dunlap was taken. There were also rubber bands, survey tape, and clear plastic, as well as other items, and they tested positive for blood.

At the Joe Thomas Road campsite, Cappleman reminded the jury, there were several witnesses who had seen Hilton, plus a number of artifacts found at that location. They included more cigarette butts with Hilton's DNA, allergy medications, batting or stuffing from a sleeping bag, and more.

Witnesses who had seen Hilton at that campsite included cross-country runner Shawn Matthews, who saw Hilton there on November 20; Brian Bauer who saw him on Friday, December 7; and Dan Prosser, who saw him two times during the week of December 10, at the site and walking Dandy nearby.

Hilton's campsite was not one that had been prepared for camping, but was an isolated spot in the woods, Cappleman said, and the burn pit found there contained the bones from a human head and hands, too charred for DNA analysis because no living cells remained. Also found in the burn pit were pieces of zippers, buttons, rivets from a pair of jeans, and hooks and other hardware from a brassiere. Also in the burn pit was a bead, matching the beads found at other sites, which Cappleman said had come from Dunlap's granddaughter, Haley.

Cappleman reminded the jury again of the items found

in Hilton's van: tobacco, cigarettes and cigarette butts, rolling papers, paper towels, with the same design as those found at the Florida campsites, survey tape, more dog food, more sleeping bag batting, a baton, nicotine gum, sheeting, maps, and books that had been purchased in Tallahassee, with one titled *Head Hunters*. Several of the items had been covered with blood, and many bore Cheryl Dunlap's DNA, including a black nylon belt and items of clothing. A new pair of replacement boots were in the van, just like the ones that bore bloodstains from Cheryl Dunlap, and a backpack provided one of the most damning pieces of evidence: a bead that matched those found in Cheryl Dunlap's car and from the fire pit at the Joe Thomas Road campsite.

"All the pieces of the puzzle begin to converge to reveal a picture of the real Gary Michael Hilton," Cappleman said. "Not the man sitting at the defense table, but a strong, articulate, intellectual, dangerous man. Ms. Suber may try to convince you the picture is not as it seems—just a pile of inferences, with Gary Hilton merely a victim of circumstances. But nothing she can say can mask the real Gary Michael Hilton. What does it take to saw off a human head? No words can describe it.

"My job is ending. Yours is just beginning. The evidence will lead you to a guilty verdict."

With that, Georgia Cappleman's closing presentation to the jury was finished, and Judge Hankinson called for a break before proceeding with the defense's remarks.

The jury and the judge left the room, but there was a flurry of activity around the defense table. Hilton was consulting with his attorneys and seemed to be nervous and very serious as they whispered.

The bloggers watching the proceedings on the WCTV live streaming video began quickly speculating that the defense might be talking about the possibility of entering a plea. During the trial there had never been this amount of activity during a break, and some bloggers pointed out that Hilton appeared "shook up." Suber left the courtroom, and the others on the defense team remained around Hilton, continuing to whisper to him.

Nothing was done, however, once the judge and jury returned and court was back in session. Ines Suber began her presentation for the defense. Her strong accent, always distracting, was even more pronounced than usual as she began speaking to the jury.

Suber began by addressing the jury: "Mr. Hilton wants to thank you for your attention during this case." She continued, "What we have in this case is sole circumstantial evidence—no prints, no reliable DNA, untrustworthy statements—absolutely no direct evidence Mr. Hilton committed murder."

The first set of circumstantial evidence, Suber said, was on the prosecution's "fancy posters full of trash," trash collected at campsites, Dumpsters, "a lot of trash. So what does this trash prove to you? Marvin Stephens said there were no fingerprints found in this trash."

Suber said the state contended that Cheryl Dunlap intended to go to Leon Sinks, but there was no evidence that was her plan. The witnesses who saw Cheryl at Leon Sinks couldn't see her face. "How can we infer from that, that it was her plan [to go there]? The state says she was taken from Leon Sinks, says she was kidnapped from there. The witnesses assumed the photo in the newspaper was the woman they saw. They didn't see Mr. Hilton at Leon Sinks. What evidence did the state present that proved he did it, or did it at Leon Sinks?

"Remember the person who said you pay to get into the park? Are we now to infer that Cheryl Dunlap did not pay to get into the park?" (Cheryl's car was found outside the park.) "The state does not put reliable, trustworthy evidence in front of you. Use your common sense."

Suber said the car had been processed for prints and everything was analyzed, but nothing was found in the car. No prints, zero evidence Mr. Hilton was there. What evidence did they bring you here? Nothing that matched Gary Hilton, the defense attorney maintained.

"Because they don't have any prints, they called their witness to say she saw Mr. Hilton by the car. Was she reliable and trustworthy? The first time she talked to the police, she described the individual as being six feet to six feet two inches tall, medium build, wearing a denim blue shirt—a man in his forties, with dark brown hair, no glasses, no hat. At that time she was considered so correct, law enforcement compiled a lineup on December eleventh. She picked a man out of the lineup. A few years has passed, until now. You don't turn from forty years till now to point at Mr. Hilton."

In Suber's deposition of the witness in question, she said the woman told law enforcement she was wrong after seeing Hilton in the newspaper. Suber claimed the witness had completely changed her story: "Is that reliable to you? Mr. Hilton does not have to prove anything. It is pretty scary that the state would put that kind of evidence in front of you to even consider. Use your common sense."

Regarding the witness who had talked to Hilton at Glenda's store, then passed him twice on the forest roads, Suber claimed the witness had first said Hilton was wearing a dark blue shirt, then changed to the striped shirt seen in the ATM videos.

"She talked to Mr. Hilton, if you are to believe her. There were no prints on the phone at Glenda's. The defense has to prove nothing. That's the law. You agreed during jury selection to follow the law. Use your common sense."

Suber told the jury that there had been no evidence presented about the mask presumably used at the ATM.

"Now, they come with a bayonet found at some mountain, some trail, contending that is the tool that punctured Cheryl Dunlap's tire. Clay Bridges says Mr. Hilton made a statement. He claimed Mr. Hilton had told him that he dropped a bayonet. How many bayonets were there in the whole world? And Mr. Cecci said he went to a trail, a place we don't know where, and found a bayonet."

Then Suber went to the items found in the Dumpster: "Prints on that? No, we don't even know whose blood that is. The state said there was no direct evidence on that. We don't know the weather conditions [items had been exposed to previously] when things were found there.

"Now, the state knows they have problems. They can't tie these things to Mr. Hilton. There was no prints or reliable DNA. So what do they do? They hire a tool mark examiner, Jeff Foggy, who has never testified in any court on tool marks. He is a firearms specialist, not a tool mark specialist. At the time he tested the bayonet, he had only tested about fifteen other tools, and none was a bayonet. He agreed that when an analyst is trying to replicate something, it should be as close as possible [to the items involved originally].

"Did he use the same tire, trying to replicate in the test? No, instead of the [same company and type] as on Cheryl Dunlap's car, he took some type of tire, placed it on a table, and made punctures. Use your common sense."

Suber said that Cheryl Dunlap's car had been searched three times after being found on the side of the road, and no beads had been found on the floorboard. She implied that the beads found at the campsite and in the backpack could have been planted.

"The car was towed to Leon County from Wakulla County," she said, "So, lo and behold, comes Amy George and now she finds sixteen beads, maybe from a bracelet or necklace. A witness said they had never seen Cheryl Dunlap wearing the beads. Were they the granddaughter's beads? We don't know. And that granddaughter has a mother, who could have come here and testified about the beads. Use your common sense as to why they were not brought to the courtroom."

Suber also pointed out that there was no proof that the head and hand bones recovered from Hilton's campfire pit belonged to Cheryl Dunlap, and said that a forensic anthropologist could not even say whether or not they belonged to a woman or man. She also called into question the metal items found in the fire pit.

"Who came to testify those were bra hooks? Hooks and zippers can be attached to any kind of clothing. See mine?"

Suber showed the jury a zipper in her skirt, attempting to make the point that the burned zipper and hooks in the fire pit could have come from anywhere other than Cheryl Dunlap's intimate undergarments and clothing.

By this time the jurors were fidgeting in their chairs, and a reporter for the *Tallahassee Democrat* who was posting Twitter messages from the courtroom wrote that the jury was looking bored, restless, and tired. The bloggers were posting a number of irate messages about Suber's constant mispronouncing of Cheryl Dunlap's name, calling her "Dinlap" and "Dunlop" so often that Suber finally apologized to the jury, but she kept on mispronouncing it all the same.

With a few more remarks ending with the phrase she had attempted to drive home to the jurors numerous times during her presentation, Suber's final words to the jury were "Use your common sense."

* * *

In her final rebuttal Georgia Cappleman made what was arguably her best, hardest hitting case against Gary Michael Hilton during what had been a highly effective prosecution. She systematically tore apart all of Ines Suber's arguments.

"The defense says there is no evidence in this case. It's all circumstantial, just a bunch of garbage," Cappleman told the jury. However, she said, witnesses had put Hilton there at numerous locations in the forest, at Cheryl's car, and at the Dumpster in Georgia, where so much evidence had been found.

"The defense says the state has no evidence of kidnapping. Don't worry about [other] evidence—it's just an elaborate charade to get you to convict the wrong man, they say. The DNA is contaminated. Don't worry about the bayonet, they say. All the evidence is all garbage, they say.

"The camera doesn't lie, folks," Cappleman said, and proceeded to play for the jury the numerous audio clips with Hilton himself making damning statements that were recovered from the memory stick of his camera. Some of the items had not been previously heard in court, and these were shocking to both the jury and the courtroom viewers.

"We're gonna get some good pussy one of these days, boy," Hilton apparently was speaking to his dog. "She was no good. She was nasty."

Seven minutes later on the recording, he said, "I have guns hidden. . . . I killed them with this. . . . I killed those bitches.

"We're going to the park, but first I got to hide this someplace else."

Thirteen minutes more into the tape: "We gotta ride a little. I gotta hide that stuff."

Seventeen minutes and forty-five seconds into the tape: "I'm just going back in there to hide some stuff, that's all."

Twenty minutes and thirty seconds, with the camera briefly showing a flash of the sky and tall pines: "Gotta do something with this here."

Cappleman turned to the jury. "Can we trust Mr. Hilton's words? 'Killed them. Guns hidden. Nasty. Hide stuff. . . .'"

She reminded the jury of the conversations overheard by Caleb Wynn, the corrections officer, when Hilton was heard to say, "If the state would give me life, I'd tell them where the head is," and Hilton saying the only thing he regretted was getting caught. He admitted to using the bayonet, and said, "All the questions would be over with, if I could get life."

Cappleman noted that Hilton had given Clay Bridges a description of the bayonet and told him where it could be found, and it was retrieved from that location.

During this time the defense made a constant stream of objections—all of which were overruled by the judge.

"Hilton destroyed Cheryl Dunlap's fingerprints. You can't identify the head and hands because they were burned to destroy the evidence. He dumped her body in the woods to be riddled with maggots. She died an unimaginable death."

Cappleman had the complete attention of the jury as she made her final statement regarding Gary Michael Hilton: "Today is his day for justice. There is only one verdict that does any justice in this case. Please find him guilty."

At 12:30 P.M., the jury was sent out to begin their deliberations, after getting their final instructions from Judge

Hankinson. At around two o'clock, they sent the judge a request to hear once again the videos with Hilton's voice talking to his dog, and also segments of the audio of the transport from Georgia back to Florida, when he spent around four and a half hours on a rambling monologue.

Ines Suber immediately objected to them being played, renewing her objection to the videos as evidence. Judge Hankinson cut her off midsentence, and she immediately renewed all her objections concerning the transport audio. Hankinson stopped her again, saying the only items that can be played are those already in evidence. Then the jury was brought in to hear what they had requested.

During the time they were listening, the jurors strained to hear what Hilton was saying, and some were staring intently at him as he rocked back and forth, pursed his lips, looked down, and at some points seemed to smile.

The jury left the courtroom at 4:05 P.M., and five minutes later the bailiff came out and announced a verdict had been reached. The jury filed back in and Judge Hankinson was handed their decision: They had, indeed, done as Suber had requested and had used their common sense. Gary Michael Hilton was found guilty of first-degree murder, kidnapping, and grand theft. The only charge he had managed to dodge was grand theft auto. The jury would now decide what sentence they would recommend to the judge; it would now be up to them whether or not they would ask Judge Hankinson to impose the death penalty.

When the next day of the trial began, the start of the penalty phase, defense attorney Paula Saunders began the morning with a series of objections and motions, claiming the defendant was not getting a fair trial. Saunders wanted to have some of Hilton's statements thrown out, including remarks made during interviews, such as "You either kill them, or you get caught," "Blood Mountain is a good place to hunt," and his remarks about stalking women in the mountains, and referring to himself as a "pro." The defense attorneys said those statements were prejudicial and were not relevant to the murders of either Cheryl Dunlap or Meredith Emerson, and cast Hilton in the role of a serial killer.

Judge Hankinson appeared to be out of patience with the defense, and SA Meggs said that Hilton's remarks were "highly relative to the issue here today."

Saunders brought up the Aileen Wuornos case several times, trying to keep out aggravating factors, saying the state was "introducing a lot of hypothetical and highly prejudicial things into this case," but the judge denied all objections, ruling that Hilton's statements about Meredith Emerson and all of the other cases would be heard by the jury.

The judge, the defense, and the prosecution discussed correct jury instructions, and Hankinson said he would give standard instructions. When the jury was brought in, he told them, "You have found Gary Michael Hilton guilty of first-degree murder. Now the state and the defense will present evidence so you might determine if aggravating circumstances exist to justify the death penalty, or if mitigating circumstances exist to justify life in prison."

The jury would give an advisory sentence, he told them, but it would ultimately be up to him to pass sentence.

After short introductory remarks by Willie Meggs and death penalty specialist Robert Friedman, on behalf of the defense, the state called its one and only witness, Special Agent Clay Bridges. Bridges once again related his career experience and qualifications for the jury: nearly twelve years with the GBI, following nine years of uniform patrol in Clarksville and Gainesville, Georgia.

Bridges played a key role in the massive investigation of the Meredith Emerson case. He interviewed Hilton at the Union County, Georgia, Sheriff's Office, and later in UCSO vehicles with Sheriff Scott Stephens, Hilton and his attorney, and the attorney's investigator.

Hilton's van had been taken and the evidence was being collected, Bridges said. Hilton had given directions to Meredith Emerson's body and confirmed the suspicions of law enforcement that she was dead.

"We spent one to one and a half hours in the car on the way to Blood Mountain," Bridges said. "We found the body nude, on top of the ground, decapitated, with bleach burns, covered with brush and leaves. We could not find the head."

Bridges said Hilton took them to the location where he said the head could be found.

"He said he removed the head and clothing to cover up evidence."

Hilton had said he lost his baton during the struggle with Meredith Emerson.

"Seth Blankenship saw Hilton and Meredith on the trail and noticed his baton and bayonet," Bridges said. "Later he saw water bottles and a leash on the trail and turned them in to the store at the bottom of the trail."

Hilton told officers that he had lost the bayonet when Meredith fought with him. Bridges sent Mark Cecci to go back with a metal detector to the location Hilton had indicated and look for it; Cecci found it.

"We wouldn't have known where to look for it if Hilton hadn't told us," Bridges said.

During the second interview Hilton had with Bridges—a voluntary debriefing that lasted around four and a half hours and was videotaped—Hilton talked about a wide range of subjects: hiking, equipment, his childhood, his time in the army, the end of the world, the San Andreas Fault, Meredith Emerson's murder, and more. He talked about chains and padlocks, and how he chained Meredith in his van. He initially denied raping her, but he later said she "owed it" to him. Hilton also said on the videotape, "I'm the one who killed her."

However, he then attempted to place the blame for her death on his former employer John Tabor, saying, "The reason she's dead is that when I called him, she was alive, in the van." Hilton had phoned Tabor asking for money because he hadn't gotten as much as he wanted from Meredith. "I lost money on that deal," he said, referring to the money he spent on gas, driving around from one ATM to another, trying to get the PIN numbers, which Meredith gave him, to work.

Tabor refused to give him any money, Hilton said. "If he hadn't been . . . If he hadn't said . . . Instead of trying to trap me, on the second or third day before she was killed . . . These people are such *women*."

Hilton then repeated, over and over, his theory on taking prisoners: "Once you've taken someone, you either kill them, or get caught. You either kill them, or get caught. If you're already caught, there's no reason to kill them. You either kill them, or get caught."

Hilton said he had forty dollars and several days' worth of food: "So I had to kill someone."

On the videotape Hilton described killing someone and the methods for finding a victim: "It's dreadful. Nothing sexual, so fucking dreadful that all you can do is do your duty and go on. One reason I chose to kill for money was partly sociopath rage against society. When you go out to kill someone, if you're seen by one single person on the trail, that day is screwed. Blood Mountain is a good place to hunt because it's the most used day-hiking trail in the state of Georgia. It's a good place because there's a huge selection [of victims], but it's bad because of so many people. The way you do it is to lurk with binoculars."

Hilton told the officers about his fight with Meredith Emerson, which he said he almost lost: "It was not my finest hour. I'm better than that. I had to fight her twice, then secure her to a tree. I went back and the stuff I dropped (the dog leash and water bottle) was already gone."

He said there came a point [when taking a victim] that "they fight, then submit."

He told the officers, "A martial artist stays calm and has confidence in his proficiency—you must have. I've been there a million times."

Hilton said it took planning, training, and equipment to take a victim successfully. He told that he tried to reach out and make himself a person to his victims, not an inhuman monster, and he said that he had started hunting in September 2007.

When the video ended, the prosecution had no further questions for Special Agent Bridges. Hilton had answered them all—in his own words.

The cross-examination took the defense only a short time. Robert Friedman asked Special Agent Bridges if he had a list of the medications Hilton had been on at the time of the Georgia guilty plea. Bridges said he did not have such a list.

Since Bridges had been the only prosecution witness,

Friedman began introducing evidence prior to calling witnesses. He submitted a reprimand received by Hilton's doctor, Dr. Delcher, a well-known endocrinologist connected with Emory University, from Georgia's Composite State Board of Medical Examiners, in May 2009. Friedman had a court reader read the letter of reprimand into the record for the jury. Following Meredith Emerson's murder, the board had publicly reprimanded the doctor for continuing to give Hilton prescriptions for more than the FDA-recommended dose of Ritalin. Delcher had noticed what he called Hilton's "manic spells" and "rapid speech" and took no action, despite his patient's obviously deteriorating condition. He was suspended from practicing psychiatry and had to take a class in medical ethics. Friedman also entered into evidence two prescription bottles from October 2007 found in his van, one for Effexor and one for Ritalin, with some pills remaining in each of the bottles. Also entered into evidence were honorable discharge papers from his two tours of duty with the U.S. Army.

The first witness to be called for the defense was Dr. Joseph Wu, a medical doctor at the University of California, Irvine, College of Medicine. His testimony was delayed for a few minutes because he planned to deliver a PowerPoint presentation on Hilton's brain scans. There was a problem, however, with the audio in the courtroom, and a loud buzzing noise filled the room.

"I don't know about y'all," said Judge Hankinson, "but that's going to drive me crazy."

The problem was remedied when a laptop power cord was moved from some wires it overlapped, and testimony began.

Dr. Wu was a specialist in brain imaging and said he had been paid $6,448 for his testimony. He had conducted a positron emission tomography (PET) scan on Hilton several months earlier.

Wu blamed Hilton's problems largely on damage he claimed to have found on the right side of Hilton's brain and his frontal lobe, which Wu said had been injured in 1956. He showed the PET scans of Hilton's brain, which he had made, pointing out the areas he said showed damage. If not for the injury caused by being hit in the head by a falling Murphy bed, when he was ten years old, "his life trajectory would have been entirely different."

Wu said of Hilton, "This is someone very bright who is crazy. It started in the military, and he was never able to do much more than be a telemarketer—never able to make much of himself. He became addicted to drugs, alcohol, and quaaludes, and had an impaired ability to control his impulses.

"He became homeless at around age fifty and became depressed, with episodes of extreme fatigue. Dr. Delcher tried to help him have more energy, and started him on a low dose of Ritalin in 2005—from twenty milligrams up to eighty milligrams."

This, Wu said, caused an extreme increase in some of Hilton's symptoms, and he became manic, hyperaggressive, energetic, with clouded and impaired judgment. Delcher had noticed pressurized speech and flight of ideas, but the physician did nothing.

John Tabor had stated that he noticed more and more bizarre behavior in Hilton, worsened by his Ritalin dosage being increased.

"I think this was horrible clinical malpractice," Wu said. "Delcher was practicing gross mismanagement." Otherwise, he said, "I don't think any of these things would have occurred."

When manic depression goes untreated, Wu said, it gets worse. "Delcher continued to pour Ritalin into this guy," he said, leaving Hilton's mania to accelerate.

Wu said that Hilton's brain damage, emotional abuse, and Ritalin abuse created what he called "a perfect storm. Mr. Hilton had not engaged in violence until he had Ritalin poured on top of him, year after year, while his mania was uncontrolled."

The defense witness told of some incidents from Hilton's early life that he believed had contributed to his problems. The tension between Hilton and his stepfather, Nilo Dabag, had escalated to the point that at age fourteen Hilton shot him and was consequently admitted to a psychiatric hospital, then placed in foster care. Gary was arrested for vagrancy at age sixteen, and then claimed to have been sexually abused by the attorney who represented him on that charge.

Wu said that Hilton had three strikes against him: the head trauma, the emotional abuse he suffered during his childhood, and the mismanagement of his Ritalin use.

When Willie Meggs cross-examined the doctor, he pointed out to him that Gary Hilton was aggressive prior to his Ritalin use. Dr. Wu replied that Gary shot his stepfather and started fires before being prescribed Ritalin, but he wasn't killing people at that time.

"Does Ritalin make people kill?" Meggs asked.

Wu replied, "No."

Four jurors had questions for Wu, and had sent them to the judge, who asked Wu if, in his opinion, Hilton knew right from wrong.

The doctor answered, "In the extreme state of behavior, it's not clear if Mr. Hilton would know right from wrong, but he was aware of his actions."

Meggs asked Wu then, if a person didn't know right from wrong, would the doctor expect that person to try and cover his tracks so he wouldn't get caught by law enforcement? Wu said he wasn't sure, and really didn't know.

The next witness for the defense was Dr. Charles Josh Golden, a neurophysiologist who had given Hilton a number of tests to determine both his IQ and his personality profile. Golden reported that Hilton's verbal scale test scored 120, which put him in the upper 10 percent of the population. His nonverbal reasoning test was 105, considered an average score.

On his working memory and ability to repeat, Hilton landed in the upper 2 percent of the population with a score of 131, which indicated that he had an excellent memory. His verbal memory test score was 117 through 129, in the top 10 percent of the population.

The category test posed no problem for Hilton; Golden reported the test, which determines the ability to figure out puzzles, was not at all difficult for Hilton.

Then came the patterns test, which Hilton grew very frustrated with while taking. In that computer test, which is designed to never let the person being tested figure out the pattern, Hilton became frustrated because he thought he should be able to do it.

Hilton also did very poorly on the cognitive performance test (CPT), which measured attention and impulse control, but his greatest downfall came with the Rorschach inkblot test.

"Mr. Hilton had tremendous problems with the test," Golden said. "He was trying to impress us with his ability and intelligence, but [the test showed] he couldn't control his emotions. He has very poor interpersonal relationships. He prefers isolation, and his interactions tend to be fantasy-based. He gave poor-quality answers, more typical of an eight- or ten-year-old, not an intelligent adult."

In his opinion, Golden said, Hilton's diagnosis required both symptoms and history. In Hilton's case, he said, he believed his problem was schizoaffective disorder, including depression. Hilton was self-diagnosed with multiple sclerosis, but there was no medical evidence that he had it. His symptoms were those of severe depression and manic depression, Golden told the jury. Hilton, he said, was hypermanic, had delusions, hated his stepfather, and did not do well in school, despite his intelligence.

Golden also told the jury that Hilton, in his opinion, had antisocial personality disorder, which can't be caused by a brain disorder. He said that Hilton had a hypofunctioning frontal lobe, which he believed had led to his personality problems, or an organic personality disorder. He told the jury that the frontal lobe of the brain allowed a person to be able to control his emotions. He said that Hilton hid his brain defect well because of his abilities in other areas and by self-medicating and avoiding other people. The Ritalin that Hilton took made him irrational, hyperaggressive, suspicious, and sleep-deprived. It caused him not to understand why he did the things he did, Golden said.

"We clearly have a brain injury that led to the personality problems," but Hilton "knew right from wrong, no question." He was under the influence of an "extreme emotional disturbance" and was experiencing a lack of emotional control.

Following the defense's questioning of Dr. Golden, Judge Hankinson called for a short break.

Friedman walked back over to the defense table. "Am I doing okay, Gary?" he asked the defendant.

Hilton replied, "You're doing great. Thanks a lot."

Chapter 24

When court was called back into session following the break, it was the prosecution's turn to question Dr. Golden. State Attorney William Meggs asked him again about the results of Gary Hilton's IQ test, and Golden repeated that Hilton's overall IQ was 120, which put him in the top 10 percent of the population.

Meggs asked if Hilton had been tested for malingering, or deliberately trying to look bad "when you know you're normal." Golden denied that Hilton had been malingering during his testing. He said that Hilton did not have insight into his problems. Hilton had psychopathic tendencies, and Dr. Golden stressed that any amount of Ritalin would be too much for someone with Hilton's problems.

When asked if Hilton was capable of love, Golden said, "There is no question in my mind, he loves his dog."

Golden said he had been paid $14,000 for one hundred hours of work on the case.

The final defense witness of the day was Dr. Abbey Strauss, a psychiatrist whose specialty was the treatment of disorders. Strauss said he met two times with Hilton for psychiatric evaluation, once in February 2009 and again in December 2010. He also said he had been provided with a "tremendous amount of material" to read in connection with Hilton's evaluation.

Strauss tended to lay much of the blame for Hilton's mental and emotional condition on Gary's deceased mother, saying Hilton had a "horrible" childhood, and never bonded with his mother. Strauss said that the women in Hilton's life were not loving or caring to him, and his mother rejected him when he was five or six years old. Hilton told him that his mother talked to him about her sexual activities with her boyfriend.

When Gary was fourteen, he went into foster care following an incident when he shot his stepfather. He told Strauss that he felt like a "nonbeing." Strauss said that, in his opinion, Hilton had an Oedipus complex because of the rejection Gary experienced from his mother, not sexual in nature, but caused by his unmet need to feel safe and loved.

Strauss said he believed that Hilton's killings started when he was in his sixties, and he blamed the Ritalin for that.

On the second day of the penalty phase of Gary Michael Hilton's trial, the defense continued to call witnesses in hopes of convincing the jury to recommend life in prison instead of the death penalty. First to take the witness stand was Dr. William Alexander Morton Jr., Professor Emeritus of Pharmacy, at the University of South Carolina, in Charleston. Dr. Morton specialized and served as a consultant in psychopharmacology.

Morton told the jury that he had met with Hilton the previous year, observed his behavior in Hilton's home videos, and had reviewed his prescription and medical records. He had prepared a PowerPoint presentation, which he had titled, "Approach to Evaluating Gary Hilton's Medications and Behavior."

Morton restated several points that had been made by the defense witnesses the previous day: the public reprimand of Dr. Delcher, and John Tabor's description of Hilton's increasingly bizarre behavior and speech. Morton pointed out that on the GBI's taped interview of Tabor, he had mentioned Hilton's becoming harder to deal with, more excitable than usual, threatening, demanding money, hostile behavior, and becoming more and more bizarre during a period of three months in 2007, when Hilton's Ritalin use reached more than one hundred milligrams per day.

In Hilton's home videos, made when he was abusing Ritalin, he exhibited rapid, rambling speech and was seen singing and posing for the camera, saying he would be "buzzing soon." He also stated, "I'm fucking wrecked," and "I'm tripping," and "I'm tripped out."

During their interview Hilton told Morton that Ritalin made him feel great. He could talk forever on it, and he felt "bulletproof." Morton said Ritalin abuse could cause a person to experience symptoms of hypersexuality, impulsiveness, feel no need for sleep, experience feelings of paranoia, irritability, hostility, violence, racing thoughts, hypervigilance, and manic symptoms.

At the time of Cheryl Dunlap's death, Morton said, Hilton was taking both Ritalin for fatigue and Effexor for depression, as well as adding six to eight cups of coffee to the mix each day. Both the drugs could have very serious side effects, he said, and Hilton should have been monitored carefully by Dr. Delcher, "but he didn't do a thing about it.

"In my professional opinion," Morton said, "Mr.

Hilton's drug combination would produce both profound and psychotic side effects."

Morton then echoed the words of the earlier defense witnesses, saying that when Ritalin and Effexor were combined in a person with Hilton's other conditions: "You're adding gasoline to the fire."

After a short break Dr. Morton was cross-examined by Willie Meggs, who asked him how much he was being paid for his testimony. Morton said his rate was two hundred dollars per hour, and he didn't know yet what his total amount of hours would be: probably twenty or thirty.

Morton said he asked Hilton if he was using cocaine, and Hilton denied it, but Meggs said, "Don't you know he used practically every street drug in his earlier life? We don't know if he was taking Ritalin at the time of the murders."

Morton said Hilton's dosage of Ritalin had been increased up to eighty milligrams within one month of getting his initial prescription, and sixty milligrams was the FDA's recommended maximum dosage. Hilton wanted more, Morton said, so Gary knew he was abusing it. He took it depending on how he felt, Morton said; when he didn't have much money, he took less.

There were no further questions for Dr. Morton, and the court was dismissed for a lunch break.

After lunch the jury remained out while the defense set up for review by the judge and the prosecution a slide presentation by its next witness, Chris Ellrich, an investigator with the public defender's office.

The prosecution made many objections when the

slide presentation—"The Life History of Gary Michael Hilton"—began to play.

On a large screen the first slide was a photo of Hilton's mother and father at the time they were married, followed by a photo of their marriage license, then Hilton's birth certificate. The next photo—Gary as an adorable ten-week-old baby—brought an immediate objection by the prosecution, which was sustained. A subsequent photo of Gary at five months of age was allowed, but the next four slides—Gary at six, nine, and fourteen months, and at two and a half years old—were objected to. The objections were all sustained.

"I want to hear the relevance of these photos," Judge Hankinson said. When the defense answered that they were intended to show that Hilton had grown up in alleged poverty, Hankinson said, "They show him all happy and smiling. Objection sustained."

Childhood photos of Hilton continued to be shown, and the objections to them continued to be sustained. In many of the photos designed to show Hilton's early poverty, his surroundings did not reflect poverty, and his demeanor, indeed, was that of a happy, normal child. Other photos showed one of Hilton's report cards, another was of him playing drums in a band he was with in high school, and other photos showed him with his dogs. Other photos showed him in the army, and living in a storage building with his dog Ranger.

After he viewed the presentation, Judge Hankinson ruled that the jury would only be allowed to see photos without sustained objections, and he said the jury would not be allowed to see any of the photos with sustained objections: "It has no relevance whether he was a cute baby or not. It certainly doesn't have anything to do with what the jury is deciding."

Since the judge had ruled that the jurors would not

be allowed to see most of the photos, there were not many left; so the defense decided not to show their slide presentation, after all. Instead, they began with the first of several videotaped testimonies: Victorine Rowe had lived next door to Gary and his mother in Tampa in the early 1950s, when Gary was a child. She said that one morning she had heard Hilton's mother screaming, "My son! My son!" Several neighbors had come running, only to find that a Murphy bed had fallen and hit Hilton on the head, gashing it badly.

"The whole neighborhood was upset. It was horrible," she said. "There were bloody towels everywhere. It was a terrible morning. The little boy was crying, and his mother was frantic." One of the neighbors took Hilton and his mother in his car to the hospital; and when they returned, "his whole head was bandaged up, like a cap."

Rowe said she had never even known their names. "I think they left the apartments right away. They were only there a couple of days."

On cross-examination the representative for the prosecution asked Rowe if she knew why she was being questioned about the accident and what Hilton was charged with.

"I knew he was in some kind of trouble," she said. When she was told about the murder charges, she said, "Oh no!"

The next videotaped testimony was from Thomas Perchoux, of Hialeah, who had allowed Hilton to stay at his home after the shooting incident with Nilo, Gary's stepfather. Hilton's mother, Cleo Hilton Dabag, and Perchoux's wife worked together, and Cleo had come to Perchoux and his wife to ask if Gary could stay with them for a while. Perchoux, who was a Boy Scout, Cub Scout, and Girl Scout leader, and was very experienced with young people, agreed.

"He and his stepfather didn't hit it off—could have been jealousy. I don't know," Perchoux said. The time Hilton had spent in their home had been without problems, he said, and he and Hilton went fishing. Hilton rode along with him sometimes on his job, and he got along very well with his wife, and played with their baby son.

"Normal teenage behavior," Perchoux said, describing Hilton. "No worse than anybody else's kids. He hadn't reached an age where he was getting an attitude." Gary always respected him, he said; but Perchoux added that while Gary was staying there, Cleo and Nilo never came to visit the boy, and Gary didn't go to visit them, either.

Following Thomas Perchoux's videotape, the defense told the judge that they planned to play a long interview that had been recorded with Hilton's mother prior to her death of cancer. It was made by GBI agents during the investigation of Meredith Emerson's murder. The jury would return from lunch and hear a detailed description of Hilton's life from childhood through his adult years, as told by Cleo Hilton Dabag.

Chapter 25

Agents from the GBI, led by Special Agent Matt Howard, had made a trip to visit Cleo at her home in Florida. She was quite ill at the time they visited her, the day after Hilton had made his plea deal in the murder of Meredith Emerson. Cleo subsequently died of her illness; and Hilton, hearing his mother's voice on tape talking for two hours about him, showed no visible emotion. His constant rocking back and forth, however, became slightly faster. He looked down and made even more of the lip-pursing, sucking mouth movements that he had made continuously throughout the trial. And as the interview progressed, he fidgeted in his chair more than usual. The fidgeting increased as time passed.

In the interview, after telling Cleo that Hilton had entered a plea the previous day, Howard told her that he and the other law enforcement agents who had been involved in the case were trying to learn as much as possible about Hilton to determine what had caused the crime.

"Gary did what he did, and in one case we have a very polite guy most of the agents have a personal relationship with. And on the other hand, we have this incident he did," Howard explained.

Cleo tended to ramble a bit as she recalled bits of information, and Howard kept her on track as best he could. She was on oxygen at the time, and she told Howard that her memory had been somewhat affected by chemotherapy.

She began by telling the agents that Hilton had been "hiking all over the mountains out West. He sent me lots of pictures." Howard asked to see the pictures, but Cleo told him she'd had to throw most of them out when she moved years earlier and had no place to keep many of her belongings.

Hilton's father, William Escoe Hilton, was originally from Arab, Alabama. He had never been a part of his son's life. He had another family, Cleo said, and when the double life he was living was exposed, the marriage ended. She and her son were on their own, until she married Nilo Dabag when Gary was nine years old.

The incident with the Murphy bed had happened prior to that, she said; she told the agents about the bed falling on top of him and almost taking off the back of his scalp. "It took over two hundred stitches," she said, recalling how horrified she had been about the accident.

Gary was a good child who never complained much, his mother said. "He hardly ever cried," she told the agents. He did well in school, when he wanted to, and he didn't fight or have problems. When he was in the sixth grade, though, he would customarily finish his work early, and then he would disrupt the class with talking and moving around. He went after school to the Boys Club, which Cleo said he enjoyed a lot, and won a sharpshooter award there. He liked playing with little cars throughout his entire childhood, she said, and she told the agents that she had a photo of Hilton taken on the day he joined the army, writing a letter to his girlfriend with some of his little cars around him on his desk.

Nilo Dabag was in the horse business; and after he and Cleo married, Gary enjoyed helping with the horses. But Nilo was jealous of him, she said, and resented her for paying too much attention to her child. He never physically abused the boy, but Cleo said there was a lot of verbal and emotional abuse.

"Nilo had a terrible temper," she said. As a result, Gary wasn't very demonstrative or affectionate toward his mother.

"Would he tell you he loved you?" Howard asked.

"He wasn't really like that," Cleo said. "He and I were very close, but I think he was worried about how my husband would act." Cleo said she had left her husband seven times because of the friction between him and her son. Nilo would yell and break things in front of Gary.

"He was so sensitive," Cleo said of her son, telling the agents that at one point he had overheard her talking with Nilo about expenses, saying they were going to have to "tighten their belts for a while." At the end of the week, Gary came to her and handed her all of his lunch money in an attempt to help the family finances.

One incident that Cleo was very reluctant to talk about was the shooting episode when Gary was fourteen years old. Her brother was there, visiting with her, during the videotape session. She didn't want him to know about it. She told the agents she didn't want to talk about the shooting in front of him; so he left the room for a while, allowing her to speak privately.

"I've never talked to anyone about this," she said. "I don't want [my brother] to get the wrong impression about my son."

The shooting happened during a time when Cleo and Nilo were separated, she said. When he'd leave, he'd come back later and beg, promise Cleo and Gary all kinds of things about how he'd do better from then on. On one occasion, after a separation, Nilo had come back to the home. Gary had borrowed a gun from a neighbor, unbeknownst to Cleo, and he told Nilo, "Mom doesn't want you here," and said he was going to shoot him if he didn't leave. Nilo dared him to shoot, and held up a mattress in front of himself. Gary shot him in the lower gut. Following that incident, Gary Hilton went to a juvenile detention center and had psychiatric care.

Cleo expressed a great deal of regret about the incident, because Gary's counselor at the detention center told her that her duty was to her husband. The counselor told her to get Gary a room or an apartment. "I shouldn't have listened," she said, but she sent him away to stay with the Perchoux family, and she stayed with Nilo.

"I realize now that my duty was to my son," she said.

When Cleo next left Nilo, she got an apartment, and Gary came back home.

The only girlfriend she could remember her son having was a girl named Sandy, whom Gary had liked a lot throughout high school.

Hilton dropped out of high school only a few weeks from graduation, Cleo said, because he played drums in a band and they were offered a job at a Miami Beach nightclub. Soon he decided to join the army, even though he was only seventeen years old. He was happy to go, his mother said, and a friend joined up at the same time. They left together and went to boot camp together.

After his time in the military, Hilton married for the first time, a girl named Ursula, and they lived in a house behind Cleo and Nilo. Hilton, his wife, and Cleo would go to a cabin in the Keys on weekends when Nilo was out of town, and Cleo said they all enjoyed spending time there. All seemed to be going well, until their divorce.

"He sort of fell to pieces after they separated," she said; then he moved to Atlanta. "He got a nice apartment there," Cleo told the agents, "and I'd go up to visit him every few weeks."

Eventually, Gary married a woman with two children, she said, whom he seemed to like. They were married only a short time; she didn't know why. "He wasn't saying much then." But she had stopped going up to visit him because he had started using drugs. She never knew whether he had stopped his drug use or not, she said.

One of the last times Cleo had spoken to her son, he had called her from jail after being arrested. At that time, she said, Nilo had fallen for a lottery scam and they'd had to scrape together everything they had to repay the $10,000 it had cost them. When Hilton called, hoping she could bail him out, she told him they were broke and did not have the bail money. Gary called her after he finally got out of jail and asked why she didn't help him. Cleo told him about the fraud and that it had cost them $10,000 to cover it.

"You had ten thousand dollars and didn't come bail me out?" he asked her. Then Hilton hung up the phone, and she never heard anything from him again.

"I didn't know if he was dead or alive. I haven't seen him since '86 or '87."

Cleo told the agents that she didn't want to say anything that would hurt her son.

"He may have done something wrong, but he's still my son."

Not even hearing the voice of his deceased mother speaking of her concern and support for him brought any sign of emotion from Hilton. He kept on rocking back and forth in his chair, moving his mouth, and looking down.

The message board reacted to Hilton's mother's interview: Well, that certainly didn't sound like a cold, uncaring mother to me.

She sounded like a good, loving mother, wrote another.

It was becoming clear that the defense was, for all intents and purposes, throwing Cleo Dabag under the proverbial bus. In their effort to save her son's life by putting a great deal of the blame on her for his problems, she was being portrayed as something she clearly was not.

The next witness in the courtroom was Nilo Dabag's sister, Maria, who had been brought up from Argentina by the defense to testify about Hilton's childhood. She was accompanied to the witness stand by a translator, who interpreted the questions and answers for her. Maria Dabag was a stern-appearing, very serious woman who took a no-nonsense approach to her testimony.

Maria knew Hilton when she visited her brother and Cleo, she said. She lived with them for a time when Gary was sixteen, she stated. She prepared food for him and did things for him, and she called him "a very grateful child."

"Nilo had a very strong personality, very aggressive," she said. "He was very dry, and he didn't associate with the boy much," Maria said. "The boy bothered him."

When asked about Hilton's mother, Maria said, "I never saw Cleo show love for him, hug him, kiss him, show any affection. No, she was very cold. She chose Nilo over him. She was selfish and cold. The boy grew up alone."

When Willie Meggs cross-examined Maria, he asked her how long she had stayed with her brother's family, and she said she stayed for around three months the first time she visited them. From that time on, she visited nearly every year.

SA Meggs pointed out to the jury that Hilton was not

living at home during the time Maria had said she made her first trip to her brother's home.

When the next witness was called, Hilton smiled and looked around to greet Sandy, his high-school girlfriend, as she came to the stand. Sandra Carr said that the Gary Hilton she knew had been funny, outgoing, and smart; although he was an underachiever for someone with his intelligence and ability. She said that he had taught himself the drums and she thought he played very well.

"He was there for me when I needed him," she said. "I had problems with one of my parents, and he came and got me and helped me get to a safe place."

Sandra said that when Gary was fourteen, there had been an altercation between him and Nilo.

"After that, he went to foster care. He seemed more relaxed then."

Hilton came to see her before he went into the army, she said, "and after that, I never saw him again."

Sandy, the girl Hilton had been so fond of as a teenager, looked over at him for the first time as her testimony ended, and gave him a small smile.

Next up for the defense was Roy Cave, from Hillsboro, Oregon, Hilton's high-school friend who was a fellow band member in the Majestics.

"We played at parties and nightclubs," Cave said. "I thought we were pretty good."

Like most bands of that type, Cave said, they broke up many times. When Hilton went into the army, so did Cave. They went together and stayed together through boot camp. Then they were separated, and Cave said he saw Hilton once more in Germany in 1966.

On cross-examination SA Meggs had only two questions for Cave: "Were you ever in a combat situation? Did your training cause you to have any kind of 'rage against society'?"

"No," said Cave.

When Cave left the stand, Hilton smiled at him, turning to watch his old friend walk by on his way out of the courtroom.

The next witness brought the most reaction from Hilton that he had shown at any point during the trial. When Stefanie Durham, of Jacksonville, Florida, came into the courtroom, Hilton grinned widely at her. She looked back at him with obvious affection. Stefanie had been thirteen years old when her mother and Hilton lived together for two years.

"He was absolutely like a father figure to me," she said, "making sure I ate, got to where I needed to go, helped me with my homework." She said Hilton had given her medicine when she was sick, had taken her to basketball games, and described him as "giving, caring, eccentric, fun, funny, and outgoing."

Stefanie's feelings for Hilton were very positive, and so was her testimony. She repeatedly stressed that he "absolutely" was good, kind, loving, and caring to her during the time he and her mother were together, and she glanced at him repeatedly during her testimony.

When Meggs cross-examined her, he asked her if she was familiar with an arson case that Hilton had been charged with during the time she knew him, and she answered, "No."

The jury had a question for Stefanie. They wanted to know how her mother and Hilton had met, but Stefanie said she didn't know.

As she left the stand, she and Hilton smiled at each other. Then, later in the trial, she was seated directly behind him and spoke with the defense attorneys at length during the next break.

After Stefanie Durham's testimony the next interview was a taped statement made on the phone by a Duluth, Georgia, police officer who was unable to be present in court because he was waiting to be deployed to Afghanistan. It concerned an incident that occurred on February 25, 2006, when the officer received a call concerning a suspicious person at the Riverbrooke tennis courts, in one of Duluth's better neighborhoods. When he arrived, he said, Hilton was there with his dog in a white van. Hilton seemed "agitated, confused, out of it," and the police officer said Gary appeared "unstable."

Next up was James Scott Gillespie, of Marietta, Georgia, who said that he had been at the Copper's Creek trout fishing area on Thursday, June 7, 2007, with a group of people. They came into contact with Hilton when they walked into his camp and saw him sitting on a rock, slumped over, sharpening a knife. He was rocking back and forth, Gillespie said, muttering to his dog, and he never spoke to them.

Then came another recording, this one from October 25, 2007, made from the dash cam on a police car. It showed Hilton's van driving at night down a long stretch of road, then being pulled over because, according to the police officers in the car, Hilton was "driving all over the road."

When Hilton got out of the van, they wanted to know if he had been drinking. Hilton assured them that he had not been, and said his driving had been erratic because he was smoking a cigarette and petting his dog. When the officers wanted to know if he was on any medication, he told them that he was on "all kinds," including Ritalin. He kept assuring them that he had only been "messing with the dog" and smoking a cigarette at the same time, and he would pay closer attention to his driving. At the time he was wearing a purple cap with a pom-pom on top, and it was only two to three days after the murder of John Bryant.

It was unclear to the message board bloggers just what the point of this statement was. Several of them wrote that it seemed to them to be more beneficial to the prosecution than to the defense.

Forest Service officer Mary King next took the stand and said she had met Hilton, around 7:40 P.M., in November 2007, off Silver Lake Road. He was walking with Dandy when she stopped to perform a welfare check on him, and he was very resentful of her intrusion and accused her of "hassling" him, saying that he didn't like the government. She made a notation in her logbook that indicated "signal 20," which meant "crazy person."

When Willie Meggs cross-examined King, he had several questions. King told him the stop was made close to the Thomas/Wallace road locations, and said Hilton was very negative and hostile. There was a large knife in plain view on him, she said, and she told him his license tag was nearly expired. She also told him he would have to leave his campsite soon because hunting season was about to begin. Hilton told her he'd be leaving the forest soon, and she took no action about him.

The final presentation by the defense was a video interview with Jinhee Lee, a lady who operated a dry cleaner/Laundromat in Duluth, Georgia. Hilton, she said, was a good customer, who came often to the Laundromat.

He was accompanied by Dandy, whom, she said, she was very fond of. She never knew Hilton's name—only the dog's name, she said.

Hilton came regularly to the Laundromat; then he stopped coming for a while, starting back in 2007. At that time, she said, he told her that he had been in the mountains. Lee commented several times about Hilton always wearing the same type of clothing, synthetic outdoor/camping-style clothes.

When Hilton returned to the Laundromat after having been away, she noticed he was shaking and said she could see a change in him. She asked him if he was okay and he told her he had multiple sclerosis, and he took a pill while he was in the Laundromat.

"I couldn't believe it when I saw him on TV several months later," after Meredith Emerson's murder, she said. "What happened to his dog?"

The interviewer assured Lee that Dandy had been adopted and was being well taken care of.

Following the videotaped testimony of Ms. Lee, the defense rested.

When the prosecution called their first rebuttal witness, clinical psychologist Dr. Greg Prichard, it was already past five-thirty in the evening, and the jury was growing tired. They'd had a long day and had heard from many witnesses, watched videos, and listened to tapes. Now there would be more testimony, but at least Prichard, with his down-to-earth delivery, was much more easily understood than some of the other expert witnesses who had testified.

Prichard began by confirming with the prosecution that his specialty was forensic psychology and he was being paid at the same rate as other expert witnesses, two hundred dollars per hour.

SA William Meggs began by asking Prichard what his opinion was on the diagnosis the other experts had given about Hilton's mental and emotional condition.

Prichard immediately said that he disagreed with the diagnosis of most of those who had testified. He didn't believe that Hilton had suffered a brain injury from being struck on the head by the falling Murphy bed, or by most of the other diagnoses presented by the defense. Instead, Prichard said, he believed Hilton was a psychopath.

Psychopaths, Prichard said, exhibited a cluster of behavior and personality traits that were extremely dangerous when combined. Psychopaths, he told the jury, were impulsive, callous, glib, facile, talkative, and with no emotional connections. They were selfish and self-centered, believing "the end justifies the means." They were also subject to having antisocial personality disorder, which Prichard said was a disorder shared by 75 percent of the population in prisons.

Prichard pointed out that Hilton was not taking Ritalin when he shot his stepfather, and that according to his army dismissal papers, he had been counseled five times in the military and was relieved from assignment to a special weapons platoon because of "undesirable character traits." The records said he had been doing well until he began hearing voices and having increasing anxiety. He told his commanding officer he had come into the service on false pretenses, and the report said he had a "conflict of personality," but no mention of a diagnosed mental illness.

Between the age of twenty-one and the present time, Prichard said, Hilton had been arrested on criminal charges multiple times. Prichard said he had interviewed Hilton's second wife, who told him that within six months of marriage, Hilton had her quit her job and work for him, picking up checks for businesses. She told him she soon realized Hilton was posing as a charity.

During their marriage Hilton admitted to her that he had touched her nine-year-old daughter sexually and had also pulled out his penis and asked her young son to touch it.

When he admitted doing so, he said, "Well, they're not my children."

Concerning the murders of Meredith Emerson and Cheryl Dunlap, Prichard told the jury to "listen to what Mr. Hilton says" for psychopathic traits, such as:

"I started hunting in September."

"Blood Mountain is a good place to hunt. There's a large variety of people who come there."

"She was doomed from the start. I had to kill her."

"That's the one (Meredith Emerson) I'm going to get."

Prichard also reminded the jury about Hilton's involvement with the movie *Deadly Run,* his statements made on the way to Florida, and the fact that Hilton had offered information on Cheryl Dunlap's murder for personal gain. There were constant objections from the defense during his testimony—all of which were overruled—and Prichard concluded his remarks with his analysis of Hilton's behavior and its causes.

"He clearly knew right from wrong and the criminal nature of his conduct," Prichard said. "He tried to avoid detection by his treatment of his victims' bodies and the mask he wore at the ATM. The primary issue for Mr. Hilton is a personality and character issue present for his entire life. He's a psychopath. That's what generated the murders, and nothing else."

When Prichard's testimony for the state concluded, an exhausted jury was dismissed at six-thirty on Friday evening, with instructions to come back at ten-thirty,

Monday morning, when Prichard would be cross-examined by the defense.

When the third day of the penalty phase of Gary Michael Hilton's trial began, the jury was not due to take their places until ten-thirty, but the arguing between the defense and Judge Hankinson began bright and early, at eight-thirty in the morning. The defense immediately moved for a mistrial on the grounds that Dr. Prichard, during his testimony the previous day, had improperly criticized the testimony of the other experts appearing for the defense. Judge Hankinson denied that motion, and told the defense that there had been no evidence that Prichard had attacked the credibility of the other doctors. He had merely given his own opinion and had not maligned the others.

Then the defense again moved for a mistrial, saying that the prosecution had violated a court order when Dr. Joseph Wu was questioned about Hilton's involvement in the movie *Deadly Run.* The prosecution countered by claiming that Wu was the first one to bring up the movie when he said that Hilton was "clearly delusional" when he claimed to have been involved in the film.

"The state has disregarded the earlier court order, not to mention the movie," Ines Suber said.

"Dr. Wu opened the door for the state to introduce the movie, because he brought it up first," Willie Meggs countered.

"The prosecution brought it up first with Dr. Wu," Suber claimed, and asked again for a mistrial and sanctions. "The defense didn't bring it up during direct examination. The prosecution did, during cross-examination," Suber stressed. "We have the movie. Mr. Hilton received no credit for any involvement in it. The state violated the court order, and a mistrial is required."

Hankinson denied the request for a mistrial, telling Suber, "When it first came up, the defense made no objection. Now, [to object] one week later, there's no basis for a mistrial."

Then, before summoning the jury, the judge ordered both sides to go over the jury instructions again, page by page; then he asked if there were any objections. When there were none, Hankinson sent the bailiff to bring in the jury.

Defense attorney Robert Friedman began his cross-examination of Dr. Greg Prichard by pointing out that Prichard didn't conduct a clinical interview of Hilton, but rather had based his conclusions solely on a record review, Hilton's taped interviews, and interviews with Hilton's mother, his ex-wife, and his former boss John Tabor.

"In many forensic cases evaluation is not possible," Prichard told Friedman. "I could not evaluate Mr. Hilton face-to-face. I wasn't allowed to, so I had to rely on a great deal of data to generate my conclusions. Ideally, you always want to [meet with] the person."

Friedman asked if Prichard wasn't able to interview Hilton "because the state didn't follow the rules?"

Prichard told him he did not know.

Friedman then brought up Hilton's criminal record.

"There were not any prior convictions of violence prior to the Emerson and Dunlap cases," Freidman said. "There were arrests for aggravated assault and arson, but no convictions, no records." As to the allegations by his ex-wife about child abuse: "Again, there were no charges filed and no records."

The jury had questions for Prichard, wanting to know the difference between personality disorders and mental disorders. He explained that mental disorders are due to a neurochemical imbalance, and personality disorders are not biologically driven. They are a disorder in a subject's character or personality.

The jury also wanted to know if the records Prichard had examined showed who had filed the complaint against Dr. Delcher for improperly prescribing Ritalin for Hilton.

Dr. Prichard said he didn't know.

The next step in the trial was about to begin. The jury would hear closing arguments from both sides; then they would retire to the jury room for their deliberations. Hankinson ordered the doors to the courtroom locked during final jury instructions and closing arguments so the jurors wouldn't be distracted by people coming and going from the room.

Hankinson told the jury that according to Florida law, he would make the final decision on sentencing Hilton, but he was required to give their recommendation "great weight." He told them not to be influenced one way or the other by Hilton's decision not to testify, and he said it would take a majority vote to recommend the death penalty.

After the judge spoke to the jurors, State Attorney William Meggs began his closing arguments by telling the jury, "Jury duty is a high, high calling. Your job is to weigh the aggravating and mitigating circumstances and make a decision, not because of sympathy or anger."

Meggs spoke to the jury about duty, saying that the late

American hero Pat Tillman had given up a lucrative pro football contract to join the military because he wanted to do his duty to his country. "Doing his duty cost him his life," Meggs said.

The prosecutor told the jury about aggravating factors that, he said, had been proven beyond every reasonable doubt. The first, he said, was the murder of Meredith Emerson, for which Hilton had been convicted. The second aggravating factor was the kidnapping of Cheryl Dunlap. And the third was the fact that Hilton went to great lengths to conceal Cheryl Dunlap's murder.

"The defendant cut her head off. We don't have any teeth. Remember his statements, 'If you take them, you have to kill them, or you get caught,' and 'I have to go do something with these.'"

The fourth aggravating factor, Meggs told the jury, was the fact that the murder was committed for financial gain, proven by Hilton's use of Cheryl Dunlap's ATM card. And the fifth, one of the most extreme factors, was the fact that it was a heinous, atrocious crime.

"We have every reason to believe that Cheryl Dunlap knew she was going to die," Meggs said. "She was chained around the neck so she couldn't escape from the van, and knew she was going to die, and there was nothing she could do about it."

Meggs reminded the jury of the deep bruise that medical examiners found on her back. He told them Cheryl had lived for forty-eight hours: until Hilton got to the ATM, and the PIN number she had given him had worked.

The sixth aggravating factor to be considered, Meggs said, was the fact that the murder was committed in a cold, calculated, premeditated manner. He reminded the jury of Hilton's own statements: "They fight, and then they submit." "I'm out of money. I'm going to have to kill somebody." "This shit just got me caught." "When you go out to kill and you're seen, you're screwed," and other remarks Hilton had made during interviews.

Meggs told the jury that the testimony of the defense's own experts contradicted one another, and said the defense was trying to blame everybody but Hilton for his crimes. Cleo Dabag, he said, was a good mother who did the best she could under difficult circumstances, and her testimony proved that Hilton had just the opposite of a bad childhood. Most of the defense's other witnesses meant very little, Meggs said, and one of the defense's expert witnesses had been fined $15,000 for wrongfully prescribing OxyContin.

"Weigh all these factors very carefully," Meggs told the jury.

Speaking of his final witness, Dr. Greg Prichard, Meggs said, "He talked in a plain, common-sense manner," and he told the jury that Prichard was correct in his evaluation of Hilton: "He's a psychopath, who doesn't care about anything other than himself.

"Folks, I ask you on behalf of the state of Florida— your duty is clear. You must weigh the aggravating circumstances against the mitigating circumstances. Thank you for doing your duty, and your duty is about to come down to you in a very strong way. I'm asking you to vote for Gary Michael Hilton to be put to death. God bless you. Go vote and do your duty."

Chapter 26

Defense Attorney Robert Friedman had his work cut out for him, following such a strong closing argument by William Meggs. Friedman began by telling the jury that there had been three major mitigating factors that had been proven by the defense to have caused Gary Hilton to commit his crimes: his head injury, the childhood abuse he was alleged to have suffered, and his overprescribed Ritalin use.

Friedman spoke about Hilton's childhood abandonment, being placed in foster care after shooting his stepfather, Nilo, and the fact that a counselor told Cleo to leave Gary for Nilo. After being rejected by his mother at an early age, Friedman said, Hilton had enlisted in the army at age seventeen, where he eventually began to suffer auditory hallucinations during his second tour of duty.

"He was a loner," Friedman said, "and never bonded with humans as he did with his dogs."

Friedman pointed out that there had been no convictions for violence until after Hilton started seeing Dr. Delcher, who prescribed a larger-than-recommended dose of Ritalin. John Tabor had noticed a decline in Hilton after the Ritalin use began, and even Dr. Delcher had noted Hilton was having severe symptoms in July 2007, Friedman said, but the doctor did not change his medications.

Friedman stressed, over and over, about the symptoms and side effects of Ritalin, saying it pushed Hilton over the line and his problems were caused by mental illness, which was compounded by the use of Ritalin and Effexor.

Hilton had been deprived of a relationship with his biological father, suffered maternal deprivation, and lack of the normal mother/child bonding, Friedman said. Hilton had been put in foster care as an adolescent, grew up in a poor family, suffered traumatic brain injury as a child, and suffered from several mental defects.

Friedman summarized the testimonies of all the defense's expert witnesses, reminding the jury of Hilton's PET scan information, and the tests that showed Hilton as having an IQ that was in the top 10 percent of the population, but emotionally thinking like an eight- or nine-year-old child. Friedman spoke of Hilton's alleged schizoaffective disorder, which was said to have existed for a long time and was accelerated by his medications.

"No one gave him a sense of love anytime in his life," Friedman told the jury. "On behalf of Mr. Hilton, I'm asking all of you to recommend a life sentence in this case."

Judge Hankinson then turned the case over to the jury, ordering that all the evidence in the case would be sent back into the jury room with them. They left the room to decide whether they would recommend life or death for Gary Michael Hilton. It was two forty-seven in the afternoon when their deliberations began.

After the jury left, Hankinson addressed the defense and prosecution, saying, "I appreciate the professional job that has been done on both sides. This case has been very vigorously litigated—but in a professional manner—and I thank you for your service."

After the jury had left, some of the spectators also left the courtroom; many remained, talking among themselves. The attorneys and court personnel did the same, milling around and going back and forth out of the courtroom. Paperwork was shuffled, packed into boxes and briefcases, and colleagues spoke with each other. No one seemed to want to get too far away from the room, and there was a general sense that the jury might not be out for long. The guilty verdict had taken a relatively short time, and that might also be the case for a sentencing decision.

Chapter 27

Around four o'clock, only about an hour and fifteen minutes after they had left the courtroom, the jury returned with their verdict. Everyone quickly took their places and listened intently as the foreman handed the jury's decision to Judge Hankinson, who read it aloud: "'In the *State of Florida* versus *Gary Michael Hilton*. A majority of the jury, by a vote of twelve to nothing, advise and recommend to the court that it impose the death penalty on Gary Michael Hilton, so say we all.'"

There was no sudden uproar in the courtroom, and the only real surprise in the decision was the fact that it had been unanimous. Judge Hankinson told the court that there would be two more court actions; one for him to hear any other information in the case that the defense might present, and the other for him to announce his final sentencing decision. The date for those actions would be announced later, he said, when the defense and prosecution attorneys agreed on a time.

Then Hilton was escorted from the courtroom.

* * *

Newspaper and media-outlet reporters eagerly asked the prosecutors for statements as they began to leave the room.

Prosecutor Georgia Cappleman told the press that the state was very pleased with the death penalty verdict, especially since it was unanimous. She said it was apparent that the jury saw what needed to be done.

"They brought justice, and that's what Mr. Hilton got today, and what Ms. Dunlap and her family got."

"If there was ever a case for it, this was it," State Attorney William Meggs told the press about the unanimous verdict. He told the reporters that he greatly appreciated the law enforcement personnel in both Georgia and in Florida for their hard work over a long period of time, which resulted in the verdict just received. "They dug up the National Forest. They crawled in Dumpsters recovering evidence. Those folks deserve a lot of credit."

Cheryl Dunlap's immediate family was absent from the courtroom throughout the trial, but one cousin, Gloria Tucker, had sat through every day of the trial. She said she was very satisfied with the verdict, saying that Hilton would now know how his victims felt before they died, knowing that they were doomed.

"He needs to know now that he's going to face death," Tucker said.

She also told the reporters that her cousin had been such a good, loving person that she might not have wanted Hilton to die.

"Cheri was such a loving person, who always looked for the good in everyone. . . . I'm not sure she would be as happy as we are, but it's good that he won't be able to hurt anybody else."

The jury's unanimous decision echoed the feelings of the residents of Cheryl Dunlap's hometown of Crawfordville and the citizens of Wakulla County. Many of them spoke to reporters following the trial, and all were glad that Hilton would face death for what he had done to Cheryl Dunlap and for the suffering her family and friends had endured because of her murder.

"We don't know how many other people he has killed, and probably never will," one man said, adding that there was no rehabilitation for a person who committed such crimes.

Others said they were thankful that there would finally be some closure for the family, but it wouldn't bring Cheryl Dunlap back. And all were in agreement that the right sentence had been recommended. A Crawfordville resident said that because of the hideous nature of the crime, "[Hilton] didn't show Cheryl any mercy, so I don't think he deserves any mercy," adding that he thought Hilton should be executed the same way that he had killed his victim.

One man spoke bluntly, echoing the sentiments of many other people who had been interviewed about Cheryl Dunlap's murder over the past three years. "I think they're taking too long in killing him," the man said.

Among the people who had watched Hilton's trial on live streaming video from WCTV was a large group of Meredith Emerson's family and friends, who were keenly interested in the verdict. They felt that a death sentence was not only justice for Cheryl Dunlap, but for Meredith as well. When Hilton bargained his way to a life sentence in Georgia by leading authorities to Emerson's body, many felt that he was not getting what he deserved for her murder.

When Meredith's parents agreed to the Georgia plea bargain, they were made aware that Hilton would be immediately charged with capital murder in Florida as soon as his Georgia case was finished, and they had been told there was overwhelming evidence that Hilton had murdered Cheryl Dunlap. Many others, who did not know at that time that Hilton would be facing the death penalty in the Florida case, were glad when they learned that Hilton had been arrested and would be tried for Cheryl's murder. Thus, Meredith would finally get justice.

Julia Karrenbauer, Meredith's former roommate, told the press that she thought Hilton not only deserved the death penalty, but a whole lot more. She said she felt her friend Meredith had stopped a serial killer, which was the only comfort that those who loved Meredith could take from losing her so tragically.

Chris Hendley, Meredith's former boss, told the media that he was relieved when Hilton's sentence was announced, and he wasn't surprised. He had expected the verdict, he said.

There was another large group of trial watchers following the WCTV video, and they were the family and countless friends who were hoping for justice in the case of Irene and John Bryant, murdered in North Carolina in October 2007. It had long been known that Gary Hilton was the prime suspect in their murders, and their son Bob said that he felt the sentence was "just and appropriate." But although the U. S. Department of Justice had kept a tight lid on the Bryants' case, releasing no information since 2008, Bob Bryant's sister, Holly, said the family had been told that anything Hilton said in his Florida trial could be used against him when he went on trial for her parents' murder. And he would indeed go to trial—the U.S. DOJ had told her—as soon as the Florida trial was over. The death penalty would also be sought in that trial; Holly said she had been assured of that.

A spokesperson for the U. S. Attorney's Office still

claimed that nothing had been filed against Hilton in the case and the U.S. DOJ could not comment, but John and Irene Bryant's family had been told that action would soon be taken. Holly said the family had been informed that there was DNA evidence linking Hilton to the murders of her parents.

Bob Bryant told the press that he was disappointed with the time it was taking to pursue his parents' case, but he understood that Hilton couldn't be indicted for the crime until the Florida trial was finished, because of the guarantee of a speedy trial. The Florida case would have interfered with preparing a case in North Carolina, he said.

And if the bodies of any of the other missing persons considered possible victims of Gary Hilton were found, he might face even more charges. In one case in particular, that of missing hiker Rossana Miliani, shortly before she dropped out of sight in Cherokee, North Carolina, she had been seen with a man fitting Hilton's description. Her grieving family desperately needed closure in her disappearance, and they believed Hilton could be involved. A great many other people in law enforcement felt the same way; but with no remains yet located, Rossana Miliani's legal status would remain in limbo. For the time being, she could only be classified as a missing person, not a murder victim.

A few days after Hilton's guilty verdict and the jury's death sentence recommendation, it was announced that final evidence and victim impact statements would be heard on April 7 at 9:00 A.M. at a Spencer Hearing in Judge Hankinson's courtroom 3A. At Spencer Hearings, both sides would be given the opportunity to present any last-minute evidence to the judge, and statements would be given—both in person or by letter—by Cheryl Dunlap's friends and family. Just as the trial had been, the Spencer Hearing also was scheduled to be carried on live video feed on the Internet. Many of the interested parties who had watched the trial by that means were also planning to go online to see the April 7 hearing.

Chapter 28

When the morning arrived for Hilton's Spencer Hearing, his appearance had changed, yet again. He looked quite different than he had only a month earlier. He had gained some weight, and his hair was cut very short. Instead of a suit, he wore his jail clothing. He had also grown a short beard, and his coloring appeared a little less pale than it had looked a month earlier. He didn't look nearly as frail as he had during his trial. One thing had not changed, however; he still rocked back and forth in his chair and made constant chewing motions with his lips.

When Judge Hankinson entered the courtroom and took his seat at the bench, he called the hearing to order and said that the proceedings had been set in order to "give either side the opportunity to present any additional evidence they may have."

Prosecutor Willie Meggs told the judge that there would be three witnesses who would like to read their victim impact statements to the court, and others who had sent letters to be presented to the judge; then the state would have a brief argument.

"I have received the letters," Hankinson told him. "I have not read them yet."

Hilton's attorney Robert Friedman told the judge that the only aspects of the victim impact statements that should be permissible as evidence were those pertaining to the victim, not anything about Hilton—such as his character or speculation about him. Friedman then proceeded to read a long list of objections from the large number of letters that had been submitted to the court, giving the name of the writer and reading aloud what they had written that the defense considered to be unacceptable.

In a letter from Cheryl's friend Tonya Land, Friedman objected to her use of the phrase: "fear and mistrust in the community."

Nancy Hedman, another friend, used the words "may justice be served in this crime" which also brought an objection from Friedman.

Friends Amber Collins wrote that Crawfordville had *lost its sense of safety and civility;* and Hannah and Ashton Collins spoke of Hilton's not just taking Cheryl's life, he took a mother, grandmother, friend, and mentor. After reading their words, Friedman objected to them.

Friends and neighbors James C. Misso and Nancy Duran wrote letters that Friedman said he objected to almost in their entirety.

Scores of other church friends, family members, and co-workers sent letters to the judge. The last sentence of Steve Alt's letter, which said there would never be anyone who could replace Cheryl, and Aletha Arkley's written comment that Hilton's sentence could *make a bold statement to any other offender* were both objected to by Friedman.

Kimberly Smith wrote, *Justice will bring a level of comfort,* and Jennifer Glaubius penned, *He needs to pay for the hurt he has caused.* Friedman objected to both of these statements, as well as an entire letter from Michael L. Brown, Ph.D.

All the following individuals also wrote letters with sections that brought objections from Friedman, although he was reading each of them aloud for the judge to hear: Toby Peters wrote, *grieved by her senseless murder;* Scott Volk penned, *I am confident that to her last breath, Cheryl was praying for her abductor;* Robert Gladstone wrote, *No doubt, Hilton found out what kind of person Cheryl was;* Gaby Godfrey put on paper that *My life changed and I was honored to know her. Her legacy will live on forever.*

Friedman also objected to almost all the content of letters from Tom Barry, Becca Anderson, Kasie Forbes, Ben Godfrey, and Marsha Misso. In total, there were over two dozen letters, and the defense had objected—to one extent or another—to all of them but one.

When the defense's litany of objections finally ended, Meggs told the judge, "Given the fact that we're aware that the purpose of victim impact statements is to give what the victim meant to the community, the court can consider the statements, what sentences will be imposed, and the court can readily distinguish parts admissible for death or kidnapping or grand theft. The state doesn't think the court will be 'inflamed' by the statements. The victim's family and friends have a right to be heard. The state asks that the letters be made part of the record and that the live statements be allowed to be heard."

Friedman then asked that various other rulings be considered as to victim impact statements, in an attempt to get much of the letters and live statements disallowed, but Hankinson told him, "We will continue with these letters. It seems odd to have only heard the portions of them that the defense has objected to. The court can consider the letters in their entirety. All objections are denied."

Hankinson then told the prosecution that he would allow the witnesses to speak, reading their letters to him, and Friedman said that he would have a standing objection to the letters.

While all the legal maneuvering concerning the victim impact letters and statements was taking place, there was a great deal of discussion about the case taking place on the video feed's message board, just as there had been during the trial. One writer said that he had been following John Cagle, the Georgia investigator, on the Internet. Cagle was one of the key investigators in the Meredith Emerson and Patrice Endres cases, among very many others, and was keenly interested in the outcome of Hilton's Florida trial. The writer said Cagle had indicated that he thought as soon as the sentencing of Hilton was finished, North Carolina would step in, indict him and move forward with their case.

This would surely be welcome news for the family of John and Irene Bryant.

Chapter 29

"The state calls Mrs. Emma Blount."

When Emma Blount, Cheryl Dunlap's aunt, stepped to the microphone to read her statement to Judge Hankinson, it was immediately apparent that she was very emotional and would not have an easy time maintaining her composure.

"This is the hardest thing I've had to do," she said before beginning to read her letter.

"'I'm Cheryl's aunt,'" she began. "'Cheryl's mother was in a nursing home at the time Cheryl was murdered, and when she was told what had happened, she withdrew,'" Blount said. "'She died thirteen months later.'"

Blount went on to tell of Cheryl's work with patients and family members at the nursing home, and said Cheryl had told her of going often to the forest.

"'She said she was safe at the National Forest,'" Mrs. Blount said in a choked voice.

"'She was compassionate, loving, quick to help, and loved mission work. She had worked hard to complete nursing school. Her children have been cheated out of her love and devotion,'" Blount told the judge, growing more emotional. "'She was always happy and smiling.'"

At this point several people on the message board noticed and commented that the court reporter appeared to be crying as she steadily continued taking notes.

Cheryl's best friend, Laura Walden, was next to read her letter: "'I miss her smile, her laugh; she was a friend, a sister, a counselor, and a shoulder to cry on. When I realized she was gone, I felt empty and void. I loved and respected her because of her honesty, integrity and loyalty that never wavered. I depended on her to be there. I miss her terribly; she was gone too soon. May her light continue to shine brightly in those of us she touched.'"

Gloria Tucker, Cheryl's cousin, was the last to read her letter to the judge: "'Cheri had so much compassion for people. She went to her patients' homes after their benefits had run out, and she went to disaster areas to help people.'"

Tucker then spoke powerfully about the crime that took her cousin's life: "'She must have been so afraid and lonely during that time with Hilton. Hilton sentenced his victims to death. What will it take to stop him? The solution is to carry out the sentence speedily. He must pay with his own life.'"

Robert Friedman immediately rose to his feet. "Parts of the last victim impact statement we object to, specifically the mention of terror, captivity, death sentence, et cetera."

Judge Hankinson then pointed something out to Friedman that he should probably have realized earlier.

"All you're doing is repeating these things for me to hear again," the judge told him. He asked Friedman if his client wished to speak, and Friedman told him that Hilton did not.

Then it was time for the state to give their final argument for the death penalty to be imposed.

Willie Meggs told the judge, "The state doesn't ask the court to impose the death penalty lightly. There are six aggravating factors to consider."

Meggs then listed the six factors:

1. Hilton previously confessed to Meredith Emerson's murder;
2. Cheryl Dunlap's murder was done during the commission of a planned kidnapping;
3. The murder was done to avoid arrest, according to Hilton's own statement, and great pains were taken to avoid Cheryl Dunlap being identified;
4. The murder was done for financial gain;
5. The crime was heinous, atrocious, and cruel, with "cognition of impending death by the victim in the case," and was wicked, vile and pitiless;
6. The crime was cold, calculated, and premeditated. "He had a plan, detailed his plan, had time to reflect on his activity."

"Your Honor, the state feels the jury's recommendation [of the death penalty] should be given great weight. We hereby ask the court to impose the death penalty in this case."

Chapter 30

When Robert Friedman stood up to tell the judge of the statutory and nonstatutory mitigating circumstances in Gary Hilton's case, he was ready to pull out all the stops in an effort to save his client from the death penalty.

The statutory mitigating circumstances, Friedman said, were the facts that Hilton was "impaired" at the time of the murder, and was under extreme stress at that time.

Friedman named a list of ten nonstatutory mitigating circumstances, which included yet another repetition of his prior claims that Hilton was raised in an abusive home, had been abandoned by his father, suffered from maternal deprivation, was put into foster care, was from a poor family, suffered a brain injury, and had severe mental defects.

The defense attorney also told the judge that "no weight should be given to the 'avoiding arrest' aggravating circumstances." He said that the state was relying on what occurred in the Emerson murder.

"Much of the state's presentation is replete with errors and factual inaccuracies," Friedman said. "The DNA evidence, the medical examiner's statement . . . speculation, relying on Emerson and inaccurate facts.

"The court should give no weight" to the state's arguments, Friedman said. "The mitigation clearly outweighs the aggravation in this case. The court should impose a life sentence."

Judge Hankinson sat for a moment, considering the situation.

"I don't particularly want to hear more," he said. "Does the state have more?"

Both sides told the judge they did not have anything further.

"The next session of this court will be held on Thursday, April twenty-first, at ten A.M.," Judge Hankinson said. "We are recessed till then."

As everyone rose to leave the courtroom, Hilton leaned over, patted Friedman on the back, and said, "Hey, good job."

When sentencing day came, there was a larger crowd waiting in the courtroom than there had been on many days of the trial. Cheryl Dunlap's aunt, cousin, and other friends and relatives were present, along with the Leon and Wakulla County sheriffs and many of the other law enforcement personnel who had been closely involved in the case for so long.

Gary Hilton entered the courtroom several minutes early, cuffed and shackled and wearing jail clothing. He was immediately surrounded at the defense table by his attorneys. Ines Suber sat down beside him and spoke to him intently, leaning in closely. Hilton smiled, nodded, and looked relatively relaxed as he turned around to see the spectators and looked directly at the TV cameras. If he was apprehensive about his sentencing, he did not show it at that time.

Judge Hankinson entered the courtroom. After stating for the record the purpose of the hearing, he said, "Some judges have read their entire sentencing orders, but I don't think that's necessary today. I have written my orders and copies will be provided to both sides."

Hankinson then told the court that he was prepared to give his order.

"Mr. Hilton, rise, please."

Hilton stood up, along with his defense team.

"'The court has considered and weighed the aggravating and mitigating circumstances in this case, and the court finds, as did the jury, that the aggravating circumstances outweighed the mitigating circumstances.

"'Accordingly, it is ordered and adjudged that you, Gary Michael Hilton, be sentenced to death for the murder of Cheryl Dunlap. This sentence is subject to automatic reviews by the Florida Supreme Court.'"

Hilton, for the first time, showed some small sign of emotion, blinking rapidly.

"Mr. Hilton, you have thirty days to file an appeal.

"May God have mercy on your soul."

The judge ordered Hilton to be fingerprinted in the courtroom; then he was immediately taken out by his escort of deputies. There was complete silence in the courtroom for a moment; then the observers quietly began to leave. Some of Cheryl Dunlap's family wiped their eyes; others smiled. There was no air of celebration—only a quiet vindication.

Leon County sheriff Larry Campbell called Hilton a remorseless, calculating person who had come "shuffling into court like he's some poor little old grandfather, and he's not. He's a damned monster."

Cheryl Dunlap's cousin Gloria Tucker said she had been certain the judge would impose the death penalty, and was happy that Hilton would not be able to hurt anyone else. Cheryl's aunt Emma Blount said it was a relief that Hilton would never be able to harm anyone else's child.

"Cheryl was completely, totally committed to God, so I know she's in Heaven," Blount said.

After years of delay it finally had taken only six minutes for justice to be received for Cheryl Dunlap. Hilton left the courtroom, however, very much aware that yet another family, another community, and another large contingent of friends from around the nation would be waiting for him in North Carolina, ready to seek a similar verdict in the murders of John and Irene Bryant.

Gary Michael Hilton's time in court was far from over.

Acknowledgments

The police didn't know whether Meredith Emerson was alive or not during their massive search for her. They were hot on her abductor's trail and prayed that, with a little bit of luck, they would catch up before it was too late to save her. The police actually had come face to face with Meredith's abductor on a couple of occasions but had no way of knowing who he was. Or that he had any connection with the missing young woman.

The search for Meredith's abductor melded into searches for a murdered North Carolina Couple, and the abduction and killing of Cheryl Dunlap, a beloved missionary/nurse in North Florida. The U.S. Coast Guard, U.S. Park Service, the Georgia Bureau of Investigation (GBI), Federal Bureau of Investigation (FBI), and dozens of police and volunteer agencies scanned a five-state area from the air, ground and under the water. Thousands of volunteers from the Rocky Mountains in the west to the beginning of The Appalachian Trail in Maine were on the look-out for the missing people.

It was a huge effort, and naming everyone who was instrumental in the creation of this book would go on and on. I would like to extend special thanks to Special Agent Clay Bridges of the GBI who gave several lengthy interviews to the author, and who made sense of a time-line and search that drew from such wide and varied sources.

Special thanks to Stephanie Finnegan for superb copy editing, Richard Ember for encouragement, and to the always up-beat, inventive, and empathetic Michaela Hamilton, Executive Editor of Kensington Publishing Corp., who makes it all work.

Health issues made it impossible for me to attend Gary Hilton's trial or to write anything after that. The task of completing this book was thrown unexpectedly to Sheila Johnson, a Pinnacle true crime writer, who picked it up in mid-stride and continued seamlessly to the finish line. Sheila shares authorship of this book, even though she modestly downplays her role. Thanks to Sheila and all of the others who contributed their time, thoughts, and well wishes.

                                                          Lee Butcher